Schelling and Spinoza

Schelling and Spinoza

REALISM, IDEALISM, AND THE ABSOLUTE

Benjamin Norris

Published by State University of New York Press, Albany

© 2022 State University of New York

All rights reserved

Printed in the United States of America

No part of this book may be used or reproduced in any manner whatsoever without written permission. No part of this book may be stored in a retrieval system or transmitted in any form or by any means including electronic, electrostatic, magnetic tape, mechanical, photocopying, recording, or otherwise without the prior permission in writing of the publisher.

For information, contact State University of New York Press, Albany, NY
www.sunypress.edu

Library of Congress Cataloging-in-Publication Data

Name: Norris, Benjamin, author.
Title: Schelling and Spinoza : realism, idealism, and the absolute / Benjamin Norris.
Description: Albany : State University of New York Press, [2022] | Includes bibliographical references and index.
Identifiers: LCCN 2022005755 | ISBN 9781438489537 (hardcover : alk. paper) | ISBN 9781438489544 (ebook) | ISBN 9781438489520 (pbk. : alk. paper)
Subjects: LCSH: Schelling, Friedrich Wilhelm Joseph von, 1775–1854. | Spinoza, Benedictus de, 1632–1677. Ethica. | Metaphysics. | Realism. | Idealism.
Classification: LCC B2899.M48 N67 2022 | DDC 193—dc23/eng/20220422
LC record available at https://lccn.loc.gov/2022005755

10 9 8 7 6 5 4 3 2 1

We can say that in putrefaction the universe is calculated; yet even more importantly, the universe that is sensed or speculated, whether as an idea or a materialized form, is the calculus of an infinite rot.

—Reza Negarestani, "Undercover Softness: An Introduction to the Architecture and Politics of Decay"

Speculation . . . frightens human understanding, which fears the destructive character of its own operation.

—Jacques Derrida, *Glas*

For Chuck, Daniel, Sondra, and Marilyn

Contents

Preface	xi
Introduction: A Crack in the Abyss	1
1.0 A Note in the Margins	1
2.0 Schelling and Spinoza	5
3.0 Realism and Antirealism in Jacobi and Contemporary Philosophy	13
4.0 Idealism beyond Antirealism	19
5.0 The Plan	23

Part I

Chapter 1: Reason, Realism, and Faith in Jacobi and Kant	29
1.0 Introduction: Rationality, Totality, and Antirealism	29
2.0 The Difference Between Jacobi's and Kant's Critiques of Spinoza	30
3.0 Jacobi's Realism	46
4.0 Conclusion	55
Chapter 2: Weak Weapons and the Fight Against Dogmatism	57
1.0 Introduction: Letters to a Friend	57
2.0 Criticism	59
3.0 Dogmatism	67
4.0 Subjects and Objects	72
5.0 Conclusion	86

Part II

Chapter 3: Spinoza and Schelling on Identity and Difference 91
   1.0 Introduction: Spinoza, the Undeniable Predecessor 91
   2.0 The Need for Identity 94
   3.0 Thinking through the Most Monstrous Thought 111
   4.0 Conclusion 126

Chapter 4: Realism, Idealism, and Parallelism 129
   1.0 Introduction: Against Abrasive Philosophy 129
   2.0 Idealism, Elimination, and Amplification 132
   3.0 Realism *sive Natura* 144
   4.0 Conclusion 159

Part III

Chapter 5: Divine Indigestion 167
   1.0 Introduction: Identity Crisis 167
   2.0 The Strictures of Beginning 171
   3.0 The Doubling of Absolute Identity 184
   4.0 Conclusion 200

Chapter 6: From Freedom to Pantheism 203
   1.0 Introduction: An Unfamiliar Schelling 203
   2.0 Freedom and Flowers 205
   3.0 The Tripartite Tripartite Soul 216
   4.0 Revelation and Reconciliation 225
   5.0 Conclusion 235

Conclusion: The Poverty of Thought and the Madness of Living Well 237

Notes 245

Bibliography 279

Index 289

Preface

This is a book about F. W. J. Schelling. More specifically, it is a book about how Schelling takes up the metaphysical themes of Spinoza's *Ethics*. It is a book about Schelling as a metaphysician, a systematic philosopher, and ultimately as a reader. It is a book about a love affair that I contend occupied Schelling throughout the entirety of his philosophical journey. Schelling loved Spinoza, and this much is clear from his early writings on the possibility of a form of all philosophy to his last lectures on positive philosophy, mythology, and revelation. There are countless high-quality works on Spinoza and his legacy, and there is now a growing number of fascinating, high-quality studies on Schelling. This book seeks to begin bridging the gap between these two bodies of work in order to address the continuing role the notion of immanence plays in our philosophical present. The conversation between these two thinkers depends upon an unabashed interrogation of the Absolute. Due to their respective obsessions with the unconditioned, Schelling and Spinoza both force us to reconsider the viability of any metaphysics of transcendence. Further, Spinoza can teach us something about the nuance of Schelling's realist commitments, and Schelling can assist in pushing Spinoza beyond his own boundaries in order to better understand the metaphysics of existence monism, the necessary and reciprocal relation between realism and idealism, and the possible future of any metaphysics of immanence.

Narrating the love story of Schelling and Spinoza elucidates something of our contemporary impasse. We are faced not with the dramatic moment of nihilism, but with the banality of irrealism. Though nihilism and irrealism are not unrelated, as Jacobi contends, they are also not the same. Nihilism entails an ontological element, an epistemological element, and an ethical element. In addition to denying existence, the nihilist also denies truth and goodness. In nihilism there is nothing, nothing to know, and nothing to believe in. The place we find ourselves is one in which there is all too much to believe and no shared epistemic or ontological criteria according to which these beliefs can be evaluated. Unlike Davidson's characterization of Kuhn's scientists who are merely words instead of worlds apart, no dictionary can extricate us from this dilemma. In short, we live in worlds where belief reigns supreme and casts knowledge into the dumpster along with reality. Schelling's love for Spinoza was equally a love for reason's ability to tell us something about the world in which we find ourselves. Schelling was steadfast in rejecting faith as a profitable philosophical notion. Though for Schelling the Absolute is not exhaustively rational in the same way it is for Spinoza, the relation between human knowing and existence is not as obscure as we might assume. In the end, what reason tells us about reality is strange, counterintuitive, and even frightening. However, this fearful strangeness is one that we share with each other, with the natural world, and even with what Spinoza and Schelling call God. Thus, when faced with the choice of faith or fear, we must embrace fear if we are to know the world once again as a shared reality in which one can strive to live well with others. At least there is no comfort in fear, and we have run out of time for comfort.

When citing Schelling, I have made use of available translations. I have also provided references to the *Sämmtliche Werke* when possible in accordance with the traditional formatting with roman numerals indicting the division followed by volume number and page number. All references to Spinoza's *Ethics* follow the common convention with roman numeral to indicate the book, lowercase letters to indicate definitions ("d"), axioms ("a"), and propositions ("p") followed by the appropriate numerical reference. References to Kant's *Critique of Pure Reason* also follow the traditional formatting.

An exhaustive list of those who deserve to be acknowledged for making this book possible would surely exceed my word limit, so I must restrict myself to the following. I would like to thank Omri Boehm and James Dodd for their feedback on earlier versions of the project. I would especially like to thank Adrian Johnston for his assistance and generosity. Additionally, I owe a great debt to the anonymous readers at SUNY Press. I'd also like to thank all my friends who put up with my rants about Schelling and Spinoza late into the night made possible by the hospitality of kindness of Dien Huynh. Further, without the love and support of my family, none of this would have been possible. And finally, an indescribable amount of gratitude is due to Kelly Flannery and Leo McHairy who made my life feel full during the toughest times of working through this project.

This book is dedicated to my grandparents. They were with me as I began this long process but were all unable to see the completion of this work. Schelling maintains that there is a materiality to the immortal soul, and I hope that this book can be a small part of their legacy.

Introduction

A Crack in the Abyss

1.0. A Note in the Margins

The central hypothesis of this book is that Schelling's philosophical project can be fruitfully interpreted as what he referred to as "ideal-realism [*Ideal-Realismus*]"[1] in the 1800 *System of Transcendental Idealism*.[2] To make this case, I take Schelling's engagement with Spinoza as my guiding thread. In the formulation "ideal-realism" we find two familiar terms, but we find them in a unique conjunction. The familiar yet still enigmatic terms *idealism* and *realism* are immediately invoked by this conjunction, yet there is a silent third that makes the formulation possible. Schelling's deliberate use of the hyphen shows that he is referencing not mere idealism, nor mere realism. Instead, he points our attention toward the possibility of some unity of the two that is dependent upon both a binding and a separating. For the early Schelling, realism and idealism are the only two consistent philosophical perspectives.[3] However, this does not imply that each alone is a *complete* philosophical perspective. Consequently, realism and idealism need each other because neither alone can constitute a systematic philosophy.

If it is the case, as Hegel suggested, that "with Spinozism everything goes into the abyss but nothing emerges from it,"[4] then after Spinoza one must carve out a space through which philosophy itself can emerge from this abyss. Throughout the chapters that follow, I turn to Schelling in order to mark this space within the abyss. In some of his earliest publications, Schelling uses dogmatism as a synonym for realism, and in 1800 Schelling claims that "a consistent dogmatism is to be found only in Spinozism."[5] This valorization of Spinozism as the most consistent dogmatism echoes similar sentiments expressed by Kant, Jacobi, Fichte, and Hegel. However, whereas these thinkers generally saw Spinozism as a dead end, Schelling adds, "but as a real system Spinozism again can endure only as a *science of nature* [*Naturwissenschaft*], whose last outcome is once more the principle of transcendental philosophy."[6] Schelling here is articulating a version of Kant's claim that if we remain Spinozist, neither nature nor freedom can receive the philosophical treatment they deserve.[7] Spinozism is the highest form of dogmatism, and in this form it provides the philosophical ground for a science of nature.[8] The science of nature that emerges from Spinozism in turn points toward the necessity of reconsidering the place of the "principle of transcendental philosophy." So, in short, to ground the principle of transcendental philosophy in a science of nature one must begin with Spinozism but not end therein. Many years after the publication of the *System of Transcendental Idealism*, while lecturing on the history of philosophy Schelling claims that Spinozism is a vortex "around which everything moves, or rather the impoverishment of thought, from which thought has sought to emancipate itself by the succeeding systems without yet being able to do so."[9] Schelling is clear that one does not just move past Spinozist realism by embracing a Kantian inspired idealism. One must develop an immanent critique of Spinozism in order to find an exit therefrom. It is exactly this that Schelling performs as he traverses his own *Identitätssystem*, which I will refer to as the identity philosophy.[10] He begins this period of his writings with a valorization of Spinoza's monism yet ends it with a critique of Spinoza's dualism.[11] The nuanced differences we can find in the identity philosophy offer deep practical insight into Schelling's strategy for traversing Spinozism more generally.

Explicating Schelling's ideal-realism by way of his encounters with Spinoza is not an arbitrary decision. In fact, my motivation for this approach is located in Kant's final writings. Upon the disorganized and uncompleted pages that are now collected as the *Opus postumum*, Kant inscribed a quick note in his margin: "*System of Transcendental Idealism*, by Schelling" Kant scrawled upon the edge of one of the pages.[12] There is no direct evidence that Kant owned a copy of this particular work, so the exact reason for the explicit reference to Schelling's 1800 text is unclear.[13] Perhaps Kant is leaving a note to himself, marking down a brief reminder to acquire a book he had heard of but had yet to read. However, there is contextual evidence that the placement of Kant's note is not completely coincidental. Following this note in the margin, Kant writes in the main body of the manuscript that "we can know no object, either in us or as lying outside us, except insofar as we insert in ourselves the *actus* of cognition, according to certain laws."[14] He then continues "the spirit of man is Spinoza's God (so far as the formal elements of all sense-objects is concerned) and *transcendental idealism is realism in an absolute sense*."[15] When taken in conjunction with the above note in the margin, Kant here binds together Schelling, Spinoza, transcendental idealism, and realism.[16]

The passage of the *System of Transcendental Idealism* in which we find Schelling's usage of "ideal-realism" links Kant's above comments regarding transcendental idealism as realism in an absolute sense to the concerns of the young Schelling. Schelling writes,

> If I reflect merely upon the ideal activity, there arises for me idealism, or the claim that the boundary is posited solely by the self. If I reflect merely upon the real activity, there arises for me realism, or the claim that the boundary is independent of the self. If I reflect upon *the two together*, a third view arises from both, which may be termed ideal-realism [*Ideal-Realismus*], or what we have hitherto designated by the name of transcendental idealism.[17]

This passage is an effective lens through which we can understand Kant's claim's that transcendental idealism is a realism "in an absolute sense" as it frames Schelling's project of overcoming Spinozist monism while avoiding a one-sided subjectivist idealism. When combined with Kant's *Opus postumum*, Schelling's above cited reflection on idealism, realism, and ideal-realism establishes the following transitive relationship: "realism in an absolute sense" = transcendental idealism = ideal-realism. I take the liberty of translating "realism in an absolute sense" into the idea of "absolute realism." By absolute realism we are not to understand an overinflated realism that excludes what are generally thought to be the concerns of idealism. In the broadest sense, absolute realism is a metaphysical system within which the identity of identity and nonidentity (what both Schelling and Hegel call "the Absolute") is *real* and not merely ideal. Importantly, the "merely" here is not used pejoratively. Absolute realism is *not* an anti-idealism and this is precisely what allows it to be absolute.

Schelling's ideal-realism is not a mere metaphilosophical classification; it is buttressed by a unique metaphysical framework. Because, as Hegel notes, in Schelling's thinking "philosophy and system coincide,"[18] any comments on realism and idealism must equally apply to the real and the ideal as they appear therein. Taking this one step further, we can apply the coincidence of philosophy and system to the hyphen in "ideal-realism" as well. The metaphysical expression of this hyphenated unity ought to be read as a shorthand for what Schelling and Hegel articulate as the dynamic self-relation of identity and nonidentity. It is precisely this strange form of self-relation that Schelling will come to call "Absolute identity" as opposed to the simple identity of Spinoza's monism. One way of understanding this claim is that the hyphen is a graphic representation of the indifference point between idealism and realism that binds the two together while preserving the distinctiveness of each. In other words, the hyphen is the site of the absolute synthesis, of the *Wechseldurchdringung,* of realism and idealism. The emphasis upon the function played by the hyphen in this formulation is intended to bring into focus the excess generated by the differentiated incongruity of the real and the ideal. In other words, highlighting the hyphen seeks to show how the fracture internal to the Absolute is in fact an excess or abundance (insofar as the Absolute contains both what it is and what it is not) and not a lack.

Schelling's hyphenated ideal-realism calls into question any efficacy for the categories of immanence and transcendence that scaffold the debate between realism, antirealism, and idealism. The dualism between immanence and transcendence is itself made intelligible by strict demarcations of interiority and exteriority. Each in turn depends upon the construction of a monistic, self-enclosed ontological register to which all things are either internal (immanence) or to which some things are external (transcendence). The notion of a hyphenated unity signaled by Schelling's deliberate usage of the hyphen in "ideal-realism" necessarily pushes past any conceptualization of either realism or idealism that relies on or presupposes a monistic ontological register. Though Schelling's notion of identity in the identity philosophy begins in close affinity with Spinoza (the advocate of a monistic ontological register in its most radical form) Schelling comes to realize what Spinoza could not: *Identity is not identical,* and unity is never simple. Further, we will see that identity is not the same thing as monism or immanence. Instead, identity is absolute and therefore consists of both what it is and what it is not. If Spinoza's metaphysics can be seen as clean and orderly, then Schelling's must be understood as messy with blurred lines and shifting boundaries. The absolute identity of the identity philosophy is also a kind of fractured identity. Because the identity of the Absolute is a fractured identity, it entails a complex process of involution, differentiation, and augmentation. For this process to occur it is not enough that the ideal be real or the real be ideal. Instead, the two must be intertwined in a series of becomings. This becoming ideal of the real effected in conjunction with the living reality of the Idea can only be properly expressed by the hyphenated unity of ideal-realism, that is, a realism in an absolute sense.

2.0. Schelling and Spinoza

I'm interested in reconstructing a version of Schelling's philosophical project through the lens of his critique of Spinoza. This reconstruction is not motivated by a desire to show Spinoza as the wellspring from which all of Schelling's philosophy flows, a claim that is clearly false. One of the primary debates surrounding how we ought to read Schelling centers around questions of continuities and discontinuities in his work. Though on the surface Schelling's project seems to consist of distinct phases, some argue that there is a deeper continuity to the project rendering any discussion of Schellingean "phases" obsolete. Regardless of whether Schelling's philosophy is a single unified whole or a series of disparate parts, his fascination with Spinoza remains consistent. Schelling continuously returns to Spinoza as a resource, but we can trace significant differences in the lessons he draws from Spinoza. Allowing Schelling's own engagement with Spinoza to act as the guiding thread of this book brings to light both continuities and discontinuities within Schelling's philosophical development without hermeneutical privileging one interpretive strategy over the other. Additionally, my focus on Spinoza connects directly to my decision to emphasize the importance of realism throughout Schelling's project over the concept of naturalism. Much of the contemporary interest in Schelling comes from the conviction that his project can broaden our understanding of naturalism. Some commentators argue that Schelling's naturephilosophy can be seen as providing the underlying foundation for all of Schelling's work.[19] Though it is not false to emphasize the importance of the naturephilosophy—something Schelling himself does—I believe that the generalization of the naturephilosophy that follows from this approach universalizes something Schelling intended to be more localized.[20] Schelling argues in the introduction to the 1801 *Presentation of My System of Philosophy* (hereafter *Presentation*) that the identity philosophy endeavors to demonstrate that the early naturephilosophy was compatible with his transcendental philosophy, and not that transcendental philosophy was reducible to naturephilosophy. Though he attributes primacy to the idealism of the philosophy of nature in the essay "On the True Concept of Philosophy of Nature and the Correct Way of Solving its Problems" (hereafter "On the True Concept"), this does not imply that the philosophy of nature was a self-sufficient philosophical system.[21] In his attempt to demonstrate the continuity of his previous works Schelling turns to Spinoza in the *Presentation* not because he is a naturalist, but because his radical monism captured the most sublime form of realism. However, as we will see, this radical monism is precisely the reason Schelling will endeavor to leave Spinoza behind. Further, Schelling's critique of Spinoza's parallelism allows us to understand more precisely the complex relation between realism and idealism that Schelling articulates in and beyond the identity philosophy.

The philosophical influence of Spinoza on Schelling is not a settled matter. Vater describes Spinoza as "a lens or a filter for all of Schelling's appropriations of past thinkers."[22] Bernstein suggests that there is a "perpendicular relation that holds between the philosophies of Schelling and Spinoza."[23] Lawrence (who does explicitly acknowledge "Schelling's life-long fascination with Spinoza") suggests that "Schelling's Spinoza is a kind of honorary Greek."[24] Regardless of the imagery invoked to map the relation between Schelling and Spinoza, two things are immediately clear. On the one hand, it is not possible to reduce Schelling's work to a modified Spinozism and even less so to an unqualified, dogmatic one. Doing so overlooks Schelling's idealism. On the other hand, it is impossible to deny the profound and continued influence that Spinoza has within Schelling's vast body of work. Doing this would neglect Schelling's transformation of what he once called "the most sublime and perfect realism."[25] The influence of Spinoza on Schelling has not been ignored in the secondary literature.[26] Many works contain a few comments on Schelling and Spinoza, usually in a brief subsection dedicated to the pantheism controversy or in a discussion of the influence of Spinoza's account of intuitive knowledge on Schelling's notion of intellectual intuition.[27] This approach leads to the assumption that Schelling's relation to Spinoza was simple, static, and continuous.[28] For example, Richard depicts Schelling as a faithful Spinozist conceiving nature "in Spinozistic fashion,"[29] and Deleuze claims that "Schelling is a Spinozist when he develops a theory of the absolute, representing God by the symbol 'A³' which comprises the Real and the Ideal as its powers."[30] Alternatively, in his seminal lectures on Schelling's *Philosophical Investigations into the Essence of Human Freedom* (hereafter *Freedom* essay) Heidegger suggests that "if Schelling *fundamentally fought against* a system, it is Spinoza's system."[31] There is a consensus that Spinoza was of unique importance to Schelling, and there does seem to be some further consensus in recent Schelling scholarship that Schelling was either with or against Spinoza. For example, Wirth follows more in line with Richard's approach and uses Spinoza to connect Schelling to contemporary philosophy and Deleuze in particular.[32] Alternatively, Bowie shares Heidegger's assertion that it is Spinoza against whom Schelling consistently struggled.[33] Commentators such as Woodard and Nassar split the difference by outlining what Schelling borrows from Spinoza and what he leaves behind.[34] A more fine-grained analysis shows how Schelling labors both within and against the Spinozist system throughout his work—from his early essays all the way through to his final lectures on positive philosophy and the philosophy of revelation.

In the first two parts of this work, I will primarily be examining texts and lectures all composed in a short yet extremely productive period of Schelling's career. This period spans roughly from the 1795 *Philosophical Letters on Dogmatism and Criticism* (hereafter *Letters*) to the brief 1804 work *Philosophy and Religion*.[35] In this short span of time, Schelling composed works on this history of philosophy (most notable, the *Timaeus* commentary); he undertook explorations in transcendental philosophy (largely but not exclusively in the Fichtean tradition); he wrote and collected individual and collaborative experiments in nature-philosophy; and finally he undertook the geometric construction of a philosophical system grounded solely in the principle of identity. Focusing on this period may seem odd insofar as Schelling's most well-known engagement with Spinoza is in the 1809 *Freedom* essay. In fact, he calls this with marked excitement his "once and for all . . . definite opinion about Spinozism!"[36] However, understanding the role Spinoza plays in the earlier excursions of Schelling's career deepens our understanding of his critique of Spinoza in the 1809 publication.[37] The context provided by these earlier works allows us to expand our understanding of the relevance of both the problems of Spinozism and the importance of Schelling's philosophy in the present day. Unlike commentaries that argue for Schelling's relevance by demonstrating resemblances between Schelling and the philosophers that followed in his footsteps either intentionally or unintentionally, I believe that the relevance of Schelling can be demonstrated through his critique of Spinoza alone. But again, I am not interested is proposing Spinoza as the key to Schelling's complex philosophical project. Instead, I argue that the contemporary relevance of Schelling's philosophical project is in large part dependent upon the *success* of his critique of Spinoza. That is, the future of Schellingeanism relies on the surpassing of a certain type of Spinozism.

In the *Freedom* essay is also Schelling's most vivid description of the relation between realism and idealism. While reflecting upon his own philosophical development, Schelling transitions to his final and definite opinion of Spinozism. He writes of his earlier work that

> [a] mutual saturation [*Wechseldurchdringung*] of realism and idealism in each other was the declared intent of his efforts. Spinoza's basic concept [*Grundbegriff*], when infused by spirit (and, in one essential point, changed) by the principle of idealism, received a living basis in the higher forms of investigation of nature and the recognized unity of the dynamic with the emotional and the spiritual; out of this grew the philosophy of nature [*Naturphilosophie*], which as pure physics was indeed able to stand for itself, yet at any time in regard to the whole of philosophy was only considered as a part, namely the real part that would be capable of rising up into the genuine system of reason only through completion by the ideal part in which freedom rules.[38]

Schelling often signals to his readers that his works are reconciliatory in their intent, but the precise nature of these reconciliations are by no means immediately apparent. In the *Philosophy of Art*, Schelling also invokes the term *Wechseldurchdringung* in the following claim: "*Kunst demnach eine absolute Synthese oder Wechseldurchdringung der Freiheit und der Nothwendigkeit* [Therefore, art is an absolute synthesis or mutual saturation of freedom and necessity]."[39] What is interesting about this occurrence is the association of *Wechseldurchdringung* with an "absolute synthesis." Extending this association, we can view the search for a mutual saturation of realism and idealism as striving for an absolute synthesis of the two doctrines. In the above quotation from the *Freedom* essay Schelling explicitly links his earlier attempts construct an absolute synthesis of realism and idealism to the transitional role played by Spinoza in the quest for "higher forms" of the investigation of nature. Spinoza's articulation of thinking and being in a univocal ontological register intendeds to collapse realism and idealism by placing thinking and being on an equal ontological ground. However, this *Grundbegriff* (the idea that "all things are contained in God")[40] on its own was insufficient and needed an idealism through which it could become a living basis for a philosophy of both nature and of freedom. Spinozism itself is not a *philosophy* of nature because it is incapable of realizing nature's a priori status. This claim is obviously consistent with the one discussed above in the *System of Transcendental Idealism*. Thus, it must be emphasized that this discussion of Spinoza, realism, and idealism in the *Freedom* essay is the *conclusion* of Schelling's prior engagement with Spinoza and not a novelty. Schelling continues his discussion of Spinoza and pantheism by turning to idealism. He writes:

> [I]dealism itself, no matter how high it has taken us in this respect, and as certain as it is that we have it to thank for the first complete concept of formal freedom, is yet nothing less than a completed system for itself, and it leaves us no guidance in the doctrine of freedom as soon as we wish to enter into what is more exact and decisive.[41]

Here, Schelling once again articulates the codependency of realism and idealism: the philosophy of nature grows from Spinoza's realist articulation of the ontological unity of thinking and being, yet in order to prepare itself for what it must become if it is to become real, the principle of idealism must be introduced *into* realism and not just added onto a realist framework. In other words, the mutual saturation of realism and idealism is not the result of a simple addition of one thing to another.

Without setting aside this criticism of realism, Schelling simultaneously argues that idealism alone is an ineffective guide to the decisive and exact nature of freedom in its exemplary localization in the human. "Mere idealism," Schelling explains, "does not reach far enough, therefore, in order to show the specific difference [*Differenz*], that is, precisely what is the distinctiveness, of human freedom."[42] So, realism needs idealism to become the *philosophy* of nature, but idealism too is insufficient to articulate a doctrine of specifically human freedom. From this impasse, Schelling concludes that "idealism, if it does not have as its basis a living realism, becomes just as empty and abstract a system as that of Leibniz, Spinoza, or any other dogmatist."[43] Schelling then generalizes this claim, writing:

> The entire new European philosophy since its beginning (with Descartes) has the common defect that nature is not available for it and that it lacks a living ground. Spinoza's realism is thereby as abstract as the idealism of Leibniz. Idealism is the soul of philosophy; realism is the body; only both together can constitute a living whole. The latter can never provide the principle but must be the ground and medium in which the former makes itself real and takes on flesh and blood. If a philosophy is lacking this living foundation, which is commonly a sign that the ideal principle was originally only weakly at work within it, then it loses itself in those systems whose abstract concepts of aseity, modifications, and so forth, stand in sharpest contrast with the living force and richness of reality.[44]

This passage is a further example of how it is idealism that expands the naturalist framework such that it can move past previous misconceptions of both nature and freedom. Realism is the flesh and blood, idealism is the soul, and only together can they accomplish their shared aim. This shared aim is systematic understanding of human freedom, the place of freedom in nature, and the relation of these to the Absolute. These remarks from the *Freedom* essay represent both a conclusion and a transition for Schelling. They conclude Schelling's earlier analysis of the reciprocal needs of realism and idealism. Further, they signal a transition through the systems of abstract realism and idealism (represented most pointedly by Spinoza and Fichte), and toward an analysis of the progressive revelation of God in and through reality. Thus, despite its transitional position away from the identity philosophy and to the analysis of the progressive revelation of God in nature and history, the *Freedom* essay itself depends upon the notion of ideal-realism as the capstone of its edifice.

Schelling's general critique of Spinoza at first appears as somewhat simple. Spinozism forecloses a robust account of dynamic nature and specifically human freedom, but these are symptoms of a larger issue. Spinozist monism, Schelling maintains, is lifeless. "The error of his system" Schelling writes of Spinoza, "lies by no means in his placing of things *in God* but in the fact that they are *things*. . . . Hence the lifelessness of his system, the sterility of its form, the poverty of concepts and expressions . . . hence his mechanistic view of nature follows quite naturally as well."[45] The immanence of Spinoza's system is inherently flawed not because it is a pantheism but instead because it is a *lifeless* pantheism. By positing the thing as the fundamental unit of existence, Spinoza appears to be committed to the kind of somatism that renders becoming subordinate to being.[46] In the simplest possible terms, this means that insofar as Spinoza's God or nature—*deus sive natura*—privileges products over processes, it only is and can never become. In other words, substance can never become subject because it can never be alive. Briefly, we must understand that for Schelling, life is a complex interrelating of unity and differentiation. It is not, as he explicitly points out in the 1810 "Stuttgart Seminars," a hylozoism that "postulates a *primordial* life in matter."[47] Life is not something primordial or something given. It is instead something generated by a fundamental conflict omnipresent in nature, humanity, and the Absolute itself. In the *First Outline of a System of the Philosophy of Nature* (hereafter *First Outline*), Schelling writes of life (both vegetative and Life with a capital "L") that it is not "anything other than constant awakening of slumbering forces, a continual decombination of bound actants."[48] The *System of Transcendental Idealism* deepens our understanding of this awakening and decombining through the introduction of the notion of struggle. Schelling claims that "life must be thought of as engaged in a constant struggle against the course of nature, or in an endeavor to uphold identity against the latter."[49] Life in its "natural" form is an expression of the constant struggle between identity and dissolution, or between self-maintenance and self-laceration. This claim is echoed in the *Freedom* essay when Schelling writes "where there is no struggle, there is no life."[50] This struggle is further connected to the mechanism of contradiction. In the 1815 draft of the *Ages of the World*, Schelling claims that "all life must pass through the fire of contradiction. Contradiction is the power mechanism and what is innermost of life. . . . Were there only unity everything would sink into lifelessness."[51] Life, in short, is an expression of actual conflict between actually existing contraries. For this kind of conflict to be possible, there must be both unity and duality. As Schelling explains in *On the World Soul*, "[W]ithout opposing forces, no motion is possible. Real opposition is only thinkable, however, between *magnitudes of the same kind*. The original forces . . . would not be opposed to one another were they not originally *one and the same (positive)* force, which only acts *in opposite directions*."[52] The actuality of life is dependent upon real opposition, but the intelligibility of this opposition is made possible by a unity between contraries. The exclusion of unity (the unifying endeavor to "uphold identity") eliminates the possibility of real conflict. The exclusion of duality (the decombining of bound forms) denies the reality of actually existing contraries.[53]

With this general logic of the dynamics of life in mind, the next question we must ask is why Spinoza's monism is necessarily lifeless and what follows from this lifelessness. It may appear at first as if the lifelessness of Spinoza's pantheism is the result of a mereological error. How could the sum of finite, discrete parts ever come to equal a dynamic, and therefore living, whole? It is true that the reduction of the finite to the thing eliminates the possibility of any living or organic unity between parts and whole. However, concluding any discussion of Schelling's critique of Spinoza here yields only weak dividends. First, this mereological approach implies a bad reading of Spinoza (for whom the notion of finite, individual things was simply absurd), and second, this mereological problem alone is not sufficient for understanding why Schelling believes Spinozism excludes the possibility of *both* productive nature and transcendental freedom. A second candidate for the lifelessness of Spinoza's monism would be its necessitarian implications. If the goal is to allow for a philosophical account of both nature and freedom, then it seems sufficient to reject necessitarianism in favor of a richer modal metaphysics. However, were this the case, Schelling would not claim that "Spinozism is by no means in error because of the claim that there is such an unshakable necessity in God, but rather because it takes this necessity to be impersonal and inanimate."[54] It is not necessitarianism per se that one must reject. Instead, Schelling comes to the unorthodox conclusion that Spinozism is lifeless and inanimate because it is irreducibly dualistic. Because of the irreducible dualism between thinking and being, there can be no reality of conflict within Spinoza's monist metaphysic, and it follows from this that the minimal condition for a theory of life is absent from Spinoza's most sublime realism.

3.0. Realism and Antirealism in Jacobi and Contemporary Philosophy

Explicating Schelling's ideal-realism as an absolute realism allows us to call into question the dualism between realism and idealism that remains constitutive of contemporary philosophical discourse. The primary source of this erroneous dualism is the assumption that all idealism is necessarily antirealism. This belief that idealism is an antirealism is one with a long history as well a recent resurgence in a somewhat novel form. In general, when idealism is taken to be antirealist in its nature, then realism is viewed as an antidote to the errors of idealism. For the post-Kantian German Idealists, it is Jacobi who frames this dilemma most succinctly. Jacobi takes transcendental idealism to be nothing short of madness. Jacobi's challenge has by no means been overcome by the history of philosophy separating Jacobi and us. In fact, the fear of idealism's madness provides a punctual framing of a narrative that brings together the debate between realism and antirealism in analytic and continental philosophical circles. Further, these contemporary debates regarding realism and antirealism demonstrate that Jacobi's dramatic diagnosis of idealism is more timeless than his contemporaries might have hoped. I want to tell this story in a bit more detail, as it provides some context for the contemporary relevance of the reading of Schelling I propose herein.

Jacobi delivers his diagnosis of idealism as madness succinctly in his dialogue "David Hume on Faith or Realism and Idealism." The dialogue takes place between the characters "he" and "I." "He" makes the following claim with which "I" subsequently agrees:

> You forget *Wahnsinn*, "madness" or being "out of one's senses," a word, whose meaning strikes upon me quite forcefully at the moment. We say that a man is out of his senses when he takes his images to be sensations or actual things. And

thus we deny that he is rational, because his representations, which he takes to be things, lack *the thing*, or *the sensible truth*—because he *regards* something as actual which is not.[55]

The two interlocutors find common ground in the idea that the idealist flirts with madness when individual representations are granted sufficient reality onto themselves. Thinking of this kind risks the loss of the thing. Without the thing, without the sensible truth, without actual content, philosophy is indistinguishable from hallucination. In order to combat this madness generated by the fervor of philosophy's unbounded rational pursuit, Jacobi turns not to irrationalism (as is often assumed) but instead to realism. Against those who would dismiss Jacobi as an unsophisticated reactionary, we can see that he in fact offers a deep insight into the persistent problem of idealism. Recent continental philosophy (what I will describe below as "postcontinental" philosophy) is largely motivated by a rejection of the allegedly antirealist epistemological commitments of a wide range of views that rely on contextualism or coherentism. The postcontinentals represent a renewed interest in metaphysical and ontological realism. Another more contemporary way of framing Jacobi's fear has to do with the role of mind-dependence in the constitution of reality. Brock and Mares broadly define realism through the following two theses. "Realism about a particular domain is the conjunction of the following two theses," they write, "(i) there are facts or entities distinctive of that domain, and, (ii) their existence and nature is in some important sense objective and mind independent. Let us call the first thesis the 'existence thesis' and the second thesis the 'independence thesis.'"[56] The existence thesis plays an important role in recent forms of New Realism,[57] but of primary importance for Jacobi is the second of these two theses. Idealism, Jacobi claims, takes images and sensations not to be of things that are ultimately mind independent. Instead, the idealist attributes reality to these sensations and images themselves thereby erasing the need for any mind-independent foundation for their actuality. So, without the independence thesis, representations can have no traction on the world as it actually is. To embrace the existence thesis while rejecting the independence thesis strongly implies a two-world metaphysical picture in which there are existing but inaccessible things, on one side, and our subjective representations of these things, on the other. The challenge the independence thesis brings with it is the problem of access. If it is wrong to take one's own sensations and representations as objectively real on their own, how are we to bridge the gap between the subjective and the objective?

Christopher Norris argues that antirealism has become the norm in both analytic and continental philosophy. The general claim is that any philosophy that relies upon holist or coherentist theories of truth is susceptible to the charge of antirealism. Following the insights of thinkers such as Quine,[58] Wittgenstein,[59] Davidson,[60] and Rorty,[61] the doctrine of an immediate correspondence between the conceptual and the nonconceptual constitutive of previous empiricisms was no longer a viable epistemic option. As these twentieth-century criticisms of empiricism demonstrate, truth can no longer be grounded in an immediate correspondence between thought and world. Instead, the truth value of any claim must primarily be assessed in relation to the coherence of a conceptual scheme and not in relation to some extraconceptual, scheme-independent content. Norris frames the central shared claim of the antirealists as "the idea of scientific 'truth' or 'reality'" is "relative to—or constructed within—some culture-specific discourse, framework of enquiry, historical paradigm, conceptual scheme, or whatever."[62] Or, as Bhaskar frames the same point, "the postmodernist says basically that reality is a social construct. Reality is a construct of discourse, the text, the conversation, or, if you like, people or even power relations."[63] The inheritance of this generally contextualist and allegedly postmodernist framework led to the dogma that truth can only be articulated within a self-referential network of discursive claims and commitments. Again, this antirealism is of a specific sort. It does not directly deny the existence of reality internal to discourses, texts, language-games, conceptual schemes, etc. Instead, it pushes aside the independence thesis. Consequently, if there is nothing material about the material inference, then this kind of constructivism is nothing but a new form of fatally bloated idealism.

This transitions us to the resurgence of realism in recent continental philosophy. In an attempt to resist the antirealist trend he saw during the close of the twentieth century by putting forth a kind of scientific realism (in the critical realist tradition), Norris offers readings of Derrida's work, and the essay "White Mythology"[64] in particular. Norris's strategy is intriguing in large part because of the role Derrida plays in the common narrative of the development of postcontinental theory. I draw the term *postcontinental* from Maoilearca's 2007 *Post-*

Continental Philosophy: An Outline, (a work that, he observes, "may have been written too early").[65] Justifying his addition of the prefix *post* to the by no means homogenous discipline of continental philosophy, Maoilearca writes that the outline

> concerns a new relationship between the perception of Continental philosophy and immanence. It examines the shift in European thought over the last ten years through the work of four central figures, Deleuze, Henry, Badiou and Laruelle. Though they follow seemingly different methodologies and agendas, each insists upon the need for a return to the category of immanence if philosophy is to have any future at all. Rejecting both the phenomenological tradition of transcendence (of Consciousness, the Ego, Being, or Alterity), as well as the post-structuralist valorisation of Language, they instead take the immanent categories of biology (Deleuze), mathematics (Badiou), affectivity (Henry), and science (Laruelle) as focal points for a renewal of philosophy. Consequently, Continental philosophy is taken in a new direction that engages with naturalism with a refreshingly critical and non-reductive approach to the sciences of life, set theory, embodiment and knowledge. Taken together, these strategies amount to a rekindled faith in the possibility of philosophy as a worldly and materialist thinking.[66]

Maoilearca differentiates postcontinental philosophy from previous continental philosophy, on the one hand, through the shared rejection of transcendence, and, on the other hand, through the rejection of what Norris characterized as the restriction of philosophical attention to the analysis of closed, self-referential discursive systems. As previously noted, this restriction brought with it the rejection of the correspondence between the conceptual and the extraconceptual in favor of a self-referential conceptual/linguistic nexus of meanings. The postcontinental philosophers seek to move beyond both the correspondence relation between conceptual and extraconceptual as well as to combat the perceived unreality of coherentist philosophies of discourse. To do this, Maoilearca argues, they turn to the notion of immanence in order to re-embed conceptual schemes within the real in turn giving privilege to the immanence of the real over the transcendence of the ideal.

Maoilearca's analysis focuses on philosophical developments that appeared in a series of works and conversations from 1988 by the authors mentioned in the above quotation.[67] This realist thread identified "too early" by Maoilearca surged forward even more acutely in what came to be grouped under the heading "speculative realism." This general philosophical approach was articulated by Harman, Grant, Brassier, and Meillassoux during a 2007 workshop of the same name.[68] Now, and here we return to Derrida, the broad-strokes narrative of this renewed interest in realism among those working in the continental tradition of the early twenty-first century is that the generation of students following the work of Derrida and his contemporaries tired of the deconstruction of texts. *Of Grammatology*'s proclamation that "*there is nothing outside of the text* [there is no outside-text; *il n'y a pas de hors-texte*]"[69] was taken to be read quite literally. In poststructuralism, so the story goes, there is *only* the text, there is *only* the language-game, there is *only* the conceptual scheme, and this self-enclosed discursive construction is completely without relation to an independent and external reality. In his 1985 Carus Lectures, Putnam refers to this as the "extreme relativism" of French philosophy.[70] However, as works like Norris's and more recently Goldgaber's show, this reading of Derrida in particular lacks any nuance.[71] But whatever the actual attitude was, following the structuralism and poststructuralism of the twentieth century, continental philosophy once again became interested in speculative enterprises conditioned by and responsive to real, nonlinguistic constraints.[72] Though the initial four speculative realists have further parted ways theoretically, initially the project of speculative realism was to offer ontological solutions that could circumnavigate this issue of the unquestioned primacy of thinking over being.[73] Each speculative realist takes up Meillassoux's challenge to the epistemological problem he terms "correlationism." Meillassoux sees idealism in both Berkeley and Kant as artificially limiting the capacities of thought insofar as these kinds of subject-centered idealism disqualify any rational consideration of objectivity apart from its relation to subjectivity. So, much like in Norris's telling, this return to realism was a push back against a philosophical milieu dominated by the analysis of subjectively and socially determined conceptual structures of intelligibility. The moral of this story is that in attempting to understand how we subjectively come to know the world we have erased the very objective world we wish to know.

The debate between realism and antirealism is scaffolded by the largely uncontested philosophical dualism of immanence and transcendence. I already noted Maoilearca's isolation of immanence as a key shared commitment of postcontinental philosophy. Robinson also turns to immanence in order to draw a strict division between two traditions or "trajectories" within continental philosophy. He classifies this demarcation in terms of a "transcendent trajectory" and an "immanent trajectory." He claims that "the transcendent (Heideggerian, Derridean, and Levinasian) trajectory corresponds with a range of 'anti' or 'non-realist' positions while the immanent (Nietzschean and Deleuzian) trajectory corresponds more with various forms of nonessentialist 'realism.'"[74] According to Robinson, the trajectory of transcendence leads to antirealism while the trajectory of immanence leads to realism. This seems to imply that the problems generated by antirealism can be solved through a more rigorous articulation of philosophical immanence. Tritten goes so far as to suggest that "post-Kantian realisms must take the form of monism: post-Kantian realisms can only exist as philosophies of immanence."[75] However, if we take Jacobi seriously, we can see that the division Robinson draws here is not so easily maintained. For Jacobi, it is *transcendence* that renders realism possible. As we will see, this is because Jacobi argues that any philosophy of immanence generates only internal, self-referential structures that relate to nothing outside of these closed systems.

Overall, these diagnoses from Jacobi, Maoilearca, Norris, Robinson, and others bind tightly the debates over realism and antirealism to the philosophical categories of immanence and transcendence. Moreover, the various positions articulated in both continental and analytic philosophy display the lack of any simple articulation of the battle between philosophies of immanence and philosophies of transcendence. The independence thesis introduces a gap between thought and being. This gap in turn must be bridged somehow, yet the options for doing so (such as intuitive knowing, experiential extrapolation, scientific investigation, a priori formalization, etc.) carry with them their own internal inconsistencies. The transcendence implied by the independence thesis generates just as many, if not more, problems than it sought to solve. In light of this, one returns to immanence, and we're back at where we started. So, in short, despite the two centuries separating contemporary philosophy from the inception of German Idealism and the subsequent backlash articulated by Jacobi, the fear of a lost world persists. The madness of idealism and the hope that realism might act as an antidote to this madness remains.

4.0. Idealism beyond Antirealism

If idealism is madness, and realism is taken to be the antidote to this madness, then it makes sense that the return to realism has pushed idealism out of favor. However, though idealism is often taken to be a variant of antirealism, closer examination shows that this association is not exhaustively correct. Take the following example. Foster outlines three possible forms of idealism that center around one of the following three claims:

(1) Ultimate contingent reality is wholly mental.

(2) Ultimate contingent reality is wholly nonphysical.

(3) The physical world is the logical product of facts about human sense-experience.[76]

Looking at these characterizations of idealism allows us to better understand the conflicting demands of the realist. Of these three claims, only (2) can be taken as fully antirealist insofar as it wholly denies the reality of the physical. Against the assessment of someone like Ferraris,[77] it is difficult to find contemporary advocates for this radially antirealist form of idealism. Claim (1) can be taken as a realism regarding the mental in its absolute equation of the mental and the real. Though it may entail the threat of antirealism due to its emphasis on mindedness, this claim does not deny the *reality* of existence. Instead, it claims that what is ultimately real is "wholly mental." Nothing can transcend the mental to which reality is entirely immanent, and this category of the mental can be broadly defined. Claim (1) may be antirealist insofar as it seems to fail the test of the independence thesis, but it does not follow that it is fully antirealist. For example, forms of panpsychism might fulfill both this criterion as well as the more traditional realist claim that there exists a world independent of *human* mindedness. In fact, by these criteria, one could argue that Spinoza himself, who fits cleanly into Robinson's "realist trajectory" of continental philosophy, would in fact be an idealist.[78] Claim (3) evokes fears of antirealism discussed in the previous section. Here we can see a more clear-cut failure to embrace the independence thesis. The problem is that what is real is real only insofar as it is constructed by "human sense-experience" or some other conceptual schematization. It is the logical schematization of sensual givens that constitutes reality. However, (3) is not *necessarily* a full-blown antirealism because it does not deny the existence of a mind-independent physical reality given through sense experience. Instead, the idea is that these givens can only be properly called real when they are related to specifically human forms of mindedness. Claim (3) may be a form of correlationism, but it is not necessarily a full-blown antirealism. When taken in conjunction with the independence thesis, we can see that antirealist pictures of idealism arise if there is nothing that transcends the spheres of human practices and schemas. Here, as Jacobi feared, it is immanence that carries with it the threat of antirealism. So, again, all of this puts on display the ineffectiveness of categories such as transcendence and immanence to justly conceptualize the debate between realism, antirealism, and idealism.

The association of idealism and antirealism is present within the literature on transcendental idealism. Take just the opening lines of Allison's influential study of Kant's transcendental idealism.[79] He writes,

> In spite of some sympathy shown in recent years for a vaguely Kantian sort of idealism, or better, anti-realism, which argues for the dependence of our conception of reality on our concepts and/or linguistic practices, Kant's transcendental idealism proper, with its distinction between appearances and things in themselves, remains highly unpopular.[80]

Allison's focus on the centrality of what he calls the "discursively thesis" to Kant's idealism nicely connects back to the discussion in the previous section. Allison defines the discursivity thesis as "the view that human cognition (as discursive) requires both concepts and sensible intuitions."[81] It is the discursively thesis that makes claim (3) above both possible and problematic. As Davidson's and Rorty's critiques of empiricism make clear, there is no clean way of assembling concepts and intuitions into a rich account of discursive understanding. However, there are plenty of reasons to be attracted to the idea that linguistic and conceptual practices play a role in the determination of our experience of the world. In addition to dispelling the more complex errors and illusions generated by the assumptions of the transcendental realist,[82] our explanatory powers simply are expanded when we incorporate a more fine-grained understanding of the discursive practices that make our knowledge of the world possible. Interestingly, Allison's suggestion above is that what is attractive about Kant's idealism is precisely the fact that it is antirealist. Philosophers following Kant found great utility in the general thrust of the discursively thesis, but they did not desire to be burdened by the unfashionable two-world ontological implications of strong representationalism. We have already seen how unappealing the antirealist entailments of this sensible and modest position have become. In short, idealism has fallen out of favor, *but not because it is idealistic*. Instead, idealism has fallen out of favor because it is *assumed* to be antirealist.

What must be further developed is an idealism that is not constitutively an antirealism. Several commentators have seen in Schelling a rejection of the subject-centered tendencies of idealist philosophy. Bowie suggests that "the move beyond 'subject-philosophy' is therefore what constitutes the way into post-metaphysical thinking."[83] Snow suggests that Schelling begins to move beyond the idealist tradition because he "eventually brings into serious question the possibility of systematic philosophy itself," and as a result, "Schelling declares that we need a philosophy that can measure itself by life; a philosophy that would take its force from reality itself and would then also produce something actual and lasting."[84] More generally, Beiser claims that "the development of German idealism consists not in an increasing subjectivism but in the very opposite: a growing realism and naturalism."[85] So, it is broadly accepted that Schelling moves toward a kind of realism and away from a subject-centered, idealist enterprise. However, this does not entail that Schelling's move toward realism is a rejection of idealism as a whole.

In a coauthored historical survey of idealism Dunham, Grant, and Watson outline an understanding of idealism that begins to formulate an idealism robust enough to fend off the attacks of antirealism. This idealism assumes neither (1), (2), nor (3) of Foster's above outline of idealisms. Dunham et al. generally avoid the role of mind-dependence in definitions of idealism. The authors summarize the two most frequent rebuffs to idealism as follows "(a) that idealism is *anti-realist* in that it argues that reality, for idealism, is something essentially 'mind-dependent'; and (b) that idealism is *anti-naturalistic,* in so far as it disputes that matter is the basis of all existence."[86] Against this trend of defining idealism only in opposition to realism or naturalism, they advocate for an idealism that is inflationary instead of eliminative. "The idealist, rather than being an anti-realist, is in fact additionally a realist concerning elements more usually dismissed from reality," they claim.[87] That which is usually dismissed from reality by the realist is the Idea itself. Consequently, an idealism that is not an antirealism, must be a realism about the Idea:

> An idealism that is a realism concerning Ideas is not therefore committed *only* to the existence of Ideas, but rather to the claim that any adequate ontology must include *all* existence, including the existence of the Ideas and the becomings they cause. Idealism, that is, is not anti-realist, but realist precisely about the existence of Ideas.[88]

Understanding what the Idea *is* in its reality necessitates an examination of what an Idea *does*. This doing can be characterized as the becomings (both ontological and logical) that the Idea makes possible. Three things follow from this shift in perspective:

> [W]hen idealism is therefore presented as realism concerning the Idea, this means: *first,* that the Idea is causal in terms of organization; second, that this is an organization that is not formal or abstract in the separable sense, but rather concretely relates part to whole as the whole; and third, therefore that such an idealism is a *one-world* idealism that must, accordingly, take nature seriously.[89]

The role of the Idea does not generate a restrictive or reductive idealism, because the Idea is fundamentally irreducible to the mental (though it does play a functional role in the mental processes of ideation). Further, this role of the Idea is not subsumable within traditional realist accounts, because the Idea is not a thing. There is not and can be no ontology of the Idea. Instead, the Idea is better understood as a no-thing. As no-thing, the Idea is best understood as a *function* that is expressed as an asymptotic process of organization and disorganization, or of forming and deforming. Thus, the happenings of the Idea are not at all unlike Schelling's description of the happening of life described above.

5.0. The Plan

This book consists of three parts, and each is made up of two chapters. Chapter 1 presents Jacobi's criticism of idealism and emphasizes the importance of the realism he puts forth as a bulwark against transcendental idealism's implicit nihilism. In order to better frame the content of Jacobi's arguments against both Spinoza and the German Idealists, I juxtapose his critique of Spinoza to Kant's critique of Spinoza. When it comes to reading Spinoza, Kant and Jacobi share much more than one might think. Jacobi and Kant both take aim directly at Spinoza's fanatical use of the Principle of Sufficient Reason (hereafter "PSR"). There is a shared worry that the totalization that follows from Spinoza's strict adherence to the PSR eliminates either freedom, nature, or possibly both. Further, Kant and Jacobi argue that a certain form of practical reasoning is necessary to overcome Spinozism. For Jacobi, this practical rationality takes the form of the *salto mortale* and a faithful fall back into the real.

Chapter 2 turns to Schelling's 1795 *Letters*. It details how therein Schelling draws from the work of Spinoza in order to fill in what he viewed as the shortcomings of Kant's *Critique of Pure Reason*. Schelling fears that Kant's transcendental idealist epistemology lacks the proper ontological foundation that would allow it to fend off the repeated incursions of dogmatism. Schelling rightly sees that the future of the critical project depends upon establishing a broader context in which idealism and realism can be reconciled or synthesized absolutely. Initially, Schelling views realism as the missing piece of idealism and idealism as the missing piece of realism. Each must in turn supplement the other to construct a fuller philosophical understanding of the common root of both realism and idealism. In the *Letters*, Schelling thematizes what he calls *realisirenden Vernunft*—which Marti translates as "creative reason" but could be more literally translated as "realizing reason"—in an attempt to reconcile the two incomplete halves of realism and idealism.[90] This *realisirenden Vernunft* is largely posited as an amalgamation of intellectual intuition and practical reason as discussed by Kant. However, by the end of the *Letters* creative reason is not explicitly integrated within the Absolute. Consequently, it remains overly subjectivist because it constricts creative reasoning to a capacity of the individual subject.

Part II moves to the role of Spinoza in Schelling's identity philosophy. A close analysis of this brief yet vitally important period in Schelling's writings demonstrates the role his shifting views on Spinoza play in Schelling's struggle against the issues inherent in the supplemental relation of realism and idealism found in the *Letters*. I first look at the monism Schelling wishes to inherit from Spinoza and subsequently outline the dualism Schelling critiques and rejects. Chapter 3 details the role of Spinoza in Schelling's 1801 *Presentation* and the discussions on the problem of identity and differentiation in the 1804 "System of Philosophy in General and of the Philosophy of Nature in Particular," also known as the "Würzburg Lectures" (hereafter *System of Philosophy in General*). Though this latter piece was not published during Schelling's lifetime, it represents a development upon the *Presentation* and not just a repetition thereof. I argue that if Spinoza's monism is to yield insight into Schelling's concept of identity and remain faithful to Schelling's claim that the PSR is at the heart of Spinoza's system, then we must read Spinoza as an existence monist who maintains that only one thing exists. Schelling turns to Spinoza's monism to demonstrate the compatibility of realism and idealism in his earlier philosophical undertakings. However, we will see Schelling move from conceptualizing identity as something simple (as the identity of identity) to something complex (as the identity of identity and nonidentity).

Chapter 4 presents Schelling's criticism of Spinoza in the identity philosophy. Though Schelling found inspiration in Spinoza's monism, he takes aim at Spinoza's doctrine of attribute parallelism and the duality of thinking and being that follows therefrom. It is this dualism between thinking and being that eliminates the necessary conditions for animation and personality in Spinoza's system. Spinoza's inability to sustain the unity of this duality as well as the mutual saturation and dynamic interpenetration of real and ideal results in the lifelessness of his system. Chapter 4 returns to the themes of realism and idealism to frame more precisely Schelling's break from the monism of both Spinoza and Fichte in order to better effect the *Wechseldurchdringung* of realism and idealism signaled in the *Freedom* essay.

Schelling himself viewed the identity philosophy as a failed project precisely because he believed it to lapse back into Spinozism.[91]

Accordingly, Part III constructs a reading of the critique of Spinoza in the identity philosophy that does not fail to make a significant move beyond Spinozism. Chapter 5 presents an account of the emergence of ordered, finite particulars from the Absolute by focusing on the notions of mirroring and doubling. The goal is to fold the metaphilosophical analysis of realism and idealism within a larger metaphysical framework that is capable of reconciling idealism and realism into the hyphenated unity of an ideal-realism. To outline this, I turn to what I take to be the primary example of the bidirectional functioning of realism and idealism by isolating the entwining notions of doubling (on the side of the ideal), intussusception (on the side of the real), and the "mirroring" through which the two are brought into a higher unity. I argue that intussusception (a folding over and taking within of a thing into itself) can provide a speculative model for conceptualizing the emergence of quantitatively distinct finitude from the qualitatively identical infinite that is responsive to the strictures put forth by Kant in the Transcendental Dialectic and that occurs prior to the taking hold of dialectical negativity.

Chapter 6 provides a concrete example of Schelling theorization of the relation between real and ideal by way of an exegesis of the final part of Schelling's 1810 "Stuttgart Seminars." Therein, Schelling takes up the ideas of freedom and evil as discussed in the *Freedom* essay and attempts to reinsert them into the philosophical system of potencies and powers upon which he increasingly comes to rely. Schelling's goal in the final part of the "Stuttgart Seminars" is to describe the historical movement from specifically human freedom to pantheism, understood as the point at which a living God has become everything. I primarily focus on the compositional pluralism present in Schelling's discussion of the human spirit in order to further illustrate the complexity of Schelling's ideal-realism. This complexity allows us to better conceptualize the kind of fractured and differentiated notion of unity upon which Schelling's existence monism relies. In these seminars, we can see Schelling's continued attempt to formulate a kind of monism, but a monism that is distinctly non-Spinozistic because of its rejection of parallelism. There is something messy about Schelling's fractured monism, and from this mess arises life and freedom.

After returning to the relation between the reading of Schelling proposed herein and the contemporary debates over idealism, antirealism, and realism, I conclude with a discussion of madness, faith, reason, and what Schelling posits as the demands of systematic philosophy—namely the demands of (1) the spirit, (2) the heart, (3) "moral feeling," and (4) "most rigorous understanding." Though chapter 1 outlines the similarities between Jacobi's and Schelling's perspectives on the problems of idealism and the possibilities offered by realism, the function of faith and the role of knowledge drives an irremovable wedge between the two. For Schelling, faith is fundamentally unable to meet all four of these demands. Consequently, faith is an impediment to the construction of a systematic philosophy. However, this rejection of faith does not entail a cold rationalism. Instead, the philosopher must become an organ of the Absolute, that is, a local instantiation of the Absolute's dynamic self-determination, in order to delve into the turbulence of primordial Being. Only by unbounding the finitude of the philosopher in this way can one coordinate the madness of the Absolute to aspire, desire, act, and know.

PART I

Chapter 1

Reason, Realism, and Faith in Jacobi and Kant

1.0. Introduction: Rationality, Totality, and Antirealism

The association of idealism and antirealism is deeply entrenched in the history of philosophy. At times, the conflict between idealism and realism contracts into a punctuation mark. This is the case with the work of Jacobi. Through an analysis of the totalizing scope of reason articulated by Spinoza and Fichte, Jacobi came to believe that all philosophy was antirealist. Though Jacobi sought to limit the scope of reason, he did not seek to do so through a complete rejection of reason. Instead, Jacobi argues that reason must be grounded in something other than itself if it is to avoid madness. He turns to the notions of transcendence and externality in order to avoid the antirealist idealism he took to be characteristic of Kantian and post-Kantian philosophy. The antirealism of idealism, Jacobi argues, finds its roots in Spinozism and the steadfast commitment to the principle that from nothing only nothing can follow. Jacobi, Kant, and Schelling all acknowledge that this formulation, the PSR, is the fundamental principle of Spinoza's *Ethics*. The general idea is that Spinoza's use of the PSR represents in an exemplary fashion the most consistent application of this principle and thereby demonstrates the consequences of a particular understanding of reason's reach and capacities. This produces two contrary perspectives. Some contemporary authors, perhaps most notably Della Rocca, applaud Spinoza for his unwavering commitment to the PSR as the backbone of rationalism and naturalism. For others, Jacobi included, it is precisely this rationalism and naturalism that must be rejected if we are to occupy a world that is not merely intelligible (as an exhaustive series of natural causes and effects) but also meaningful (a world that allows for actions of rational agents that are not mechanistically predetermined). If the world is only intelligible but never meaningful, fatalism, atheism, necessitarianism, and, ultimately, nihilism follow. Each of these epithets captures a conflict that takes place between ontological totality, the scope of rationality, and the possibility of a causal order distinct from the purely mechanistic one that follows from the PSR.

Given the common wisdom that Jacobi was largely responsible for the renewed interest in Spinoza in German philosophy, it is not uncommon to begin with Jacobi in order to frame the philosophical endeavors undertaken by the young Schelling. However, more finely grained analysis shows that Spinozism was not revived by Jacobi. Though he does not reference Spinoza by name, Kant too was concerned with the scope of the PSR and the consequences of ontological monism in the *Critique of Pure Reason* published several years before Jacobi's incendiary study of Spinoza. The present chapter focuses on the problems generated by the conflict between theoretical reason and ontological monism and the ways these problems are diagnosed and addressed by both Kant's transcendental idealism and Jacobi's realism. It seeks to better understand what it means to critique Spinozism as well as what a response to these critiques looks like. Section 2 of this chapter counterposes the critique of Spinoza's monism found in Jacobi and Kant. Both attack Spinoza's fanatical employment of the PSR, and both in their own way do so in order to preserve some notion of freedom. We will see how Kant is able to systematize Jacobi's fears regarding the universal, constitutive application of the PSR to things in themselves. Section 3 turns to Jacobi's *salto mortale* and its relation to the problem of realism. Kant and Jacobi point to the fact that if one is to overcome Spinozism, this act cannot occur theoretically or through theoretical reason alone. In other words, there is no purely idealistic resolution to the problems generated by Spinozism and idealism.

2.0. The Difference between Jacobi's and Kant's Critiques of Spinoza

Schelling's relation to Jacobi was a complex one.[1] In an 1811 letter to Karl J. H. Windischlann, Schelling penned the following of Jacobi while awaiting a copy of his forthcoming work *On Divine Things and Their Revelation*:[2]

> This man (who knows how to deceive the world so well) has an amazing arrogance joined with such an absence of compassion and courage that it takes six years' observation to really appreciate. No doubt the world will once more be preached the reprobate doctrine of know-nothing, with pious condemnations of the godlessness of our pantheism and atheism. I hope he will be attacked on many fronts. The damage he has caused and continues to cause is unbelievable.[3]

Though Schelling at times approvingly cites the work of Jacobi, the vitriol expressed by Schelling in this private correspondence is palpable. He attacks not only Jacobi's personal temperament, but he also laments the continued impact Jacobi has had on the history of thought. It is undeniable that Jacobi's controversial works published between the years of 1785 and 1787 had a profound and complex influence on the trajectory of German Idealism as a whole and Schelling in particular. Jacobi, a novelist, literary critic, and self-proclaimed nonphilosopher, ignited what is retrospectively described as the *Pantheismusstreit* or the pantheism controversy. The heavily abridged version of this controversy centers around the 1785 publication of Jacobi's *Concerning the Doctrine of Spinoza in Letters to Herr Moses Mendelssohn*. In addition to presenting his interpretation of Spinozism, Jacobi took what proved to be the step too far by claiming that Lessing had confessed to him in private that he himself was a Spinozist. Given that Lessing died four years prior to the publication of Jacobi's incendiary text, there was no way to directly verify Jacobi's disclosure. Subsequently, Mendelssohn attempted to preserve the honor of his deceased friend by defending Lessing against Jacobi's charges.[4] More recent Schelling scholarship seems to accept that it was Jacobi who brought Spinoza back into the public view, but this account is not entirely correct. Beiser, for example, details the growing interest in Spinozism prior to Jacobi.[5] What further complicates this characterization of Spinoza as a dead dog is the idea recently put forth by Boehm that the Transcendental Dialectic of Kant's *Critique of Pure Reason* is also a critique of Spinozism and the authority of reason. This indicates that the pantheism controversy was not the sole source of the resurgence of interest in Spinoza. Oddly, perhaps, it is Spinoza that unites Kant and Jacobi. We can see that the critique of Spinoza acts as the wellspring of both "sides" of the pantheism controversy. So, in short, both the idealist and the anti-idealist must wrestle with the problems presented by Spinoza's *Ethics*.

In addition to its detailed historical reconstruction of the controversy, Beiser nicely presents the impact that the controversy had not just on the individuals directly involved (most tragically Mendelssohn who died shortly after rushing his final work to his publisher on a particularly unseasonable night)[6] but on philosophy more generally. "The pantheism controversy" Beiser explains, "completely changed the intellectual map of eighteenth-century Germany; and it continued to preoccupy thinkers well into the nineteenth century."[7] Despite this considerable impact, the *Streit* itself was for a time swept under the rug of the history of philosophy. As Beiser speculates,

> [T]he reason for this neglect primarily lies with the controversy itself, in that its deceptive appearance masks its underlying significance. It has an outer shell—the biographical issue of Lessing's Spinozism; an inner shell—the exegetical question of the proper interpretation of Spinoza; and a hidden core—the problem of the authority of reason.[8]

Insofar as the controversy played itself out as a high-profile squabble between Jacobi and Mendelssohn, it was for a time ignored as a particularly pronounced moment of eccentric grandstanding. However, the implicit content of the debate itself challenged not just the authority of reason but the possibility of philosophy itself.[9] Jacobi believed that Spinozism led to fatalism and atheism. He was further convinced that philosophy's self-understanding leads to nihilism largely due to an unfounded (and unacknowledged) faith in the capacities of reason. He thus felt compelled to stand outside of philosophy in order to preserve unmediated access to the world that the philosopher claims to know.

As we shall see, Jacobi's understanding of faith is far from traditional or self-evident. In fact, it can easily lead us to stray from Jacobi's own understanding of his nonphilosophy. "The antithesis to nihilism, in Jacobi's sense, is realism," Beiser explains, "where 'realism' is defined in a broad sense as the belief in the independent existence of all kinds of entities, whether these be material things, other minds, or God."[10] In order to elucidate the constellation of problems put forth by Jacobi we must keep in mind the fact that it was not just Spinozism that incurred the accusation of nihilism but transcendental philosophy as well. For Jacobi, Fichte's philosophy is but an "inverted Spinozism" and thus just as vulnerable to an inevitable nihilistic conclusion. In other words, Fichte and Spinoza represent two sides of a single problem.

2.1. On Jacobi's Critique of Spinoza

Though Jacobi demonstrates a comprehensive understanding of Spinoza's system, his polemical work on the latter's "doctrine" may not at first appear to be a genuine philosophical engagement with the work of Spinoza but instead a thinly veiled attack on his contemporaries and what Jacobi perceived as the decline of German piety. In contemporary terms, Jacobi was nothing short of a philosophical culture warrior fighting the remnant of Spinoza in order to reclaim the wayward soul of Germany. Janssens captures this nicely when he explains, "[W]ith unrivaled clarity, Jacobi argues, Spinoza's thought shows that the common root of the Enlightenment's philosophy and politics is a rebellious and revolutionary effort to liberate man from the authority of transcendence."[11] In the end, for Jacobi, Spinozism (and the Enlightenment more broadly) was more than a philosophy; it was a way of life and even a religion.[12] This is evident in the very opening pages of *Concerning the Doctrine of Spinoza* where Jacobi claims to have asked Elise Reimarus (a "close friend of Lessing's") "how much, or how little, Mendelssohn knew of Lessing's religious inclinations."[13] In this exchange Jacobi is not concerned with particular philosophical positions but instead the entire religious worldview of Lessing. He then writes the infamous lines that began the controversy: "I said that *Lessing had been a Spinozist*."[14] Again, according to Jacobi, Lessing did not merely have philosophical leanings toward Spinozism; Spinozism was his religion and for Jacobi this was tantamount not to having a religion at all.[15]

As Jacobi frames the issue, to argue against Spinozism is not just to argue with a philosophical position. Instead, to take on Spinozism is to take on an entire worldview. Now, Jacobi was, of course, not the first critic of Spinoza, and his own criticism is not without some historical precedent. In fact, Jacobi largely agrees with the highly influential criticism of Spinoza found in Bayle's *Historical and Critical Dictionary* of 1674. Though Bayle's critiques of Spinoza's monism are generally unconvincing insofar as they boil down to the way in which Spinoza's system stands contrary to our everyday experiences and commonsense understandings of the world, the passion with which he writes of Spinoza remains emblematic of the affective tenor Spinoza managed to evoke from philosophers for hundreds of years. In the extensive entry contained in his dictionary, Bayle takes aim at Spinoza's commitment to substance monism, and this resembles a reading of Spinoza that remains common. Of Spinoza, Bayle begins "he was a systematic atheist."[16] He then puts forth in broad strokes his understanding of Spinoza:

> He supposes that there is only one substance in nature, and that this unique substance is endowed with an infinity of attributes—thought and extension among others. In consequence of this, he asserts that all the bodies that exist in the universe are modifications of this substance in so far as it is extended, and that, for example, the souls of men are modifications of this same substance in so far as it thinks; so that God, the necessary and infinitely perfect being, is indeed the cause of all things that exist, but he does not differ from them. There is only one being, and only one nature; and this nature produces in itself by an immanent action all that we call creatures.[17]

Because all things are modifications of the one substance that exists, there is no difference between this one thing and its modifications. In other words, there is no separation between the God that creates and the things that are created. Spinoza's atheism is, for Bayle and others, a product of this identification of God and world that Bayle calls "the most monstrous hypothesis that could be imagined, the most absurd, and the most diametrically opposed to the most evident notions of our mind."[18] What is not explicitly identified in Bayle's critique is that the identification of God and world is a consequence of Spinoza's commitment to the principle that from nothing, nothing can come. What Jacobi and Kant both elucidate is that the horror of Spinoza's monism is born of his steadfast commitment to the PSR. By extension, we can note a kind of irony in Bayle's characterization of the "most monstrous hypothesis" being "diametrically opposed to the most evident notions of our mind." It would seem that the notion of causality, the basic idea that for every effect there must be a cause by which that effect is as it is and not otherwise, is itself perhaps the most fundamentally self-evident notion of mindedness. What a deeper understanding of Spinoza's philosophy shows is that the most monstrous and the most evident are one and the same.

Jacobi builds upon this legacy established by Bayle's dictionary. He claims that "Bayle did not misunderstand Spinoza's system so far as its conclusions are concerned; all that one can say is that his understanding did not go *far enough back,* that he failed to penetrate the system's foundations as intended by the author."[19] Spinoza was "a Jew by birth, and afterwards a deserter from Judaism, and lastly an atheist," as Bayle begins his entry.[20] Jacobi, as he says, agrees with this characterization of monism as atheism, but he deepens the argument for why this accusation holds true. What Jacobi adds to Bayle's critique is an explicit understanding of the consequences of Spinoza's use of the PSR. Jacobi writes,

> What distinguishes Spinoza's philosophy from all the other, what constitutes its soul, is that it maintains and applies with the strictest rigour the well known principle, *gigni de nihilo nihil, in nihilum nil potest reverti* [From nothing, nothing is generated; into nothing, nothing returns]. If Spinoza has denied a beginning to any action whatever, and has considered the system of final causes the greatest delirium of the human understanding, he has done so only as a consequence of that principle, not because of a geometry applied immediately to non-physical reality.[21]

Unlike Bayle, who focuses primarily on the phenomenologically unintuitive nature of Spinoza's claim that only one thing exists, Jacobi goes straight to the heart (or soul as he puts it) of Spinoza's philosophical system. The monstrous thought of Spinoza's monism does indeed produce a form of atheism that many find unacceptable. The charge is that by denying God an existence independent of creation, Spinoza effectively eliminates the Divine all together. For this reason, Schmitt claims in a letter while referring to Spinoza's 1656 excommunication that "the most audacious insult ever to be inflicted upon God and man, and which justifies all the synagogue's curses, lies in the '*sive*' of the formula: *Deus sive natura.*"[22] It is the inclusive conjunction of God *and* nature that inflicted the greatest harm on the history of both divine existence and human intellect. However, it must be emphasized that Spinoza was not a monist in order to be an atheist. Spinoza's *Ethics* must not be read in a negative sense, that is, as a work that takes the denial of God or the world as its central project. Instead, in the *Ethics*, Spinoza unfolds the consequences of an affirmative claim regarding the universal applicability of the PSR. In other words, Spinoza's militant commitment to rationalism is primary; the more well-known commitment to monism is derivative and therefore secondary. Put simply, monism is a consequence of the scope given to the PSR and not a presupposed condition for the applicability of the PSR.

Jacobi delves most extensively into the consequences of Spinoza's commitment to the PSR in a supplement to *Concerning the Doctrine of Spinoza* that was added in the second edition of 1789. There he states the principle in two ways, first "everything dependent depends on something," and second, "everything that is done must be done through something."[23] These two taken together produce the general formulation of this principle: "Everything conditional must have a condition."[24] Jacobi in fact praises Spinoza for embracing the consequences of this fact instead of violating his commitment to the PSR. "This immediate, eternal mode," Jacobi writes, "that he believed to be expressed by the relation of motion and rest in *natura naturata*, was for him the universal, eternal, *unalterable* form of individual things and of their unceasing change."[25] Jacobi then continues,

> If this *movement* did not have a beginning, *individual things* could not have begun either. Not only were these things eternal in origin, therefore; they also, according to reason, existed *simultaneously*, regardless of their succession: for in the *concept of reason* itself, there is no prior or posterior, but everything is necessary and simultaneous, and the one and only consequence permitted in thought is that of *dependence*.[26]

Passages such as this make clear the depth of Jacobi's understanding of Spinoza. For example, he clearly connects the necessity of substance as *totum analyticum* (a totality given at once without individuated parts) and the PSR when he writes of the lack of prior and posterior for reason. Moreover, he uses the same language of conditioned and condition that can be found in Kant's Transcendental Dialectic. Thus, as we will see in the following section, Jacobi and Kant focus on the same soul of Spinoza's philosophy; they think his most monstrous thought but refuse to stop there. Instead, both realize that to combat Spinoza in the name of freedom and nature it is the limit of reason and the scope of philosophy that must be brought into sharper focus.

Jacobi rejects the reach of the PSR and the universal scope of theoretical rationality in an attempt to reclaim the doctrine of final causes or, as he refers to it, "rational freedom."[27] To do this, Jacobi (1) insists that everything must come from something, and (2) claims that the something from which everything comes must exist externally to the series of its effects. This externality must be the reason for everything that is itself without need of a reason; it must be entirely transcendent to the causal and rational order that it makes possible. For Jacobi, this transcendent uncaused cause must be God. He explains in the 1789 supplement to *Concerning the Doctrine of Spinoza*, "the *God* of the *universe* cannot just be the architect of the universe; he is also the *Creator* whose *unconditional* power has made all things *also according to their substance*."[28] We will delve further into Jacobi's utilization of a transcendent and omnipotent creator below, but for now we must understand how the criticism of Spinoza is likewise a criticism of all philosophy.

"Our philosophical understanding does not reach beyond its own creation," Jacobi writes.[29] Philosophy can only come to know that which it creates for itself. Milbank, perhaps the most influential contemporary advocate of Jacobi's attack on Enlightenment rationality, comes close to grasping this general idea:

> If pure reason can accept as real only the identically repeated according to logically necessitated laws, then a fated chain without meaning must float above an abyss identified by the fundamental law of identity: a = a. This abyss is the underlying real, and yet it is nothing; the only "something" is the phenomenal fated flux, yet as only phenomenal this is also nothing.[30]

Milbank's claim here is that when reason relates only to itself, it is groundless. It consequently "floats above" this lack of ground, this void, and therefore relates to nothing other than itself. However, it is crucial that we grasp, contra Milbank, that the fundamental law of identity is not itself the "soul of Spinoza's philosophy" according to

Jacobi. As noted above in relation to Spinoza's monism, the law of identity *follows from* the PSR. At this point, however, what we must attend to à la Jacobi is that from the philosophical point of view (that is, from the view firmly committed to the PSR), philosophy can only come to understand the content that it provides to itself. As we shall see, the unbounded application of the PSR is self-defeating in the deepest of possible ways. In striving to know all things, reason turns all things into shadows, and philosophy perilously balances itself upon an abyss. To return to Jacobi's characterization of idealism as a kind of madness, we can see how when thought lacks "the thing," the thinker is indistinguishable from the madman.

One can locate a precise formulation of philosophy's epistemic shortcomings in Jacobi's *David Hume*. Therein Jacobi discusses what could be called "concept collapse." Though he will come to a radically different conclusion, McDowell voices a similar concern.[31] In reference to the mind's capacity for the conceptual determination of nonconceptual givens McDowell writes, "[W]e need to conceive this expansive spontaneity as subject to control from outside our thinking, on pain of representing the operations of spontaneity as a frictionless spinning in a void."[32] McDowell's worry here is that there must be some kind of constraint that exists external to spontaneous conception if concepts are to be at all grounded in a relation to objects. This brings us to the problem of finitude. In a discussion of the relationship between language and representation, Jacobi emphasizes the consequences of the finite nature of the speaking subject: "But these words begotten of finite seed are not like the words of *He Who Is*, and their life is not like the life of the spirit that calls being forth from nothingness," he explains.[33] As John 1:1 would have made clear to Jacobi, the word of God creates its referent simply in the act of being spoken. Alternatively, the finite word does not create its referent from itself. It is dependent upon the actual and external existence of the things it names (the actual existence of some external constraint to which it is responsive). Jacobi then presents the consequence of collapsing the relationship between finite word and thing: "The moment we lose track of this *infinite distinction,* we remove ourselves from the source of all truth: we forsake God, Nature, and Ourselves."[34] The collapse of this *infinite* difference between the finite and the infinite cuts one off from the source of truth itself. Collapsing any externality, be it on the side of either substance or intellect, eliminates the possibility of truth. We can see that Jacobi's epistemic problem is also an ontological problem. This erasure of extraconceptual content turns the philosopher into a sleepwalker, a mere navigator of bottomless dreams: "With the philosophical dream, we only slide deeper and deeper into it, until we finally rise to the perfection of a most wondrous somnambulism," Jacobi writes.[35] Not only is philosophy incapable of producing the objects to which its concepts are supposed to correspond. It is likewise unable to wake itself from its own dream state. Jacobi too fears a philosophy that is spinning frictionlessly in a void and thus, from Jacobi's perspective, the philosopher's dream quickly becomes a nightmare.

2.2. On Kant's Critique of Spinoza

Despite Jacobi's opposition to Kantian idealism, the two share much when it comes to their critiques of Spinoza. Though composed prior to Jacobi's writings, the Transcendental Dialectic of Kant's *Critique of Pure Reason* can be read as systematizing Jacobi's worries regarding the relation between rationality and totality. Therein, Kant provides an immanent critique of the history of philosophy leading up to his own distinction between appearances and things-in-themselves. In order to do this, he presents the antinomical (that is, the equally valid yet mutually exclusive) philosophical doctrines that result from the constitutive application of the PSR. Reason seeks totality according to Kant. In fact, without reference to some notion of totality, particularity remains insufficiently understood. However, because human intellect is fundamentally discursive, it is unable to properly capture the totality sought by reason and this in turn leads one into error and illusion. Yet, this does not necessarily mean that rationality excludes the possibility of all totality, and it is precisely here where Spinoza comes into play. Though not explicitly mentioned in the Antinomies of Pure Reason, when properly understood Spinoza's notion of totality represents the most significant challenge to the critical solution offered in the Transcendental Dialectic.

In order to demarcate between the proper and improper uses of reason, Kant formally systematizes the inner workings of reason. He introduces the "logical employment" of reason in the following:

> Reason, in its logical employment, seeks to discover the universal condition of its judgment (the conclusion), and the syllogism is itself nothing but a judgment made by means

of the subsumption of its condition under a universal rule (the major premiss). Now since this rule is itself subject to the same requirement of reason, and the condition of the condition must therefore be sought (by means of a prosyllogism) whenever practicable, obviously the principle peculiar to reason in general, in its logical employment, is: to find for the conditioned knowledge obtained through the understanding the unconditioned by which its unity is brought to completion.[36]

Here, the search for unity and completion connects rationality to the construction of some kind of totality. When applied to itself, reason continues to seek the unconditioned by virtue of which each and every conditioned is brought into a complete unity. Kant continues this characterization as follows, "but this logical maxim" Kant comments regarding the previous quotation,

can only become a principle of *pure reason* through our assuming that if the conditioned is given, the whole series of conditions, subordinated to one another—a series which is therefore itself unconditioned—is likewise given, that is, is contained in the object and its connection.[37]

What this shows us is that reason is insatiable for Kant. For any given condition another must be sought and so on forever. Yet, there is a careful distinction that must be drawn between these two principles of reason. In the first quotation, Kant is discussing a task given to the reasoner. In light of any given condition, one must seek to find the unconditioned by which the given conditioned is made possible as thus and so. In the second quotation, Kant is making a related but significantly distinct claim. Therein, he writes of the *assumption* that for any given condition the "whole series of conditions" (the "unconditioned") is likewise given *in the same way* that the conditioned is given. Thus, the first quotation is subjective in its scope (insofar as it describes a task given to the reasoner). In the literature on the doctrine of transcendental illusion this subjective formulation of the principle of reason is referred to as "P_1." Alternatively, the second quotation is making an objective claim: *if* the conditioned is given, *then* so too is the unconditioned by which the givenness of any particular conditioned is possible. This objective formulation of the principle of reason is nominated "P_2."[38]

Both above principles of reason are formulations of the PSR. Reason, if it is to produce a complete and systematic understanding of the world, demands the set of conditions by which any particular conditioned is render possible. Grier formulates this point as follows:

> Although P_2 appears to be an entirely different principle from P_1, Kant's view seems to be that P_1 and P_2 express the very same demand of reason, viewed in different ways. Put most simply, P_2 just is P_1 when it is conceived by reason in abstraction from the conditions of the understanding.[39]

A large part of Kant's insight into the machinations of reason is that reason gives to itself a task it cannot accomplish. Kant argues that it is false to assume that the PSR presents the finite mind with an attainable goal. In this sense the PSR in its objective formulation represents a necessary impossibility. If an object is given to the senses, this does *not* mean that the entire series of conditions for that object is also given objectively. For example, space and time are the necessary forms of intuition that make the experience of objects possible. They are particular conditions for any conditioned object, but one must not then posit space and time as *objective* conditions of objects in themselves. This would be to move from transcendental idealism to transcendental realism,[40] a position the philosopher must avoid, for, "[W]ere we to yield to the illusion of transcendental realism, neither nature nor freedom would remain."[41] So, what is at stake for Kant is in fact twofold: in order to allow for *both* freedom and nature, we must curtail the necessary yet unattainable ambitions of reason.

Building upon Kant's analysis of the errors and illusions that result from the conflation of the subjective and objective formulations of the principle of reason, Boehm makes the case that the problems Spinozism presents were not the concern of Jacobi alone, or more specifically that it is not the case that Spinoza was a "dead dog" in Germany prior to Jacobi's controversial 1785 book. Against the common wisdom that the Leibniz-Clark debate frames the philosophical dispute presented in the Antinomies of Pure Reason, Boehm shows how the antithesis positions map more precisely onto Spinoza's substance monist metaphysics.[42] In order to demonstrate this, Boehm details the difference between a *totum syntheticum* (a totality generated by an infinite, successive series of parts that is then taken as a whole) and a *totum analyticum* (a totality that is absolute in itself and consequently forecloses the intelligibility of a successive series) in order to show the resiliency of Spinozism to the Kantian critique of rationalist cosmology. In short, though the notion of a *totum syntheticum* may generate an antinomy, this is not the notion of totality Spinoza outlines in the *Ethics*. Consequently, if Kant's arguments against transcendental realism are to succeed, they must do so elsewhere—namely, in the realm of the practical and not the theoretical.

To understand the importance of this distinction between two distinct understandings of totality we should briefly turn to Boehm's analysis of Spinoza and the First and Third Antinomies. These Antinomies are particularly relevant to our previous discussion of Jacobi as well as subsequent discussions of emergence insofar as they deal with (1) the size and age of the world (and thus the possibility of externality), (2) the problem of the creation of the world (and novelty), and (3) the possibility of distinct causal orders (one of freedom and the other of necessity).[43] Kant's hope is that any form of transcendental realism will fall prey to one side of each antinomy. The strongest possible form of transcendental realism would be Spinozism, the system that most radically traces the consequences of the PSR in its objective form. "By Kant's understanding of the term" Boehm writes, "Spinoza is the dogmatic metaphysician par excellence."[44] In the end, if Kant cannot dismantle Spinozism, then the critical project achieves far less than it is understood to. Minimally, it has not demonstrated the possibility of limiting knowledge in order to make room for faith or freedom.

The argument of the First Antinomy regarding the size and age of the world can only generate an antinomy between the thesis and antithesis if we assume that the notion of totality under consideration is the *totum syntheticum*. That is, the Antinomy is only generated if by totality we designate the existence of a whole that is constituted by parts that are given prior to the existence of the whole. Because this is not the notion of totality at play in the *Ethics*, the Spinozist can in fact maintain that Kant's argument would generate an antinomy, but that the world is still infinite in space and time insofar as its totality is given analytically. "The fact that the world is experienced as discrete is besides the point," Boehm explains in reference to Spinoza.[45]

> The appropriate order of metaphysical reasoning is directed by the intellect, not by the senses. . . . According to the intellect, the unconditioned whole is metaphysically prior to its conditioned "parts." Therefore, it must also be methodologically and epistemologically prior; therefore, a consistent notion of an infinite *totum analyticum* remains justified and, therefore, the world may be infinite and complete.[46]

The argument of the First Antinomy depends upon the idea that an infinite sequence can never be brought to completion. This argument is in turn grounded in the assumption that the only possible notion of totality is one of sequential parts or consecutive moments. Our experience of the world as seemingly discrete parts and the sequential unfolding of events in time does not matter for Spinoza. It is the insight of the intellect as guided by the PSR that matters for Spinoza and not the evidence presented by "ordinary" experience. Thus, the apparent absurdity of Spinoza's existence monism reveals itself to be rationally necessary. The world is infinite in space and time because the only logically consistent notion of the world as a totality is the world as *totum analyticum* regardless of the phenomenologically counterintuitive nature of this concept.

Let us now turn to the Third Antinomy. Through his analysis of the first *Critique*'s Antinomies, Boehm argues against Franks's suggestion that Spinozism and transcendental idealism are equally valid solutions to the Third Antinomy:[47]

> Transcendental idealism and Spinozism cannot be concurrent resolutions to the Antinomy because the Spinozist position is transcendentally real. If Spinozism constitutes a possible solution, there is no Antinomy at all, for transcendental realism does not conflict with itself. Moreover, we have seen that this (alleged) Spinozist challenge to the third Antinomy concerns the first Antinomy just the same. Unlike the third Antinomy, the first is supposed to provide a proof of transcendental idealism. Therefore, if Spinoza's cosmological *totum analyticum* is granted, transcendental idealism loses its force.[48]

We can see that just like the First Antinomy, the Third repeatedly evokes the notion of a series of causes and effects given precisely as a series or as a *totum syntheticum*. However, as I have noted several times, for Spinoza, things are not parts given sequentially that subsequently constitute a whole. This is a kind of totality that remains untouched by the criticisms contained in either half of the antinomy. It is therefore not the case that transcendental idealism and Spinozism are equally valid solutions to the Third Antinomy, but instead that the Third Antinomy, like the First, fails to mount a substantive challenge to Spinozism at all. If it cannot be demonstrated that transcendental realism is untenable, then we have no real evidence for the superiority of transcendental idealism over transcendental realism. If this were the case, the *Critique* would fail entirely and "neither nature nor freedom would remain."

"The Spinozist challenge to Kant's Antinomies, and thus Spinoza's challenge to the critique of reason in general" Boehm writes, "stands and falls with the notion of complete infinity."[49] He continues,

> [G]iven the fact that the Antinomies fail if the *causa sui* is granted—Thought and Being collapse—the ontological argument should be studied as the key to the Kantian attack on—and to the rationalist defense of—the possibility of dogmatic metaphysical thought.[50]

So, being able to maintain a separation between thinking and being, conceivability and causation, concept and object, and ultimately idealism and realism is central to moving past "dogmatic metaphysical thought." I want to emphasize Boehm's strategy for defending Kant's Critical philosophy, namely that it "depends on the relation between practical and theoretical rationality."[51] As a consequence,

> Kantians would have to insist that the only way to justify our theoretical use of the PSR is by a *normative* decree; specifically, that we strive to explain the world only because of the conviction that the way the world "is" is not the way it ought to be.[52]

In short, we shoulder the burden of reason's impossible demand due to our commitment to self-determination and the possibility of free intervention upon the way things are. Otherwise put, we seek to understand the world as it is in order to change it in accordance with how it ought to be. Boehm concludes that "it is not only that theoretical reason cannot override the practical; in fact, it is grounded in it."[53] Thus, Spinozism is a (theoretically) legitimate philosophical alternative to transcendental idealism, yet one must understand in full the consequences of Spinoza's commitment to the unlimited scope of reason's reach. Spinozism is the rival that remains even after the supposed destruction of dogmatic and precritical transcendental realisms.

Both Jacobi and Kant agree that the PSR ought to be understood as the core of Spinoza's *Ethics*. Further, as we will see in the subsequent sections of this chapter, both believe that theoretical philosophy alone is not sufficient to overcome Spinozism. However, we must also take care to differentiate between the conclusions of each. Briefly returning to First and Third Antinomies of the *Critique of Pure Reason* sharpens the difference between Spinoza, Jacobi, and Kant. Jacobi sides firmly with the Thesis position of the First Antinomy, believing that there is a beginning of the world in time and that the world is limited in space. God, the architect and creator of the world, precedes the world in time and limits it in space insofar as he is necessarily prior to and distinct from his creation. Spinoza, on the contrary, sides with the Antithesis maintaining that the world has no beginning and is infinite in both space and time. As for the Third Antinomy, Jacobi again sides with the Thesis argument's claim that "causality in accordance with the laws of nature is not the only causality from which the appearances of the world can be derived. To explain these appearances, it is necessary to assume that there is also another causality, that of freedom."[54] For Jacobi, this causality separate from the laws of nature is that of God as the first and free cause of himself and the world. Spinoza once again finds himself squarely on the side of the Antithesis, maintaining that "everything in the world takes place solely in accordance with the laws of nature."[55] Again, following Boehm, the Spinozist nature of the Antithesis arguments is not accidental but is instead essential to the structure of the Transcendental Dialectic and the *Critique* as a whole.

Insofar as they remain unchanged in the B edition, it is improbable that Jacobi himself is the target of the Thesis arguments. Despite this, Kant was acutely aware of the general *Zeitgeist* the Thesis arguments entail. As he explains,

> A certain *practical interest* in which every well-disposed man, if he has understanding of what truly concerns him, heartily shares. That the world has a beginning, that my thinking self

> is of simple and therefore indestructible nature, that it is free in its voluntary actions and raised above the compulsion of nature, and finally that all order in things constituting the world is due to a primordial being, from which everything derives its unity and purposive connection—these are so many foundation stones of morals and religion. The antithesis robs us of all these supports, or at least appears to do so.[56]

Kant knew full well the consequences of the Spinozist threat to the "foundation stones of morals and religion." There is thus a sense in which he himself does not stand far from Jacobi. Yet, the difference between the two is massive: whereas Jacobi is content with placing himself on the side of the Thesis, firmly planting himself upon the sacred foundation stones, Kant seeks to let the Antinomies stand as antinomies. So, not only is Jacobi a critic of Spinoza, but if we take Kant's formulation of the Antinomies as a rubric, he is the absolute opposite of Spinoza. Further, if we understand subsequent German Idealists (particularly Schelling and Hegel) as working through Kant's antinomies and against his doctrine of the thing-in-itself, we can see that some kind of synthetic reconciliation of Jacobi and Spinoza acts as an immanent engine for their philosophical development.

3.0. Jacobi's Realism

To understand fully the positive intent behind Jacobi's criticism of philosophy we must turn to his ontological realism. "Without God, *nothing* becomes as real and actual as actuality itself. This is the irrational conclusion which reason must reach. By contrast, only the transgression of reason by faith establishes commonsense reason which requires the priority of the actual," Milbank writes in defense of Jacobi.[57] Milbank's formulation here is quite helpful. Rationality without externality leads to the irrational conclusion that nothing itself is real and actual. Only through the interruption of reason by faith can one arrive at the proper "commonsense" conclusion that the actual is prior to rational understanding. Faith saves reason from itself and in the process rescues the actuality of the world. Milbank calls this brand of realism "fideistic realism."[58] One can only give thought real content by restricting the

PSR and the authority of reason and turn instead to "irrational" or "extrarational" faith.

Before delving deeper into Jacobi's realism let us first look briefly at the errors generated by reading Jacobi as committed most centrally to irrationalism, his "reprobate doctrine of know-nothing," as Schelling put it. Because Jacobi targeted the reach of reason while praising his own "non-knowledge" it seems plausible to assume that curtailing reason as such would satisfy Jacobi's concerns. Yet, although Jacobi continuously appeals to the necessary existence of something extrarational that cannot be "known" in any properly philosophical sense, he was not committed to the outright dismissal of reason. "'Irrationalism' often connotes a tendency towards or advocacy of arbitrariness in one's beliefs or decisions," Crowe explains, "the thought is that an irrationalist is someone who simply plumps for a particular belief or course of action without considering reasons for or against it."[59] If we dismiss Jacobi as an irrationalist, we miss the deeper insight of his work. For Jacobi, one ought not reject rational consideration outright as implicitly nihilistic. Instead, Crowe suggests that "rationality must be 'animated,' as it were, by a variety of extra-rational considerations."[60] These "extra-rational considerations" are in large part what ground us as living beings within the world: "Reason . . . is merely a refinement of our organic powers of sensation or perception," Crowe explains.[61] More specifically, it is the immediate and noninferential experience of ourselves as living beings in the world that acts as the ground for our reason. In other words, reason is not itself a transcendent faculty; instead, our sapient capacities are modifications of our sentience. Consequently, Crowe suggests that Jacobi is critical of "a paradigm of rationality on which 'reason' just means deductive or 'analytic' patterns of inference" while proposing "a more naturalistic theory of rationality that situates it more firmly in human psychology."[62] If this is indeed the case, it makes more sense that Jacobi would find a seemingly strange companion in Hume despite the latter's explicit atheism. Hume too was not content with the rationalist doctrine of necessary connection insofar as any evidence of necessary connection is always absent from experience. More broadly, Hume and Jacobi agree that philosophy becomes unhinged speculation when it loses its grounding in experience. For Jacobi, "Our natural cognition can never rise above the result of the relations of finite to finite, relations that flow into one another, back and forth without end."[63] Insofar as our reason is natural, it is by nature limited to know only the relations between finite things. Therefore, reason alone cannot bridge the infinite difference between the finite and the infinite that grounds the possibility of being, meaning, and truth without subsequently collapsing this distance and erasing the being it seeks to know.

To further understand why Jacobi would appeal to realism in order to combat nihilism let us turn to Jacobi's 1787 work *David Hume on Faith or Idealism and Realism*. Though the letter to Fichte in which Jacobi deploys the full accusation of nihilism was not written until more than a decade later, this earlier work on Hume lays the ground for Jacobi's vision of the relationship between faith and knowledge that he believes is necessary to combat the madness of idealism. Jacobi's work on Hume attempts to clarify his appeal to the idea of faith in his work on Spinoza. Contrary to Kant, who claimed to limit knowledge in order to make room for faith, Jacobi will attempt to ground all knowledge through his self-noted idiosyncratic notion of faith. "The unusual use that I made of the word 'faith' in the *Letters concerning Spinoza* refers to a need that is not mine, but a philosophy's that claims that rational knowledge does not deal just in relations, but extends to the *very existence* of things and their properties," Jacobi writes in the work's prefatory note.[64] He continues, "[A]ccording to this philosophy there is a twofold knowledge of existence, one *certain* and the other *uncertain*. This latter, [as] I said [in the *Letters concerning Spinoza*], should be called faith."[65] Philosophy "knows" existence in two ways, one of which it is certain and one through which it ought to acknowledge its own constitutive uncertainty. By calling attention to this distinction, Jacobi is not claiming that philosophy has excluded faith but instead that philosophy needs to incorporate some operation of faith if it is to make claims about anything other than the relational appearances of things. Put anachronistically, without the ground provided through faith, philosophy is empty coherentism, a web of coherent inferences that nevertheless has no real material basis. Thus, if rationalist philosophy is to understand not just how things exist in relation to other things but what these things actually are, rational knowing alone cannot disclose this ontological truth. To again quote Milbank, from the perspective of philosophy without faith, "what we truly know are only appearances—so, in effect, once more: nothing."[66]

The obvious question that now remains is how faith can serve as a vehicle to ground certainty in existence.

In contrast to faithless philosophy susceptible to madness, Jacobi explains, "As a realist I am forced to say that all knowledge derives exclusively from faith, for *things* must be *given* before I am in a position to enquire about relations."[67] *As a realist!* Jacobi claims of himself. The bulk of Jacobi's criticism can be said to be realist insofar as it extensively concerns the problem of the (experiential) given as independent of (rational) thought. Inferential knowledge of the relations between things can never by itself produce certainty in the givenness of those things, in part because a thing is distinct from the thought of that thing. As noted above, there must be an *infinite* difference between a thing and the thought of it. On the one hand, we have the problem of philosophy's ontological legitimacy, that is, its ability to say something about some *thing*. On the other hand, we have the problem of philosophy's systematic aspirations, its ability to say something about *everything*. Once again, we see that philosophy leaves itself without the resources needed to atone for its original sin. Pure reason renders the notion of the thing-in-itself necessary while being incapable of replacing veritable givenness and certainty. The finite intellect is unable to bridge the gap between thought and thing. Alternatively, faith is supposed to be noninferential and immediate. Consequently, faith must provide undistorted access to the givenness of the things that ground thoughts. Or, as Bruno puts it, "Jacobi's conception of faith thus supports a realism for which 'object' signifies transcendental reality."[68] Furthermore, faith as nonpredicative certainty does not collapse the infinite chasm between thought and thing; it allows this chasm to remain infinite while simultaneously acknowledging the necessity of an unknowable core that necessarily grounds all knowledge.

3.1. Life and the Heap of Being

In order to offer an antidote to the madness that follows from idealism, Jacobi turns to the notion of life. In Jacobi's discussion of the understanding of causality found among "ancient peoples, or the uncivilized tribes of today," he claims that "for them every cause is a living, self-maintaining, freely acting, personal power of this kind; and every effect is an *act*."[69] From this we are to conclude that were we merely rational beings, or beings characterized first and foremost by our ability to rationalize, we would never have come to intellectually map the coordination of causes and effects, a practice that lies at the very core of explicability. According to Jacobi, these concepts of cause and effect, "certainly would never have entered the language of beings who were *only capable of intuition and judgment*."[70] Only insofar as we are living beings capable of action can we come to utilize the concepts of cause and effect. He then continues, "[W]ithout the living experience of such a power in us, a power of which we are continuously conscious, which we use in so many arbitrary ways, and which we can even let go of, without distinguishing it—without this basic idea we should not have the slightest idea of cause and effect."[71] This thought lends further credence to Crowe's reading of Jacobi as offering a form of naturalized rationality that limits the reach of reason by grounding it in the life of finite beings. "'Multiplicity' and 'relation' are *living concepts* that presuppose a living being capable of actively assimilating the manifold into its unity," Jacobi explains.[72] So, both multiplicity (that thing Spinoza excludes) and relation (the only thing that philosophy can think) presuppose a "living being" that can provide unity, consistency, and ground to these central concepts.

Moreover, this life is not something that can be understood representationally. "Certainly we have the most intimate consciousness of what we call our 'life,'" Jacobi claims,

> [b]ut who can grasp it in a representation? . . . And our soul is nothing else but a certain determinate form of life. I know of nothing more perverse than to make life into a property of things, when things are on the contrary only properties of life, only different expressions of it. *For the parts in a manifold can penetrate one another and become one only in a living being.*[73]

If this is in fact the case, we can once again see why any philosophy that maintains we only have access to the world mediated through representations is devoid of the real explanatory reach of which it takes itself to be capable. Life "is the instrument of almighty love. . . . Only by this means can the blessing of life, the blessing of an existence that externalizes itself and thereby enjoys itself, be bestowed upon a multitude of beings, and a world can be called forth out of nothing."[74] Jacobi continues,

> And if it is unified, then it must be unified by *something*, and the only thing that is truly *something* is the *spirit*. But the spirit that makes the All into a One, and binds the heap of being into a whole, cannot possibly be a spirit *that is only a soul*. The source of life needs no vessel. It is not like drops that need a vessel to catch them one by one and hold them. CREATOR is this spirit. And that is his creation: to have instilled souls, founded life, and prepared immortality.[75]

It is clear that Jacobi is once again falling in step with the account of creation found in the Gospel of John. This transparent affiliation leads Ford to summarize Schelling's critique of Jacobi's God as "the God of 'ordinary theism'" that is "incapable of explaining creation,"[76] and this is largely true. For example, Jacobi claims that

> if the universe is not God but rather a *creation*; if it is the effect of a free intelligence; then the *original* tendency of each and every being must be the expression of a divine will. This expression of God's will in the creature is its original law, and the power to fulfil this law must also be given in it necessarily. This law, which is *the condition of the existence of the being itself,* its *original impulse,* its *own will,* cannot be compared to natural laws that are only the *results* of relations *and* rest everywhere upon *mediation*.[77]

Here, we return to the problem of concept collapse as it relates to the ontological problem of absolute externality. Jacobi is claiming that if there is not an infinite difference between God's will and the laws of creation, then God is bound up in the mediated, determinate relations of worldly beings. Were this the case, there could be no divine free will insofar as it would be determined in part by terrestrial relations. Further, because divine free will is the only possible source of creation, without it there could be no world at all.

If it is the case that there must remain an infinite difference between the finite and the infinite, as we can see repeatedly in Jacobi's criticism of Fichte, Spinoza, and philosophy more generally, it is clear why only faith can respect this infinite difference without giving up on the infinite in doing so. Bernstein characterizes faith as "an absolute relation to the absolute."[78] It is only this noncommunicative, rationally inscrutable, absolute relation that does not determine and thereby destroy its own ground. However, as we have seen, Jacobi does not consider faith to be reason's inscrutable other. It is instead a knowing of unknowing, a skeptical core that is the living, beating heart of all that reason takes itself to be and to be of. With this, we find a commitment common to contemporary realism, particularly in a number of continental variants. First is what was previously referred to as the "independence thesis." For Jacobi, there is necessarily a real of actually existing objects whose actuality is not dependent upon human mindedness. These objects are independent of any attempt to conceptually determine them in order to systematically know creation. Second is the commitment that this independent real of objective existence is internally organized in accordance with its own rules and regularities. In other words, it is not the mind that brings organization to the independent real. Instead, the mind comes to know by reflecting this order. As Ferraris has recently put this point, "[R]eality has a structured nature that precedes conceptual schemes and can resist them."[79] So the real must be ontologically independent of the mind in both its form and its content. Or, as Schelling puts a similar point in 1841 "*concepts exist only after nature, not before*; *abstracta* cannot be prior to that from which they are abstracted."[80]

3.2. THE LEAP BACK INTO THE REAL

Life begins to bridge from the infinite to the finite, but it is not itself sufficient for avoiding the collapse of the infinite division between the finite and the infinite. We must turn to the *salto mortale* that Jacobi argues is necessary in order to return the finite intellect to the light of the creator and deliver it from the shadowy nightmare of philosophy. The *salto mortale* is characterized as a "death defying leap." In the *salto*, a circus performer would leap from a considerable height and turn their feet over their head risking great injury and possibly death. In the air, with eyes turned only toward the sky, the performer has no knowledge of where they will land but must nonetheless believe that the world has not vanished at the moment of their leap. The performer must have faith that the world is still there waiting to catch them as they come back down. They must have faith in what they cannot know in order to be returned to an upright and no longer tumbling state. In his conversation with Lessing contained in *Concerning the Doctrine of Spinoza*, Jacobi appeals to the *salto mortale* in the context of the relation between the possibility of "intuiting the manifold in the infinite"[81] and Jacobi's belief in "an intelligent personal cause of the world."[82] He explains to his interlocutor, "I extricate myself from the problem through a *salto mortale,* and I take it that you are not given to any pleasure in leaping with your *head down.*"[83] The leap described here can be associated with what was taken as Jacobi's irrationalism. What cannot be proven demands faith. At the limit of reason, one must leap without regard to their own safety. However, as the recent scholarship discussed above argues, to pigeonhole Jacobi as an irrationalist obfuscates some of his more fundamental theoretical insights. For, again, let us recall that for Jacobi the answer to nihilism is not irrationalism but *realism.*

Proulx and Nisenbaum both take up the theme of the *salto mortale* in order to provide a thicker understanding of this central yet underdeveloped concept. Both resist the temptation to equate the *salto* with irrationalism. Both view the *salto* as a cornerstone for a form of rationality distinct from the kind Jacobi openly condemns. Proulx's explains,

> [T]his *salto* is an active leap of assent to what is intimately felt but cannot be explained; it is a choice of a certain kind of system (the system of freedom), and in this it is in part a conceptual assent to the undeniable feeling that freedom makes sense as an explanation of human experience.[84]

The *salto* contains both epistemic and nonepistemic elements. It is a "conceptual assent," but it is based upon or grounded in a nonconceptual given, a feeling held by way of firm conviction. Proulx then continues,

> [B]ut it is also an active assent, an activity that itself grounds the feeling of freedom. It is after all in the active embrace of human freedom that one is finally able to make the *salto mortale,* and it is really only in acting freely that one can feel one's freedom.[85]

Now, this is not too novel an idea. That the act of freedom precedes any knowledge of freedom is a thought to which Descartes and Fichte, for example, would likewise assent. To be, to exist, is the consequence of a positing that occurs through an act of judgment. However, for Fichte, this free act is grounded by the I's capacity for rational self-determination. Alternatively, for Jacobi, a feeling through faith must precede the act of the *salto*. We see that though the *salto* is based on a feeling, it is not itself passive. In the free act of the *salto,* freedom is both felt and grounded. Thus, instead of representing a complete rejection of reason, on this reading the *salto* is a plea for the primacy of a kind of practical reasoning.

Nisenbaum comes to a similar conclusion in her discussion the *salto*. First, she situates the *salto* as inheriting an insight from Spinoza, namely, that "Jacobi's objection to Spinoza's monistic ontology is also tempered by his appreciation for Spinoza's key insight that the Absolute cannot be apprehended reflectively, through any process of ratiocination, but that such apprehension must be achieved through *intuition* or *insight*."[86] Spinoza, on this account, also rejects the capacity of inferential reasoning alone to know God. However, Jacobi inverts Spinoza by attributing intuitive and immediate knowing to the senses and not to the intellect. Nisenbaum continues: "Assenting to a belief that is based upon a need of *reason* is different from assenting to a belief that is based upon *inclination,* since the latter only provides us with a subjective ground for assent."[87] We again see that the *salto* is a kind of self-grounding; in the leap, the thinker finds reasons for belief that are not true or false in relation to other beliefs. Thus, "we can conclude that Jacobi's aim is not to overthrow reason, but to restore reason by establishing the primacy of reason in its practical use."[88] The *salto* is not a leap out of reason but instead a leap back into the immediate world of familiar everydayness. It is not a leap into the unknown but a daring retreat into a world left behind. Recall Jacobi's discussion cited above of "ancient people" for whom the entire world was alive. It is this living world of action into which the *salto* daringly tumbles. It is this living world that grounds the possibility of inferential and conceptual reasoning and not the other way around. What we must keep in mind is that it is faith that makes the *salto* into the lost world of immediacy possible. To feel the living real upon which the rational knowledge of cause and effect is based, one must first have faith. In other words, faith is the mode of access to the ground that renders inferential knowledge referential.

Both Proulx and Nisenbaum come to similar conclusions regarding the primacy of the practical as a consequence of Jacobi's *salto*. However, neither reaches the point of connecting it with Jacobi's explicitly stated silver bullet against the nihilism of transcendental idealism, namely, realism. Frank, Beiser, and Snow all openly acknowledge the influence of Jacobi's realism on the subsequent idealists and romantics. One last step is in order if we are fully to understand the complex nexus of concepts Jacobi deploys in order to reclaim realism through faith, and this is a renewed appeal to divine creation. He writes, "It is the instrument of the almighty love, or . . . the *secret laying on of the hand* of the creator. Only by this means can the blessing of life, the blessing of an existence that externalizes itself and thereby enjoys itself, be bestowed upon a multitude of beings, and a world be called forth out of nothing."[89] Through the faith that makes the *salto* possible, one falls back into the world of immediacy that has been covered over and ultimately erased by theoretical reason. The next step is to acknowledge that this living world could come only from the "secret laying on of the hand of God." Only through this laying of the hand and the love of the Divine can something come out of nothing. This allows one to break free from the consequences of the fundamental law of rationalism. "A shiver goes down my spine," Jacobi writes, "whenever I think of this; every time it is as if I received my soul directly from the hand of the creator at that instant."[90] So, though Jacobi does advocate for the necessity of a kind of self-grounding and self-justifying practical rationality this practical rationality is not sufficient in and of itself. There must exist a living world with a mind-independent structure inscribed by the Divine into which one falls. We can see the difference between Jacobi's use of faith and the *salto mortale* on the one hand, and the notion of intellectual intuition Schelling's develops on the other. Faith does not establish a reality through a kind of self-relating production. That is, faith is not an act of creation but is instead a return to an earlier state. Faith, we are told, allows for a return to the prephilosophical world of the everyday.

4.0. Conclusion

Jacobi saw with unrivaled clarity the antirealist threat at the heart of the kind of systematic philosophy desired by both Spinoza and the German Idealists. At bottom, idealism is a mad nihilism precisely because of its constitutive antirealism. I close by emphasizing this for one primary reason. If we neglect Jacobi's realism, we obscure an essential characteristic of the way Jacobi's fears have been inherited. Only by understanding Jacobi as an aspiring realist can we fully contextualize the current debates over realism and antirealism as an extension of the pantheism controversy. This, in turn, is what allows us to see the appeal of Schelling's intervention into the problem set forth by Jacobi, and our own philosophical juncture by extension.

The fuller picture of Jacobi's work provided in this chapter frames an impasse between idealism and realism that erupts from within Spinoza's *Ethics*. Jacobi's initial epistemic observations called for an ontological solution that can be satisfied by neither skepticism nor quietism. The legacy of Jacobi is not that he was wrong but instead that he was acutely aware of the truth of idealism. Idealism is a kind of madness, and this madness is twofold. First, there is the epistemic issue regarding the possibility of knowledge, and second there is the ontological problem of existence. The world is divided into one of words and one of things, without any rationally deducible guarantee that there might be some form of friction between the two. Jacobi shares with Kant and the German Idealists the idea that theoretical rationality is insufficient for obtaining the demands it makes of itself. It must be in some way supplemented by a kind of practical rationality. Jacobi's characterization of this practical rationality relies upon an active assent to the passive reception of the transcendent externality of the real through faith. One must fall back into the real from which they came in order to place themselves within meaning, truth, and goodness. Keeping Jacobi's schema of transcendence and passivity in mind allows us to better understand what is unique about Schelling's approach to the reciprocal need of realism and idealism to which I will now turn.

Chapter 2

Weak Weapons and the Fight against Dogmatism

1.0. Introduction: Letters to a Friend

Schelling's *Letters* provides in broad strokes the coordinates of his early appropriation of Kant's idealism as well as his utilization of Spinoza's realism to counterbalance what he views as the perils of the reception of Kant's critical project. In this early text, we see what Schelling wants from both Kant and Spinoza as well as what he wishes to leave behind. Schelling's relationship to Spinoza in the year 1795 alone is complex to map. Famously, on February 4, 1795, he wrote to Hegel that he had "become a Spinozist!"[1] During the same period of time Schelling was composing *Of the I as the Principle of Philosophy, or On the Unconditional in Human Knowledge* [hereafter *Of the I*]. Therein, he praises Spinozism as "more worthy of high esteem, because of its bold consequences,"[2] and even suggests that "I hope that some happy time may be granted to me in which it will be possible to bring to realization the idea of writing a counterpart to Spinoza's *Ethics*."[3] Despite this open and enthusiastic praise of Spinoza, we can see Schelling grow more critical of Spinoza as the year goes on, particularly in the *Letters*.[4] Schelling begins the *Letters* by noting the urgency he felt at the close of the eighteenth century. In his estimation, following Kant's tribunal of reason a novel form of dogmatism rose to the surface. This was in large part because "there is as yet no sharp enough determination of the boundaries that the *Critique of Pure Reason* drew between dogmatism and criticism."[5] Thus, Schelling sees as his task in the *Letters* the firmer demarcation between critical and dogmatic philosophy. Yet as the *Letters* unfold, we see that though there is a line between criticism and dogmatism, each depends on the other in part because of this separation. By more precisely demarcating the difference between dogmatism and criticism, Schelling seeks to determine the common root from which they come. Furthermore, though they explicitly name "criticism" and "dogmatism" in their title, the *Letters* are just as much about the relation between idealism (broadly understood at this point as the philosophy of the form of intelligibility) and realism (broadly understood as the philosophy of the content of experience, or more precisely the objective genesis of the content of experience): Schelling tells us that "criticism and dogmatism are nothing else than idealism and realism systematically conceived."[6] In short, Schelling uses both Kant and Spinoza in order to articulate the necessary interconnection without subordination of idealism and realism.

"My friend," writes Schelling, "the fight against dogmatism is waged with weak weapons if criticism rests its whole system merely upon the state of our *cognitive faculty*, and not upon our genuine essence."[7] Because, as Schelling will insist, the synthetic operations of both real objective content and ideal subjective form must be genetically accounted for, neither dogmatic realism nor critical idealism can stand alone as a satisfactory philosophical position. Put otherwise, the madness of idealism diagnosed by Jacobi inevitably results from criticism without dogmatism and the elimination of freedom and nature diagnosed by Kant in the Antinomies of Pure Reason results from dogmatism without criticism. Further, Schelling shares with Kant and Jacobi the commitment that Spinozism cannot be refuted by theoretical reason alone. However, for Schelling, there is no absolute division between theoretical and practical reason. Instead, each holds a reciprocal need for the other. This conviction likewise held by Schelling leads him to develop to the notion of "creative reason," or *realisirenden Vernunft*. He writes:

> Dogmatism and criticism, starting from principles however different, must nonetheless meet in one point in one and the same problem. Only at this meeting does the time come for their proper separation; only here can they realize that the principle which they had so far proposed, was nothing but *a prolepsis,* upon which the verdict is to be given only at this point. Now only is it manifest that all the proposi-

tions which they had put forth thus far were propositions asserted absolutely, that is, without ground. Now, as they enter a new realm of *creative* reason [realisirenden *Vernunft*], it will be revealed whether they are capable of *giving* reality to those propositions.[8]

For the time being, what is essential in the above quotation is the idea that creative reason *gives* reality to the propositions of any system, be it one of dogmatism or criticism. Exactly how this works is not fully fleshed out in the *Letters*, but what we do see is that the key to solving this problem will have something to do with a creative production that gives reality in its very act of producing. What the *Letters* do extensively detail is the common problem upon which dogmatism and criticism meet in order for their "proper" separation to be drawn. This problem is that of synthesis and its relation to the "riddle of all philosophy," namely, the existence of the finite world.

Whereas the previous chapter focused on the conflict between theoretical reason and ontological monism, this chapter turns to the epistemological problems generated by a certain form of dualism. To do so, it first outlines the dyadic relation between idealism and realism presented by Schelling in the *Letters* and then looks at Schelling's attempt to bridge this dyadic relation through the appeal to a shared ground. Section 2 presents Schelling's reading of Kant's *Critique of Pure Reason* to isolate how the *Critique* produces the need for both dogmatism and criticism. Section 3 turns to Schelling's presentation of dogmatism by way of his appropriation of Spinoza. Instead of just lingering on the shortcomings of dogmatism, Schelling seeks to expose what Spinoza's form of dogmatism offers to the philosopher with systematic aspirations. Section 4 then develops the idea of productive intellectual intuition, what Schelling calls creative reason, in relation to Kant's Refutation of Idealism. Though creative reason makes few appearances outside of the *Letters*, the operation of this original synthesis remains characteristic of the dynamics of spirit, nature, and ultimately of the Absolute itself.

2.0. Criticism

Schelling's motivating concern for the *Letters* revolves around the relation between theoretical and practical reason. According to Schelling,

Kant needed to posit God as an end in accordance with the demands of practical reason that stem from the "weakness" in theoretical reason. The idea of a moral God, Schelling claims, "not only signifies nothing sublime, but signifies nothing whatsoever; it is as empty as every other anthropomorphic representation."[9] The moral God is not a God at all insofar as it is itself restricted in accordance with the moral world order: "What distinguishes criticism is not the idea of a *God,* but the idea of a God *conceived as being under moral laws.*"[10] Practical reason, for Schelling, does not serve as a stand-in or a hero that comes to the defense of theoretical reason. Instead, it is an ampliative operation that expands the scope of theoretical reason. "Thus your theoretical reason would become quite a different reason," writes Schelling, "with the help of practical reason it would be broadened so as to admit a new field alongside the old."[11] Schelling does not deny the importance of theoretical reason; instead, he locates it within a larger context of rational practices and processes.

This is the general frame Schelling is working within, yet the main body of the *Letters* concerns itself most extensively with the *Critique of Pure Reason* and not the *Critique of Practical Reason* in which many of the conclusions Schelling found so troubling are located. This is in large part because the advent of critique represents a point of no return in the history of philosophy. From critique's successes and failures grow the opposed systems of criticism and dogmatism. Schelling's overall view of the first *Critique* is nicely summarized in the following:

> The *Critique of Pure Reason* is not destined to establish any one *system* exclusively, much less to establish that cross between dogmatism and criticism. . . . On the contrary, as I understand it, the *Critique* is destined to deduce from the essence of reason the very possibility of two exact opposed systems: it is destined to establish a system of criticism . . . or more precisely, a system of idealism as well as and in exact opposition to it, a system of dogmatism or realism.[12]

Instead of reading the *Critique of Pure Reason* as a monolithic attempt at constructing a singular system of reason, Schelling takes it to be drawing a line between two distinct yet equally necessary systems. First, we should note and bear in mind the implicit association here of criticism with idealism as well as the direct association of dogmatism and realism. Second, idealism and realism are both derived ("deduced from the essence of reason") by the *Critique of Pure Reason* while being reducible neither to it nor to each other. While this quotation broadly captures Schelling's view on Kant's first critical work, we must also take careful note of Schelling's word choice here; he speaks of the "exact" opposition between criticism and dogmatism, or idealism and realism. This theme of opposition will come to play an important role in understanding the way the *Letters* unfold. The theme of opposition connects this entire discussion to the possibility of life and personality more generally.

2.1. Synthesis, Unity, Egress

According to Schelling, criticism as articulated by Kant lacks the proper tools to fully keep dogmatism at bay insofar as "the consummate system of criticism cannot confute dogmatism theoretically."[13] Kant and Jacobi both analyze the relation between theoretical and practical reason when it came to the possibility of refuting Spinozism. For Jacobi, it was imperative to stipulate the primacy of faith over reason and undertake a *salto mortale* back into the real in order to exit from the prison of Spinozism. Alternatively, for Kant, it was the is/ought distinction unavailable to Spinoza that enticed us with a practical decision to limit the scope of the principles of theoretical reason. Here, we see that Schelling understands his analysis within this lineage. Schelling continues, "[I]n theoretical philosophy dogmatism is overthrown, but only to rise again with even greater power."[14] The tribunal of reason had not quelled the fervor upon the battlefield of metaphysics. Instead, after a temporary reprieve, the combatants acquired new weapons and began to rage once again with heightened bloodlust. Schelling asks how it is that this result came to pass by showing how these two systems of philosophy (between which there ought to be an "exact opposition") can convert seamlessly into each other. As Schelling will demonstrate, the role of synthesis is crucial for answering this question.

"Criticism proceeds from the point it has in common with dogmatism," Schelling claims, "from the original synthesis."[15] The theme of synthesis is present throughout the first *Critique* and in fact forms its explicitly stated guiding question, namely, "How are synthetic a priori judgments possible?"[16] Answering this question, for Kant, would ensure the possibility of metaphysics as a systematic philosophical endeavor. To begin, all knowledge from experience (insofar as it takes the form of judgments) is synthetic. As Kant explains, "[I]n all judgments in which the relation of a subject to the predicate is thought . . . this relation is possible in two different ways. Either the predicate B belongs to the subject A, as something which is (covertly) contained in this concept A; or B lies outside the concept A, although it does indeed stand in connection with it."[17] A synthetic judgment *augments* the subject by way of an addition through some form of connection to a predicate that the subject did not itself already contain. For Schelling, the shortcoming of the *Critique*'s treatment of synthesis comes from its overly cognitive focus on the question. As a consequence, the original synthesis that stands as the common point between criticism and dogmatism "criticism can explain only by the *cognitive faculty* itself."[18] Take, as an example of this, Kant's appeal to synthesis in the B Deduction in order to prove that "it must be possible for the 'I think' to accompany all my representations."[19] Kant writes,

> [O]nly in so far, therefore, as I can unite a manifold of given representations in *one consciousness,* is it possible for me to represent to myself the *identity of the consciousness in* [*i.e., throughout*] *these representations.* In other words, the *analytic* unity of apperception is possible only under the presupposition of a certain *synthetic* unity.[20]

The unity of consciousness is only possible by way of a preexisting "synthetic unity." Thus, synthetic unity is, in the case of the unity of apperception, prior to analytic unity. Schelling will agree that synthetic unity must always precede and condition analytic unity, but he will add a further complication to this relationship. Schelling writes:

> *How did we ever come to judge synthetically?* This is what Kant asked at the very beginning of his work, and this question lies at the base of his entire philosophy as a problem concerning the essential and common point of *all* philosophy. For expressed differently, the question is this: *How do I ever come to egress [Entgegengesetztes] from the absolute, and to progress toward an opposite?*[21]

Egress from the Absolute is essential for the possibility of philosophy because "if we had had to deal with the absolute alone, the strife of different systems would never appear. Only as we come forth from the absolute does opposition originate, and only through this *original* opposition in the human does any opposition between philosophers originate."[22] It is not the specificity of philosophical practice that generates the opposition between realism and idealism. Instead, it is the "exiting" from the Absolute that constitutes idealism and realism as codependent necessities. It is this egress that establishes the relation between real and ideal as well as the relation between real, ideal, and the Absolute.

The *Critique of Pure Reason*'s accomplishments and failings are rooted in its focus on the cognitive or formal conditions of synthesis. As Schelling explains, "[I]nstead of deducing the formal and material steps of all synthesis from a principle at the base of *both* steps, the critique of the cognitive faculty explains the progress of one synthesis by that of the other."[23] The *Critique of Pure Reason* is not false or wrong due to this cognitive focus; it is simply one-sided and incomplete. The *Critique of Pure Reason* might have established the cognitive conditions for metaphysics by way of its analysis of the formal conditions of synthesis, but it was unable to demarcate the real possibility of metaphysics as a form of inquiry with actual content. For Schelling, the metaphysics of criticism in isolation can be called the metaphysics of madness insofar as it is a metaphysics of pure possibility and not reality. It is an investigation into the synthetic structures of thought that disregards or minimizes the equally important issue of the objective synthesis that renders the content of thought real, not unlike what Schelling will later call "negative philosophy."

Schelling contends that dogmatism has come to accept the cognitive point put forth within the critical project. In other words, dogmatism can accept, at least partially, the Copernican shift in the direction of fit between concepts and objects. Schelling explains:

> [W]ith triumphant evidence criticism proves that, as soon as the subject enters the sphere of the object, that is, as soon as it judges objectively, the subject emerges from itself and is compelled to engage in synthesis. Once dogmatism has admitted this, it must also admit that no absolutely objective cognition is possible, that is, that the object is knowable only under the condition of the subject, under the condition that the subject come out from its own sphere and engage in a synthesis.[24]

So again, though the analysis of the cognitive faculty is central to the critical project, it alone is not enough to stave off the return of dogmatism. Dogmatism must and, perhaps more importantly, *can* admit that objective judgment requires some form of subjective primacy. This is the source of dogmatism's particular resilience. Following Kant's critical intervention, objective conditions are knowable only as they are subjectively conditioned. Furthermore, if Kant is correct, any attempt to know objects independent of subjective conditions would be unintelligible. We thus see one way in which dogmatism adapts to criticism in order to live a renewed life. The dogmatist can grant the first Kantian point, that knowing things as they appear "for us" must necessarily fall into the confines of the subjective conditions of experience, while still attempting to think the objective conditions of objects "without us." Put otherwise, the dogmatist can adopt the theoretical prescriptions of criticism while losing sight of their practical importance.

2.2. The Tragic Fate of Synthesis

Schelling's next step in demonstrating the wellspring of dogmatism and criticism is to delve deeper into the idea of synthesis. What Schelling shows is that though the idea of synthesis is necessary to both the systems of criticism and dogmatism, in each system synthesis finds itself expressed in an opposing form. There is a tragic fate to synthesis in both criticism and dogmatism, and this fate exemplifies the problem of any one-sided system of philosophy. Schelling begins this discussion by demarcating two basic principles of any synthesis. Any synthesis is intelligible under two conditions. First:

> S_1—"that it precede by absolute unity [*Einheit*], which becomes an empirical unity only in the synthesis itself, that is, only if an opposite is given, a manifold [*Vielheit*]."[25]

and second,

> S_2—"no synthesis is thinkable except under the presupposition that it terminate in an absolute thesis; the purpose of any synthesis is a thesis."[26]

Synthesis is intelligible only if (1) it becomes empirical in the synthetic act itself by moving from absolute unity into multiplicity, and (2) if it begins and terminates in an absolute, either as unity or as thesis understood as a determinate assertion. Given the emphasis of S_1 at this point Schelling seems to be straying from Kant's critical philosophy into the realm of Fichte's idealism. Fichte spent many years developing an account of how the free, synthetic activity of the I (the *Ich*) is able to produce the world of conditioned appearances through determining and subsequently opposing itself to the not-I. "In the first synthetic act," Fichte writes, "the fundamental synthesis (of self and not-self), we have likewise established a content for all possible future syntheses."[27] The self-positing I renders empirical multiplicity intelligible through progressive synthesis. Furthermore, for Fichte the initial act provides not just the form of all future syntheses but the content as well. However central the notion of synthesis is to the work of Fichte, the discussion of synthesis in this context it is not reducible to the principles of the *Wissenschaftslehre*. To grasp how Schelling is deploying this familiar theme in order to characterize the passage from critique to the dualism of criticism and dogmatism, we must turn again to the *Critique of Pure Reason* and Kant's characterization of the tragic fate of reason. What we will see is how Schelling's distinction between these two principles of synthesis yields a similar tragic fate.

As Kant demonstrates in the Transcendental Dialectic, for reason the temptation of objective knowing is too great. When one gives into this temptation in full, transcendental illusion arises. We looked at this analysis and the role it plays in Kant's critique of Spinoza in the previous chapter. We can now look at the more general form of this critique as it applies to the functioning of reason itself. Kant tells us that "if the conditioned is given, the entire series of all its conditions is likewise given; objects of the senses are given as conditioned; therefore etc."[28] Due to this assumption, reason oftentimes becomes overambitious and trespasses its limitations. It moves from P_1, which merely dictates the subjective striving for the entire series of conditions, to P_2, the objective positing of the complete series.[29] Again, if an object is given to the senses this does *not* mean that the entire series of conditions for that object is also given objectively. In the present case, P_1 relates to S_2 insofar as both are explicitly applicable to conditions of intelligibility whereas P_2 relates more closely to S_1 because both are tied to objective conditions of existence. Schelling's claim in S_1 is ultimately similar to the presupposition Kant takes as his starting point in the Transcendental Dialectic, namely, that if a given conditioned is to be intelligible, the unconditioned must play some role in this intelligibility. Likewise, if an empirical unity is present, some absolute unity must have become empirical by way of synthesis itself. According to S_1, existent multiplicity implies a previous unity. It stands to reason that given an empirical unity one could come to know the absolute, unconditioned unity of which any particular conditioned unity is an expression. However, Schelling explains that criticism

> must admit that theoretical reason necessarily seeks what is not conditioned, and that the very striving which produces a synthesis demands an absolute thesis as a goal of all philosophy. And, for this very reason, the critique must destroy what it only just erected. For it masters dogmatism only within the domain of the synthesis; as soon as it leaves this domain (and the critique must leave it just as necessarily as it had to enter it) the contest begins anew.[30]

Like Kant, Schelling believes that there is a tragic fate of theoretical reason. It demands of itself that which it can never in principle attain. The seemingly warranted quest for the unconditioned that renders any given conditioned possible reveals itself as quixotic.

Schelling specifies his understanding of reason's tragic fate by explaining that "if the synthesis is to end in a thesis, it is necessary to do away with the condition under which alone a synthesis has actuality [*wirklich ist*]. And the condition of a synthesis is that there be *opposition*—more definitely, opposition between subject and object."[31] S_2, the condition of intelligibility for synthesis (that it end in a thesis), undermines the first condition whereby a unified synthesis becomes an empirical multiplicity through synthetic activity itself. Schelling rephrases this relation as that between subject and object: "[I]f the opposition between subject and object is to cease," he writes, "it ought to become unnecessary for the subject to step out of itself; both must become *absolute*, that is, the synthesis would terminate in a thesis."[32] What we see is that for synthesis to remain absolute, it can only do so through the act of striving; it must operate interminably. Were it to cease this interminable striving, it would abjure its ability to act as a common root between the systems of criticism and dogmatism. It is by this consequence of S_2 that the *Critique of Pure Reason* accomplishes its work of deducing "from the essence of reason the very possibility of two exactly opposed systems."[33] The first system is that of dogmatism, in which if the subject were to "disappear in the object, then, and only then, would the object be posited [*gegetzt*] under no condition of the subject's, that is, it would be posited as *thing in itself,* as absolute; but the subject would be absolutely done away with as knower."[34] The other system is that of criticism, which arises "if the object became identical with the subject, then this would become *subject in itself,* absolute subject, while the object would be absolutely done away with as *what is knowable.*"[35] Thus, intelligibility under S_2 seeks the Absolute through the reduction of synthesis by way of assimilating its dynamism into thetic stasis, either in the subject or in the object. In order to do so, an absolute opposition between subject and object must obtain, and remain primary. The synthetic common root of criticism and dogmatism must remain active and avoid termination if it is to end in neither criticism nor dogmatism alone. Were there to be a termination of the synthetic becoming that serves as the common ground for both subjects and objects, the opposition between subject and object becomes reified. However, at this point, it is only through this stagnation of conflict and the concretization of subject and object that the world becomes intelligible. There is not yet a notion of stagnation through which subjects and objects could become but moments in a larger play of forces that actively resists the kind of stagnation that results in either one-sided idealism or one-sided realism.

3.0. Dogmatism

The most common *modus operandi* when it comes to a philosophical engagement with dogmatism is to reject the dogmatist as naive and simply wrong. What is intriguing about the *Letters* is Schelling's return to dogmatism in order to outline a fuller philosophy of freedom that can account for both the form and content of experience. Instead of focusing exclusively on what is wrong with dogmatism, Schelling asks of dogmatism what it can contribute to the construction of a systematic philosophy. Understanding the structure of opposition between subject and object now takes the forefront for understanding the relationship between criticism and dogmatism. The tragic fate of synthesis terminates in the opposition between subject and object, and this opposition demands resolution. Criticism and dogmatism are not characterized by the termination of synthesis alone. What matters is where this termination occurs. At this point, Schelling argues that criticism results from the absorption of the object in the subject whereas dogmatism is the absorption of the subjective in the objective. The resolution provided by both positions is consequently one-sided. If, as Schelling suggests, exhaustive objective determination excludes the possibility of independent subjectivity, then the problem of dogmatism is largely the problem of what we now call reductive naturalism. The reductive naturalist holds that all aspects of human experience must be exhaustively explicable by way of the sum of scientific facts. In Schelling's words quoted above—that in dogmatism the subject "disappear[s] in the object, then, and only then would the object be posited [*gegetzt*] under no condition of the subject's, that is, it would be posited as *thing in itself,* as absolute; but the subject would be absolutely done away with as the knower"[36]—the knower would be reduced to the known; the subject would be annihilated in the object. What, then, are the lessons to be learned from dogmatism, and how can they be learned while avoiding this reductionist fate?

3.1. Spinoza and the Riddle of All Philosophy

The *Letters* are composed of ten separate letters to an unnamed addressee. Schelling's discussion of Spinoza begins in the sixth letter. According to Schelling, the primary concern of Spinoza's philosophy was the "riddle of the world, the question of how the absolute could come out of itself and oppose to itself a world?"[37] How, if at all, is it possible for the unconditioned Absolute to immanently come to oppose itself to a conditioned world? This question connects directly back to Jacobi's and Kant's concerns surrounding the metaphysical and moral consequences of the PSR. In chapter 1 we saw how Jacobi came to generalize his criticism of Fichte and Spinoza and apply it to the whole of philosophy. The core of this opinion is shared by both Kant and Fichte. In the *Critique of Practical Reason*, Kant writes, "[I]f that ideality of space and time [i.e., Transcendental Idealism] is not maintained, solely *Spinozism* remains."[38] Fichte concurs when he writes, "So far as dogmatism can be consistent, Spinozism is its most logical outcome."[39] What appears is an unlikely convergence of convictions between otherwise disparate thinkers when it comes to the issue of Spinozism. Spinozism is taken as the height of all previous philosophical inquiry. For Kant, if one does not accept transcendental idealism, one can only be a Spinozist.

For Jacobi, if one does not accept "non-knowlege" predicated upon the existence of something transcendent to both nature and reason, on pain of inconsistency one can only be a Spinozist. For Fichte, if one is to remain a dogmatist, again on pain of inconsistency, one can only be a Spinozist.

Insofar as the termination of the synthesis at the common root between criticism and dogmatism relates to the possibility of real opposition (as evidenced by Schelling's discussion of the fraught relation between S_1 and S_2), we now have a concrete example of how criticism and dogmatism share the problem of synthesis as their common point. As Novalis observed, "[W]e *seek* the absolute everywhere and only ever find *things*."[40] Both criticism and dogmatism seek the Absolute, but each finds only conditioned things. For the critical philosopher, these things are subjects, whereas for the dogmatist, they are objects. Now, a Spinozist would immediately object here. For Spinoza, there is no difference between the world and God, or the One and the All. This is largely what was so controversial about Spinoza's philosophical system. If God and world are one, then we are left with two equally unappealing options. Either there is no world (acosmism) or there is no God that is not determined by the worldly causal order (atheism). What follows from either option are the much-maligned doctrines of fatalism, nihilism, or reductive naturalism. Schelling, to his credit, acknowledges his advantageous framing of Spinoza's problem in a footnote. "This question is intentionally expressed this way," Schelling writes of his comment regarding the riddle of the world, "The author knows that Spinoza asserts only an immanent causality of the absolute object. Still, what follows here will show that he asserted it only because for him it was unintelligible as to how the absolute could go out of itself: i.e., because he could propose that question but was unable to answer it."[41] This strategy of reading of Spinoza somewhat disingenuously is quite fascinating. Consider, for example, Fichte's reaction to Spinoza's *Ethics*; he too claimed that Spinoza "could not have been convinced of his own philosophy. He could only have *thought* of it; he could not have *believed* it."[42] This is because his was "a philosophy that directly contradicts those convictions that Spinoza must necessarily have adopted in his everyday life, by virtue of which he had to consider himself to be free and self-sufficient."[43] Both Schelling and Fichte think that they have identified an insincerity within the work of Spinoza. Spinoza was led to think something absurd, something that he could not possibly hold to be true. Perhaps Fichte and Schelling are both taking the fact of freedom for granted in presenting Spinoza in this way. They assume that Spinoza must not have believed in what he said, because he clearly must have known through his own experience that he was free. Just like everyone else, Spinoza must have put his pants on one leg at a time *in order to* leave the house. Against this trend of dismissing Spinoza as insincere, we must consider the frightening thought that perhaps Spinoza knew *exactly* what he was doing in his *Ethics*, namely, following the consequences of the PSR to their extreme including the elimination of the fact of freedom so often simply assumed based on experience. As I claimed in chapter 1 and will discuss further in chapter 3, it is precisely from the most commonly held conviction that every effect has a cause that Spinoza draws the sum total of his most monstrous hypothesis. According to Schelling, the central tenant of the *Ethics* would be merely an admission of defeat. Unable to find the solution for his riddle, Spinoza dissolves the problem of all philosophy by melding God and world. He both articulates the core problem of philosophy and eviscerates it at the same time.

In the seventh letter, Schelling expands Spinoza's riddle into the problem of all philosophy: "The main task of philosophy consists of solving the problem of the existence of the world," Schelling explains.[44] The main task of philosophy concerns the existence of the world as a world, understood broadly as the objects of possible experience and the rules and regularities that render these objects intelligible. Neither the existence nor the categorical structure of the world is simply given. Consequently, both must be accounted for. After proposing that this is the fundamental philosophical question, Schelling turns to Spinoza as framed by way of the conversation with Lessing narrated by Jacobi that sparked the pantheism controversy. By doing so, Schelling places himself within the tradition of Jacobi's then infamous provocation, as well as in relation to the problem of the PSR. Schelling writes, "[W]hen Lessing asked Jacobi what he would consider the spirit of Spinozism to be, Jacobi replied: it could be nothing else than the old *a nihilo nihil fit*, which Spinoza contemplated according to concepts more abstract and pure [*nach abgezogenern Begriffen*] than those of the philosophizing cabbalists or of others before him."[45] It is the PSR—that from nothing comes nothing and every effect must have a cause—that serves as the spirit of Spinozism. This contextualization is far from accidental or irrelevant. While Schelling and Jacobi will take this as a starting point in approaching the work of Spinoza, it must be noted that their understandings of the consequences of this guiding thread are massively divergent. Jacobi maintains that if one is to be a consistent philosopher, they must be a Spinozist. Schelling, on the contrary, seeks to demonstrate how the philosopher must traverse Spinozism in order to meet the demands of thought. That is, to articulate a robust nature-philosophy compatible with transcendental subjectivity, one must take seriously the content of Spinozism while not remaining trapped therein. One must strive to think not just the analytic One but the emergent relation of the All to this One (the *becoming* All of the One) as well.

"I don't believe that the spirit of Spinozism could be better circumscribed," Schelling writes in reference to Jacobi's characterization, "but I believe that the very transition from the nonfinite to the finite is the problem of *all* philosophy, not only of one particular system. I even believe that Spinoza's solution is the only possible solution."[46] We have already noted that the solution Schelling finds in Spinoza is not the solution found expressly on the surface of Spinoza's *Ethics*. Spinoza denies any distinction between God and world and thereby avoids the need for a solution to the problem of all philosophy. In fact, Schelling will go on to posit the impossibility of finding such a transition with reference to Kant: "No system can realize the transition from the nonfinite to the finite," he explains, "No system can fill the gap between the nonfinite and the finite. This I presuppose; it is the result, not of critical philosophy, but of the *Critique of Pure Reason*, which concerns dogmatism as well as criticism, and which must be equally evident for both."[47] It is intriguing that Schelling locates the dissolution of Spinoza's riddle in Kant. The inability of reason to make the transition from infinite to finite, or to find the unconditioned for any given condition, is a conviction that Schelling holds throughout his work. Throughout his engagement with Spinoza, Schelling maintains at least partially a Kantian perspective. We can also note that this would seem to imply a rejection of P_2 insofar as it is not possible from the perspective of theoretical reason to begin with the objectively given unconditioned unity by which any given conditioned is made possible.

Because there could be no *reason* for the emergence of something from nothing Spinoza began with what Schelling characterizes as "a nonfinite substance, an absolute object."[48] The reference here is to Spinoza's radical form of substance monism. By beginning with the absolute object understood as a *totum analyticum,* Spinoza casts away the possibility of a subject that stands in opposition to this object. The absolute object carries with it the further consequence of causal monism: "Spinoza had done away with just that independent causality of the ego by which it is ego," Schelling claims.[49] Schelling likens this move to the desire for "self-annihilation."[50] Further, as Schelling will demonstrate, Spinoza does away with the ego's independent causality by externalizing an objectification of the intellectual intuition of the self. Schelling therefore provides a genetic account of Spinoza's philosophy as the result of Spinoza misplacing his own fundamental insight. Recall Kant's claim in the *Opus postumum* that "the spirit of man is Spinoza's God." Here, Schelling is effectively reversing this claim. Schelling establishes that Spinoza's God is just the spirit of man. The idea here is that Spinoza was initially correct, but ultimately fell victim to a kind of transcendental illusion. He rendered the subjective as objective and thereby erased the subjective origin of his insight. Spinoza hypostasized the unconditioned subject, the given condition of intuition, into the unconditioned absolute object. In other words, Spinoza took the feeling of freedom (the unconditioned subjective capacity for determination) present in himself and externalized it by turning the subjective powers of the ego over to the objective structure of substance. However, in this error of dogmatic realism, Schelling finds the resources for countering what he believed to be the overly subjectivist outcomes of critical idealism.

4.0. Subjects and Objects

Though there can be no theoretical account of the transition from the infinite to the finite, Schelling does believe that one can retroactively account for this transition in the other direction: "Philosophy cannot make a transition from the nonfinite to the finite, but it can make one from the finite to the nonfinite," he claims.[51] The desire to make this transition intelligible is a shared tendency of all philosophy. "In order that there may be no transition from the nonfinite to the finite," Schelling writes, "the finite itself must have a tendency towards the nonfinite, a perpetual striving to lose itself in the nonfinite."[52] For Schelling, dogmatism and criticism are mutually opposed expressions of the premature termination of a fundamental synthesis. For the dogmatic realist, this termination happens in the object and thereby renders all existence objective. Alternatively, for the critical idealist this termination happens in the subject and thereby eliminates all objective existence. The exact opposition between these two doctrines as well as their reciprocal tendency toward self-annihilation in the nonfinite returns us to one of the fundamental hurdles that faces Kant's critical philosophy. Namely, how is it possible for transcendental idealism to avoid being an overly subjective, problematic idealism that is unable to account for the existence of an external world? Here we come to a question of the relation between subjects and objects as well as the possibility of a common root for this relation.

In his early critique of Spinoza, we have seen Schelling summarily reject the idea of an ego without independent causality. The criteria for the independence of the causality of the ego are quite stringent. However, just because the ego has a kind of independent causality, this does not mean that it is without relation to the objects of knowledge. According to the first *Critique* and the Refutation of Idealism contained therein, transcendental idealism is not a solipsistic idealism insofar as the subject can only come to know itself if it is related to an external object that persists through time. If there is no correlation between subject and object, no matter what the characteristics of that correlation may be, there can be knowledge of neither subject nor object. In other words, there can be neither external objectivity nor subjective self-consciousness without some form of relation between these two things. Additionally, this relation must itself be an *actual,* and not merely hypothetical, relation between a real subject and a real object. This relational dependency cuts both ways. On the one hand, the "I think" that accompanies all my representations would be unknowable if it was not related to anything other than itself. On the other hand, the objects of experience remain unknowable if they do not relate to some kind of I that thinks. What this means is that the Refutation of Idealism is not merely an attempt to prove the existence of the external world. It is also an attempt to justify the intelligibility of the "I think." In other words, it is an attempt to formulate an idealism that is not necessarily an antirealism.

Outlining the modifications Schelling makes to Kant's Refutation of Idealism in the *Critique of Pure Reason* elucidates both Schelling's insistence on the necessity of a causality independent of the objective as well as the intended function of his turn to creative reason. Whereas Kant's Refutation of Idealism seeks to outline the logical necessity of a relation between subjects and objects such that the relation between subject and world can be one of actual knowing, Schelling's *Letters* attempts to formulate an ontological account of the genesis of this relation. Schelling argues that the intelligibility of finite, objective relations is dependent upon the independent causality of the ego. The focus on the notion of creative reason highlights how Schelling's usage of intuition is not narrowly reducible to that as outlined by Kant in the first *Critique*. For Schelling, intellectual intuition is not an unmediated, nonconceptual relation to a pregiven object or world. We will see that it instead relates more closely to Schelling's own idiosyncratic usage of the notion of practical reason. It is this notion of creative reason that best captures what is unique about Schelling's own deployment of intuition as an attempt to dispel the worries of problematic idealism.

4.1. Subject, Object, and Intellectual Intuition: Kant

In the *Critique of Pure Reason*, Kant famously claims that there is a nonempirical "I think" that must necessarily be able to accompany any and all of my representations if these representations are to be systematically organized into intelligible experiences. While the Transcendental Deduction attempts to show the validity of the application of concepts and categories to representations, it does not seek to establish the actuality of the objects of thought.[53] The trouble that animates the Refutation of Idealism is consequently quite close to Jacobi's overall worry about all idealism. Any successes of transcendental idealism are nullified if representations refer only to themselves and are "empty" by consequence. Kant gives two possible roads for the connection between representations and objects: "Either the object alone must make the representation possible, or the representation alone must make the object possible."[54] Kant excludes the possibility of the former option because this connection would be merely empirical. Instead, Kant maintains the latter option but with the caveat that "representation in itself does not produce the object in so far as *existence* is concerned, for we are not here speaking of its causality by means of the will."[55] Thus, the actuality of objects must be proven not in the Deduction (which is concerned primarily with validity) but elsewhere, namely, in the Refutation of Idealism.

Kant's explicit concern in the Refutation of Idealism is what he calls "material idealism," understood as "the theory which declares the existence of objects in space outside us to be merely doubtful and indemonstrable or to be false and impossible."[56] Kant terms the first "problematic" idealism and likens it to the project of Descartes. The second form of idealism he calls "dogmatic" idealism and attributes it to Berkeley. To disqualify dogmatic idealism, Kant believes it is enough to acknowledge that space is not a property belonging to objects as things-in-themselves. However, in order to take aim at the problematic idealism of Descartes, Kant believes he must develop an additional refutation that builds upon Descartes's claim that the "I am" is the only thing of which one can rightly be certain. Kant must show that, contrary to Descartes, the existence of the I think cannot be established independent of relation to any and all objects of experience.

Kant begins with this general idea: "I am conscious of my own existence as determined in time."[57] Now, Descartes makes no explicit mention of time when he speaks of his consciousness of himself, yet he would agree with Kant that the *cogito* "persists" in some sense; "[L]et him deceive me as much as he can, he will never bring it about that I am nothing *so long as* I think that I am something," writes Descartes.[58] Kant then continues, "All determination of time presupposes something *permanent* in perception."[59] If I can be minimally conscious of my own existence persisting through time, I must be conscious of something permanent in perceptual experience that is external to me. But what exactly is this permanence that renders persistence intelligible? As Kant explains, "This permanent cannot . . . be something in me, since it is only through this permanent that my existence in time can itself be determined."[60] So, unlike Descartes's idea that the reality of the I think can be determined in relation to itself alone, Kant introduces the necessity of a bilateral relation. The consciousness of the self as persisting through time cannot be determined by itself. It is therefore dependent upon something else for its determination.

So far, all this seems acceptable, but Kant's next move is much harder to grasp. "Thus perception of this permanent is possible only through a *thing* outside me and not through the mere *representation* of a thing outside me," Kant claims.[61] Here, we can see Kant formulating a version of the independence thesis. A representation alone cannot be the externality upon which the certainty of the self is grounded (minimally insofar as the "I think" in principle accompanying all my representations is the condition for the possibility for the relation between representations and their content). Grounding self-certainty in representations would presuppose the self to be proven. There must exist something independent of the self in relation to which it can anchor the experience of persisting through time. Kant then makes a bolder claim, namely, that "the determination of my existence in time is possible only through the existence of *actual things* which I perceive outside of me."[62] The permanence of self-consciousness is dependent on not just the relation to a thing other than the self, but on the *actuality* of things that endure. Beiser suggests that the actuality in question here is not of an ontological status, but is instead "only in a *formal* sense as a whole whose individual perceptions are only its parts."[63] He further suggests Kant's break with the subjectivist tradition as follows: "that intersubjective order makes possible the subjective order of my inner consciousness."[64] The idea is that because intersubjectivity precedes the possibility of subjective consciousness, the subject is never alone in its ability to determine its existence in relation to an object. However, this characterization fails to meet fully the independence thesis, and thus contains within it antirealist residue. Further, due to Schelling's somewhat open distain for epistemological solutions, it seems fair to assume that he would be more interested in an ontological solution to the problem posed by the Refutation of Idealism. Actuality and externality are thus the conditions of possibility for the time determination of an enduring self. Kant concludes his refutation as follows: "The consciousness of my existence is at the same time an immediate consciousness of the existence of other things outside me."[65] Consequently, the Refutation of Idealism encounters the related problems of realism and immediacy. Kant seems to be claiming that for consciousness of the "I think" as enduring through time to be possible, external objects must exist as actual and independent from the "I think." However, within the confines of Kant's transcendental idealism, these other things and the form of immediacy through which we have access to them remain ambiguous.

Kant's second note to the Refutation of Idealism must be highlighted in the context of this discussion. When he tells us that consciousness of the self is made possible only in relation to the enduring consciousness of something that is otherwise than and external to the self, we must enquire what exactly this externality is. Kant writes,

> We have nothing permanent on which, as intuition, we can base the concept of a substance, save only *matter*; and even this permanence is not obtained from outer experience, but is

presupposed *a priori* as a necessary condition of determination of time, and therefore also a determination of inner sense in respect of [the determination of] our own existence through the existence of outer things. The consciousness of myself in the representation "I" is not an intuition, but a merely *intellectual* representation of the spontaneity [*Selbsttätigkeit*] of a thinking subject. The "I" has not, therefore, the least predicate of intuition, which, as permanent, might serve as correlate for the determination of time in inner sense—in the manner in which, for instance, *impenetrability* serves in our *empirical* intuition of matter.[66]

This is idealism's fatal flaw; this is the site of idealism's madness. It is precisely the possibility of this type of absolute externality and independent actuality that Jacobi believes transcendental idealism, and philosophy more generally, excludes. Idealism is always without the thing Kant himself knows he needs in order to prove the existence of the "I think" that persists through time and accompanies all my representations. Consequently, if one were to appeal to the Refutation of Idealism in this form as a refutation not just of problematic idealism but of the accusation of nihilism as well, we can see that the argument is question begging insofar as Kant presupposes the external actuality of things outside of mere representations as the condition of possibility for a self that is reflectively conscious of its own endurance through time.

Just as the Refutation of Idealism seeks to establish both the possibility of the subject and the object, it also connects directly to what Kant calls nature: "That everything which happens is hypothetically necessary is a principle which subordinates alteration in the world to a law, that is, to a rule of necessary existence, without which there would be nothing that could be entitled nature."[67] So, though Kant may be largely concerned with the necessity of a logical relation between subjects and objects, this concern connects to larger ontological problems. This brings us to the possibility of intellectual intuition, an ambiguous yet essential notion in Kant's philosophy and German Idealism more broadly. Though Schelling would later attempt to downplay the role of intellectual intuition in his earlier works,[68] this notion drew many criticisms both from Schelling's contemporaries as well as many recent commentaries. We generally understand intellectual intuition as a cognitive form of access that is itself immediate and preconceptual.

Intellectual intuition can touch the world without the burdens and rules of discursive understanding. Consequently, if there is to be an antidote for the madness of idealism, intellectual intuition is the most obvious possible candidate because it offers a way to bypass the strictures imposed by finite consciousness. Through intellectual intuition, we might know the objects of experience with intuitive certainty. In short, we could think and know things-in-themselves. However, for Kant, intellectual intuition is reserved for God alone. Looking at this form of divine cognition allows us to frame more precisely Schelling's own usage of intellectual intuition. Kant explains that "in natural theology, in thinking an object [God], who not only can never be an object of intuition to us but cannot be an object of sensible intuition even to himself, we are careful to remove the conditions of time and space from his intuition—for all his knowledge must be intuition, and not *thought,* which always involves limitations."[69] Intellectual intuition is not a form of thought as we generally understand it insofar as thought is dependent upon content that exists prior to the act of being thought. Finite cognition consequently remains limited due to this dependence on something prior to and external to itself. God alone can be our model of unconditioned intuition. There is no object properly speaking prior to divine intellectual intuition, and Kant connects this form of intuition to the intelligibility of things-in-themselves. He writes,

> If by "noumenon" we mean a thing so far as it is *not an object of our sensible intuition,* and so abstract from our mode of intuiting it, this is a noumenon in the *negative* sense of the term. But if we understand by it an *object* of a *nonsensible intuition,* we thereby presuppose a special mode of intuition, namely, the intellectual, which is not that which we possess, and of which we cannot comprehend even the possibility. This would be "noumenon" in the *positive* sense of the term.[70]

The finite mind is incapable of unbounded cognition in large part because of its dependence upon discursivity. For the discursive intellect, as Nassar points out, "knowledge is based on conditions; an unconditioned, therefore, is beyond its grasp."[71] If knowledge of the unconditioned is a precondition for knowledge of any particular conditioned, it is easy to see why the discursive intellect is unequal to this task. So, again, according to Kant's criteria God alone has access to the noumenal realm by way of a form of intellection not even intelligible or conceivable by the finite mind if we assume that discursive knowing is the only form of knowing available to it.

It is the impossibility of finite intellectual intuition that renders something like the Refutation of Idealism necessary but also so deeply complex. If these noumenal relations were possible, then the question of the content of representations, of finite things existing external to the infinite, would dissolve. If only God can know things-in-themselves as actually existing, perhaps God alone can know Godself as persisting through time. Kant explains that "if, with the *intellectual consciousness* of my existence, in the representation 'I am,' which accompanies all my judgments and acts of understanding, I could at the same time connect a determination of my existence through *intellectual intuition*, the consciousness of a relation to something outside me would not be required."[72]

4.2. Subject, Object, and Creative Reason: Schelling

Kant aptly and appropriately sets up the problem of idealism, but he cuts himself off from the kind of intellectual intuition that would provide a simple solution to this problem as he has outlined it. This returns us to Schelling and his early critique of Spinoza in the *Letters*. According to Schelling, Spinoza excludes the possibility of a subject that exists independent of the absolute object. Alternatively, Kant focuses on the activity of the subject (understood here as the formal "I think" that must accompany all my representations), but in doing so he finds himself attacked by skeptics that reignited the need to fight off accusations of solipsistic idealism. Kant initially provides two options for exiting this problematic. Either (1) the Refutation of Idealism must succeed via subjective consciousness's logical relation to actual objects that exist and persist through time, or (2) the subject must be capable of an unconditioned, nonsensible intellectual intuition. Now let us turn to Schelling's engagement with this nexus of issues. Unlike the Kant of the first *Critique* who restricts intellectual intuition to God alone, Schelling will generalize the notion of intellectual intuition to the unconditioned as such, and, in part following

Fichte, he will emphasize that this unconditioned is in fact expressed *by* and *as* the subject.

We must first note that Schelling's appeal to intellectual intuition and immediate knowledge does not map neatly onto Kant's usage of the term. As Nassar points out, for Schelling (and the "romantics" more generally), "intellectual intuition is not only epistemologically significant but bears metaphysical significance as well."[73] Instead of beginning from the point of view of the first *Critique*, which attempts to deny the possibility of subjective knowledge independent of any objective relation, Schelling begins with a regress problem presented by the experience of objective relations and causal connections. He explains that "because every experience of objects depends on the experience of further objects, at core our knowledge must start from an immediate experience in the strictest sense, that is, from an experience produced by ourselves and independent of any objective causality."[74] Objective cognition depends on previous cognition of objects, and this leads to an infinite regress. If one is to avoid this regress, there must be a primary intuition that is neither of an object nor previously conditioned by any object. There must be a form of productive intuition that is able to ground the series of objective determinations. It is this that Schelling calls creative reason. This ground, according to Schelling, must be both an intuition and experience at once. It must be an experience in which the subject provides to itself both logical form and experiential content. Schelling characterizes the effect of this independent and self-produced experience as follows: "Intuition and experience, this principle alone can breathe life into the otherwise dead and inanimate systems. Even the most abstract concepts with which our cognition plays depend upon an experience of life and existence [*Dasein*]."[75] Recall that Jacobi had argued it was through the immediate experience of life in ourselves that allowed us to understand the world as an intelligible web of causal events occurring between actually existing things. It is this experience of life in us that links together God and creation while maintaining an infinite distance between the two. Schelling further spells out the content of this intuitive experience in writing, "This intellectual intuition takes place whenever I cease to be an object for myself, when—withdrawn into itself—the intuiting subject is identical with the intuited. In the moment of intuition, time and duration vanish for us."[76] Schelling here combines several of the functions of intellectual intuition described by Kant. In intellectual intuition, the self ceases to be an object, just as God's self-constituting intuition cannot be grounded in an intellectual or sensible object that exists prior to this intuition. Divine intuition is an unconditioned intuition. Further, through this type of unconditioned intuition, the self can know itself as a self that is independent of any relationship to externality. In a single act, the subject grounds itself in the act of its generation. However, unlike Jacobi, the experience of life detailed by Schelling does not refer us to something transcendent and prior to this experience (i.e., God). It instead immanently generates its content out of itself; it gives itself actuality in its very activity.

In order to understand the role life plays in Schelling's work at this time, we must return to the notion of exact opposition. Two years after the initial publication of the *Letters*, Schelling published the 1797 *Ideas for a Philosophy of Nature* (a book oddly described by Fichte as "a brilliant sketch of the essence of Leibniz's philosophy, as compared with Spinoza's").[77] In the introduction to that work, Schelling clearly states of Spinoza that "instead of descending into the depths of his self-consciousness and descrying the emergence thence of the two worlds within us—the ideal and the real—he passed himself by; instead of explaining from our nature how finite and infinite, originally united in us, proceed reciprocally from each other, he lost himself forthwith in the idea of an infinite outside us."[78] In contradistinction to Fichte, who claimed that Spinoza could not possibly have believed his own philosophy, Schelling again highlights the *misplaced truth* of Spinoza: finite and infinite (or real and ideal) have a common origin from which they emerge. Yet, according to Schelling, this common origin is "within us" in a highly qualified sense.[79] Further, the opposition between real and ideal in the depths of self-consciousness is one of identification and differentiation, the very type of self-relation characteristic of what Schelling calls life. In short, criticism and dogmatism equally extinguish the possibility of life by erasing any opposition between subject and object. Without the opposition between two actually existing contraries, there can be no dynamic conflict through which life and personality find their expression. Thus, the termination of the original synthetic unity of subject and object will always end in a lifelessness regardless of whether this termination occurs on the side of the object or the subject.

For this reason, Kant too is unable to give an account of a living God. As Schelling points out, the reintroduction of the Divine in the moral argument for the existence of God creates a conflict between theoretical and practical reason. Practical reason demands that which theoretical reason cannot know. The Third Antinomy has shown that the causality of freedom lies in the noumenal and is unable to penetrate the realm of the phenomenal. In conflict with this, the moral law demands that moral action be both possible and meaningful. This leads us back to where we began, namely the notion of "weak reason," that is, "a reason which *desires* to know one [an objective God]."[80] Schelling continues to further elucidate the above conflict between theoretical and practical reason. Theoretical reason is not sufficient to overthrow dogmatism. Further, theoretical reason alone is unable to satisfy reason's demands:

> Theoretical reason *necessarily* seeks what is not conditioned; having formed the *idea* of the unconditioned, and, as *theoretical* reason, being unable to realize the unconditioned, it therefore *demands* the *act* through which it *ought* to be realized. Here, then, philosophy proceeds to the realm of *demands*, that is, to the domain of *practical* philosophy, and only there can the decisive victory be gained—by the principle which we put at the beginning of philosophy, and which would be dispensable for theoretical philosophy if the latter could constitute a separate domain.[81]

The conflicting demands of practical and theoretical reason disrupt any balance between the two. The need of the practical in light of the findings of the theoretical push the philosopher committed to freedom to accept the primacy of practical reason. However, "no need, however urgent, can make the impossible possible," Schelling explains.[82]

Instead of constraining itself to the articulation of the moral law and the God beholden thereto, Schelling insists that practical reason must address the existential question of "Why is there a realm of experience at all?"[83] He continues, "The problem necessarily leads me beyond all bounds of *knowledge* [*Schranken des* Wissens] into a region where I do not *find* firm ground, but must *produce* it myself in order to firmly stand upon it."[84] We also find Schelling giving an argument for the primacy of practical reason over theoretical reason, but, crucially, his focus on the creative aspects of productive reason in the practical realm allows him to expand the practical beyond the ethical or the normative. The expression "creative reason" nicely differentiates this act from both practical reason and intellectual intuition traditionally conceived. The creative aspect of Schelling's creative reason downplays the problematic immediacy of intellectual intuition. For Schelling, creative reason is not a form of unmediated access to an already existing object. Instead, it relates more closely to the creative powers reserved by Kant for the Divine alone. It is a kind of practical reason that can reach beyond the confines of the normative sphere. Snow helpfully clarifies Schelling's idiosyncratic appeal to "practical reason." "When Schelling speaks of realizing a system in practical action," she writes, "he is appealing not to moral consciousness as it was understood by Kant and Fichte but rather to a pretheoretical and immediate striving of reason. He does call it practical reason, but he does so in part from conceptual confusion (since he is thinking of creative reason, and moral action is self-constitutive activity, as he understood it), and in part to distinguish it unmistakably from theoretical reason."[85]

Though Schelling's use of practical reason is idiosyncratic on the surface, it does carry with it a deep connection to Kant's moral philosophy. In the *Groundwork for the Metaphysics of Morals*, Kant claims that

> *Will* is a species of causality of living beings, insofar as they are rational, and *freedom* would be that quality of this causality by which it can be effective independently of alien causes *determining* it; just as *natural necessity* is the quality of the causality of all beings lacking reason, of being determined to activity through the influence of alien causes.[86]

Will is a form of causality unique to living, rational beings and it stands in stark distinction to natural causes. The will can stand apart from nature insofar as the will, as long as it is good, is the only thing "which can be taken as good without qualification." This is because the will acts in accordance with the objects that it itself creates. It is not guided by any goal or object external to itself. It is conditioned only in relation to the moral law, a condition that the will itself generates. "Solely the concept of freedom," Kant explains, "permits us to find the unconditioned and intelligible for the conditioned and sensible without needing to go outside ourselves."[87] The spontaneity of freedom alone allows for the self-conditioning of the unconditioned. It is, of course, not insignificant that the causality of the moral law is likened to the experience of the sublime. "Two things fill the mind with ever new and increasing admiration," Kant famously concludes in the *Critique of Practical Reason*, "the starry sky above me and the moral law within me."[88] In both cases, in relation to the moral law and the experience of the sublime, the self is not determined by any external object in contradistinction to the Refutation of Idealism.

Recall that Schelling begins his *Letters* by denying content to the idea of a moral God and further asserting that there is nothing sublime about the idea at all. Schelling opens the first letter with the following address to Kant: "You deem it greater to struggle against an absolute power and to perish in the struggle than to guarantee one's safety from any future danger by positing a moral god. To be sure, the struggle against the immeasurable is not only the most sublime that man can conceive, but is also, I think, the very ground of all sublimity."[89] This voluntary annihilation is of course exactly what we have seen in Spinoza, according to Schelling. Here again, in Spinoza we find the peak of dogmatism, albeit for different reasons. According to Schelling, Spinoza has not committed a simple error in his self-annihilation that results from handing over the independent causality of the ego to the objective causality of substance. He has in fact realized yet misplaced a deep insight regarding the possible transition from the finite to the infinite. There is no transition, but this is not because the self is lost in the absolute object. Alternatively, Kant concedes the struggle against the sublimity of freedom and thereby evacuates the life from God.

Schelling realizes the potential of Kant's idea that it is only within the practical realm that the will can create its own object from nothing and direct itself in accordance with this self-generated object. Creative reason is thus able to generate its own object and oppose itself to this object interminably, thereby creating a perpetual and sublime struggle. In this case, the sublime force of impossibility is the productive ground of actuality. Yet if this decision is to remain alive, it must remain relatively indeterminate, that is, the opposition between the productive and the determinate must remain an active and actual one. As Schelling explains, "Man ought to be neither lifeless nor merely alive. His activity is necessarily intent upon objects, but with equal necessity it returns into itself. The latter distinguishes him from the merely living (animal) being, the former from the lifeless."[90] The life proper to a human being consists of a double motion. On the one hand, the activity of the human is intentional and directed toward external objects. On the other hand, this activity can also turn inward and apprehend the subject as subject. In order for this double motion to remain, subject must remain *as* subject in opposition to the object *as* object.

In the end, we can see how both criticism and dogmatism as previously formulated end in a lifeless state insofar as lifelessness is understood as a relation without conflict or striving; lifelessness is a distinction without exact opposition. "Dogmatism and criticism can hold their own as contradicting systems only while approaching the ultimate goal," Schelling explains, "on this very account, criticism must regard the ultimate goal merely as the object of an endless task. *Criticism itself necessarily turns into dogmatism as soon as it sets up the ultimate goal as realized* (in an object), *or as realizable* (at any particular time)."[91] Kant's moral proof for the existence of God nullifies the sublime striving of the moral agent thereby eliminating real opposition between subject and object. Kant's God is not conflicted by the imperative to act morally. Alternatively, Spinoza objectifies the intellectual intuition of the subject into an empty absolute object. This too is a God without opposition and thus without life. Criticism and dogmatism come to a common end. Or, more specifically, idealism and realism become identical at the height of their "perfection." Schelling explains,

> He who has reflected upon idealism and realism, the two most opposite theoretical systems, has found by himself that both can come to pass only in the approach to the absolute, yet both must unite in the absolute, that is, must cease as opposite systems. One used to say that *God intuits things in themselves*. If this were to signify anything reasonable, it would mean that God is the most perfect realism. Yet realism, conceived in its perfection, necessarily and just because it is perfect realism, becomes idealism. For perfect realism comes to pass only where the objects cease to be objects, that is, appearances, opposed to the subject—in short, only where the representation is identical with the represented objects, hence where subject and object are absolutely identical. Therefore that realism in the deity by which it intuits things in themselves is nothing else than the most perfect idealism, by which the deity intuits nothing but itself and its own reality.[92]

God's perfect and unmediated intuition of things-in-themselves would collapse all distinction between the knower and the objects of knowledge. When the opposition between subject and object vanishes so too does anything distinctive that could be called either realism or idealism. Following from this is the elimination of any possible living interpenetration of real and ideal, which is in turn necessary to avoid lapsing into a Spinozist dogmatism, the most perfect realism.

5.0. Conclusion

Through a series of philosophical reflections on the relationship between critical and dogmatic philosophy, Schelling's *Letters* articulate his belief that idealism and realism must not stand against each other as mutually exclusive doctrines. Instead, there is necessarily a relation between the two doctrines, and the philosopher necessarily has a need for both realism and idealism. However, the relation between realism and idealism is not a simple and stable parallel one. Instead, this relation is a messy and supplementary one. Derrida explains the double meaning of the word *supplement* in his analysis of speech and writing in the works of Rousseau. "For the concept of the supplement," Derrida explains, "harbors within itself two significations whose combination is as strange as it is necessary." The first meaning of the supplement regards something extra: "The supplement adds itself," he writes, "it is a surplus, a plentitude enriching another plentitude, the *zenith* [*le comble*] of presence." Now at the same time, and this is the strangeness of the supplement, "the supplement supplements. It adds only to replace. It intervenes or insinuates itself *in-the-place-of*; if it fills to the brim [*comble*], it is as if one fills [*comble*] a void."[93] The supplement is simultaneously a response to something lacking, as well as an addition or an excess. We can see this playing itself out in the relation Schelling articulates between realism and idealism in the *Letters*. Realism needs idealism because, internally, there is a lacking inscribed within. Realism without the supplement of idealism is unable to fulfill the goal of systematic philosophy. The same holds true for idealism. It too lacks internal self-sufficiency and calls out to realism as its other. This generates a blurred semi-parallelism between the two, but because of their supplementary co-constitution, any clean-cut demarcation between criticism and dogmatism drifts beyond our grasp. This then brings us back to the common root problem.

Importantly, at this time, Schelling does not seem to indicate that there might be some third system of philosophy that enveloped both the insights of realism and the insights of idealism. Schelling formulates a version of an idea popularized by Fichte, that "the kind of philosophy one chooses thus depends upon the kind of person one is."[94] Fichte's claim here seems to suggest a predisposition in the individual to a particular philosophical system. Alternatively, Schelling returns an element of freedom to this decision between philosophical systems. "As for myself," he writes,

> I believe that there is a system of dogmatism as well as a system of criticism; I even believe that, in this very criticism, I have found the solution to the riddle as to why these two systems should necessarily exist side by side, why there must be two systems directly opposed to each other as long as there are any finite beings, and why no man can convince himself of any system except *pragmatically* [*praktisch*], that is, by realizing either system *in himself*.[95]

There must remain an exact and real (and therefore living) opposition between the systems of philosophy. In the *Letters*, Schelling claims that this opposition can only be held together "pragmatically" or within the philosopher. We are left with the following question: What does it mean to realize a system "within oneself" and how is one to do this in a way that not reducible to the side of the subjective? How can one maintain the primacy of the ego's independent causality without annihilating the objective within the subjective and thereby falling into empty criticism? So, in short, the supplementary relation of realism and idealism in *Letters* fails to provide an answer to this question without appealing to subjectivity. We can consequently characterize Schelling's solution to the problem posed by the mutual dependence of realism and idealism as flirting with a kind of subjectivism he ultimately wishes to avoid. If the *Letters* detail the first fundamental problem of philosophy (that of the egress from the Absolute), Schelling's attempt to move away from subjectivism pushes him toward a second fundamental philosophical problem for which he again turns to Spinoza as a guide.

88 | Schelling and Spinoza

This is the problem of nothing less than the nature of the Absolute. With this demand in mind, we can now turn to Schelling's identity philosophy and the role of Spinoza plays therein.

PART II

Chapter 3

Spinoza and Schelling on Identity and Difference

1.0. Introduction: Spinoza, the Undeniable Predecessor

Like the previous versions, the 1815 draft of *The Ages of the World* remains trapped in the past. At the close of this iteration of Schelling's attempt to provide a comprehensive account of the past, present, and future of the world, he takes a pause in order to reflect on his own past. "Far be it from us," Schelling writes, "to deny in Spinoza that for which he was our teacher and predecessor."[1] He continues, "Perhaps, of all the modern philosophers, there was in Spinoza a dark feeling [*ein dunkles Gefühl*] of that primordial time of which we have attempted to conceptualize so precisely."[2] The completed content of the various fragments of *The Ages of the World*, the past it seeks to know and narrate, was felt by Spinoza. As we saw in the previous chapter, according to Schelling, this "dark feeling" was intuited by Spinoza yet subsequently misplaced, resulting in the erasure of the intuiting subject. A fear of this dark feeling was both dogmatism's lesson and the source of its fundamental error.

We can take the above reference as true not just of Spinoza but of Schelling's previous work as well, particularly the ideas that occupied him following the publication of the *System of Transcendental Idealism*. These ideas form what is referred to as the identity philosophy, or the system of identity. The identity philosophy begins as the period of work in which Schelling most thoroughly and explicitly articulates his philosophy in relation to both the form and content of Spinoza's philosophy. In the 1801 *Presentation*, Schelling argues for a strong monism by way of a geometrical presentation, much like Spinoza's *Ethics*. Furthermore, as Schelling himself suggests, "all further clarifications of the relation of our system to any other, especially to Spinozism and to idealism, are to be sought in the following presentation itself."[3] This reverence for Spinoza is evidence of a significant shift in Schelling's philosophical goals. In the identity philosophy, Schelling attempts what seemed impossible in 1795—namely, the articulation of a philosophy that begins from the Absolute itself. In the previous chapter, we found in the *Letters* the idea that "if we had had to deal with the absolute alone, the strife of different systems would never have arisen. Only as we come forth from the absolute does opposition to it originate, and only through this *original* opposition in the human does any opposition between philosophers originate."[4] In order to provide an account for the differentiation between the systems of realism and idealism, one had to begin with the question, "*How do I ever come to egress* [Entgegengesetztes] *from the absolute, and to progress toward an opposite?*"[5] The philosophies of realism and idealism only become opposed to each other once thought leaves the Absolute through this egress in question. Consequently, the possible coexistence of identity and opposition, of unity and differentiation, is of central importance for understanding the relation between realism and idealism.

Despite the overwhelming and self-identified overlap between the 1801 formulation of Schelling's identity philosophy and Spinoza's *Ethics*, it would be wrong to read the identity philosophy as either a monolithic endeavor or an uncritical adoption of Spinoza's metaphysics.[6] Tracing the shift in Schelling's perspective on Spinoza during this period elucidates other changes within the identity philosophy as they relate to what Schelling calls the Absolute. In the 1804 lectures *Philosophy and Religion*, Schelling explicitly voices both an admiration for and a dissatisfaction with Spinoza: "The last echoes of the old, true philosophy were heard from Spinoza," he remarks, "he led philosophy back to its proper subjects although he did not steer clear of the pretense and tawdriness of another, albeit different, kind of dogmatism."[7] Through his deep insight into the dark feeling of the past, Spinoza brought philosophy back to its true course even if he himself was not able to fully avoid the pitfalls of tawdriness and dogmatism. It is clear that the identity philosophy is bookended by two distinct perspectives on Spinoza; we begin with deep admiration and end with a kind of disappointment. By following the convergences and divergences in Spinoza's and Schelling's respective accounts of the identity of the infinite Absolute and the differentiation of finite particulars allows us to better understand the contours of this love affair.

Of primary importance in the present chapter will be developing the strongest possible argument for existence monism derivable from Spinoza's fundamental commitment to the idea that from nothing, nothing can come, that is, to the PSR. Though this approach might appear anachronistic, it is warranted insofar as we have already seen how Schelling follows Jacobi in his characterization of the PSR as the core of Spinoza's philosophy.[8] Taking the PSR as central to the entirety of Spinoza's metaphysical system yields a more dry and sober Spinozism than is fashionable in more recent continental commentaries. However, only in its strongest possible form does Spinoza's monist metaphysics yield insight into the relation Schelling acknowledges between the identity philosophy and the system of his undeniable predecessor. Section 2 looks at the relation between Spinoza's account of monism and Schelling's concept of identity.[9] I outline how Spinoza's monism is not presupposed in advance but instead follows from his commitment to the PSR. Alternatively, Schelling begins with existence monism as an expression of the Principle of Identity $A = A$. Consequently, for Spinoza, the scope of the PSR is unlimited, whereas for Schelling the scope of the PSR is more localized. Subsequently, section 3 traces the divergences between Spinoza's and Schelling's accounts of the self-differentiation of the infinite into finite particulars. Adopting Spinoza's strongest possible form of monism brings with it the phenomenologically unintuitive claim that finite things do not exist. Spinoza and Schelling must both account in some way for the apparent existence of individuated particulars without violating their commitment to the idea that only one thing can be said to properly exist. It is the divergence in these accounts of differentiation that brings to light the significance of Spinoza's and Schelling's perspectives on the scope of the PSR. The overall goal is both to outline the significant similarities between Spinoza's *Ethics* and Schelling's identity philosophy while also generating a minimal difference between the two that can be expanded upon in later chapters.

2.0. The Need for Identity

Schelling's quest for unity, which seems to come to its peak in the identity philosophy, is by no means a novel aspect of his philosophical project. For example, in *Of the I*, he writes that the "last ground for all reality is something that is thinkable only through itself, that is, it is thinkable only through its being [*Sein*]; it is thought only in as much as it is. In short, *the principle of being and thinking is one and the same*."[10] Determinate thoughts and beings are only possible in relation to a Being that can be thought through itself alone. Like in Hölderlin's fragment *Judgment Being Possibility*, there is a Being whose actuality precedes the division into subject and object by way of judgment.[11] Schelling expresses a similar thought from the perspective of the philosophy of nature. In the *First Outline* he speaks of a formless fluid that is "the most original product of Nature."[12] He continues, "The *whole* of Nature, not just *part* of it, should be equivalent to an ever-*becoming* product. Nature as a whole must be conceived in constant formation, and everything must engage in that universal process of formation."[13] Nature is neither subject nor object but is instead the infinite process through which subjects and objects are formed and deformed. Now, both *Of the I* and the *First Outline* contain references to Spinoza, but Spinoza's *Ethics* is not explicitly taken up as a model or a map. In fact, in the preface to *Of the I*, Schelling warns that though some readers "could jump to the conclusion that the author is trying to repeat Spinoza's errors, even though they have been refuted long ago." He continues, "For such readers (if that term may be applied to them) I want to say . . . that this essay is meant to annul explicitly the very foundations of Spinoza's system."[14] Though Schelling might have wished to annul the foundations of Spinoza's system, presumably the dogmatic elimination of the subject discussed in the *Letters*, his views on holism and the primacy of unity forbid Schelling from fully casting Spinoza aside. Schelling maintains a *need* for identity, and it is this need that returns him to Spinoza in the *Presentation*.

Schelling's need for identity in the identity philosophy at first arises as a method for reconciling the apparent dualism present in his writings that came before it. The *Presentation* opens with a warning from Schelling: "No one should think," he writes, "that I have altered my system of philosophy."[15] Though this claim is questionable, Schelling then accurately reminds his readers that "for many years I sought to present the one Philosophy that I know to be true from two wholly different sides—[both] as philosophy of nature and as transcendental philosophy."[16] As we saw in the previous chapter, dogmatism and criticism were two different philosophical perspectives that arose from the shared synthesis that sits at the root of thinking and being. Here, we see Schelling taking a decisive step forward in thinking the relationship between the two systems, hence the inaccuracy of Schelling's initial claim to the reader. He continues, "I never concealed from myself or from others the fact that I take neither what I term 'transcendental philosophy' nor what I term 'philosophy of nature,' each in isolation, to be the system of philosophy itself."[17] This remark brings forth several important facts. First, any attempt to read Schelling's work (at least up until the *System of Transcendental Idealism*) as exclusively transcendental philosophy or philosophy of nature would focus on but one aspect of Schelling's broader philosophical aspirations. Secondly, and more interestingly, in a sense it is not until the *Presentation* that Schelling begins to do what he considers to be "philosophy."

In the previous chapter, we saw how Schelling turns to Spinoza in an attempt to find a realist ground for transcendental idealism. Here, in 1801, he likewise emphasizes the realism made possible by Spinozism. In fact, he goes so far as to suggest,

> It seems to me, as I hope the following presentation proves, that until now realism in its most sublime and perfect form (in Spinozism, I mean) has been thoroughly misconstrued and misunderstood in all the slanted opinions of it that have become public knowledge.[18]

Spinozism: the most sublime and perfect realism. This sentiment is consistent with the one voiced in the *Letters*. However, we do see a significant shift taking place here. In the *Letters*, Schelling approvingly quoted Jacobi's then famous characterization of the "spirit" of Spinoza's philosophy, namely, that from nothing, nothing can come. Schelling now claims that the commonsense and public dismissal of Spinozism that followed from this characterization are distortions of the most sublime and perfect realism. Further, not only is Spinozism the most sublime and perfect realism, the *Presentation* is a *proof* of this. We can see that Schelling conceives of the *Presentation* as a type of homage to Spinoza. Schelling is not just using Spinoza as a resource. Instead, he is taking him as a model, and Schelling says exactly this:

> Concerning the manner of exposition, I have taken Spinoza as a model here, since I thought there was good reason to choose as a paradigm the philosopher whom I believed came nearest to my system in terms of content or material and in form, but I also adopted this model because the form of exposition allowed the greatest brevity of presentation and the most accurate assessment of the certainty of demonstrations.[19]

Both the form and the content of the pages that follow are best read and understood in relation to Spinoza, but are not reducible thereto. Vater and Melamed have both analyzed the influence of Spinoza on Schelling's *Presentation* and come to somewhat contrary conclusions. Vater argues that the influence of Spinoza on the text is less than it may appear:

> Despite formal similarities between Spinoza's geometric method and Schelling's numbered mathematical-geometrical construction, Schelling's direct debts to Spinoza are few: first, the Cartesian definitions of *substance* and *attribute*; second, an account of phenomena or modal being that reproduces Spinoza's teaching that nothing is intrinsically finite; and finally, a concept of "potency" or natural force modeled on *conatus*.[20]

I will primarily be focusing on Vater's second point here regarding the relation between the infinite and the finite in section 3. This is in part because it is unclear if Spinoza himself uncritically adopts Descartes's definitions of substance and attribute, and in part because (as we will see in section 3.2) Schelling's understanding of powers is opposed to Spinoza's *conatus* doctrine. However, before tracking the differences between Schelling's and Spinoza's monism's, we must grasp how Schelling takes up and subsequently overcomes the notion of simple identity articulated by Spinoza. Melamed argues that the *Presentation* transposes Spinoza's argument for substance monism into an argument for the selfsame simplicity of reason itself, indicating that the influence of Spinoza is greater than Vater initially claims it to be. Melamed writes, "At a deeper level Schelling is attempting to transform Spinoza's system by replacing God, Spinoza's ultimate reality, with reason."[21] I believe Melamed's approach to be more fruitful, especially when we take Schelling at his word concerning the relation between the *Presentation* and Spinoza, as well as his later self-critique that the identity philosophy lapses back into Spinozism. Reading Schelling alongside Spinoza allows us to elucidate how identity and difference operate throughout the identity philosophy. Looking more generally to the ways that logic (and specifically the PSR) conditions the ontological conclusions of Spinoza and Schelling respectively establishes a minimal methodological difference between the two that becomes exploitable as Schelling continues to articulate the identity philosophy.

2.1. IDENTITY: SPINOZA

In chapter 1, I claimed that Spinoza's monism—his "most monstrous thought"—was in fact *derived* from his most seemingly commonsense commitment to the PSR. Philosophical endeavors generally presuppose that some things can be explained. Spinoza refuses to arbitrarily limit the scope of explicability, and from this follows a strict adherence to the PSR. It is possible to reconstruct Spinoza's argument for monism without reference to the PSR yet doing so would neglect Spinoza's prephilosophical commitment to the project of explanation and rationalism more generally. At first glance, there is nothing radical about the commitment that for every effect there is necessarily a cause and that every causal relation between events is necessarily intelligible. It is now time to make good on this claim. To do so, let us see how a rigorous commitment to the PSR necessitates a commitment to the strongest form of monism, that is, an existence monism that holds that only one thing exists. Though the following presentation finds its ground in Spinoza's text, we will also have to move beyond Spinoza by way of recent scholarship that attempts to defend Spinoza's commitment to the PSR in order to demonstrate what this commitment fully entails. What is essential is to understand how Spinoza's existence monism *follows from* his commitment to the PSR and is not presupposed in advance. In other words, the project of Spinozism is not some grand, metaphysical defense of the odd and even frightening conclusion that only one thing exists. Instead, it is an elaboration of the modest proposition that explanation is possible.

Both Jacobi and Schelling see a version of the PSR (in the form "from nothing, nothing can come") as the essence of Spinoza's philosophy. We can rephrase this principle as follows: If a thing does not have a cause for its existence (if there is only nothing), it cannot be conceived as existing (nothing can follow). As Della Rocca argues, if we are to be consistent in our commitment to the PSR, this claim must hold true in the reverse case as well. If there is not a cause for a thing's *non*existence, then it must necessarily exist. Now, the PSR in this form is not explicitly stated in the *Ethics*, but we can at several points find intimations of it. For example, *E*Ia3 states that "from a given determinate cause there necessarily follows an effect; on the other hand, if there is not determinate cause, it is impossible that an effect should follow." If there is an effect, then this effect followed necessarily from a cause that determined it to be as it is and not otherwise. Moreover, if there is no cause then there can be no effect. We should note the hypothetical formulation of this Axiom. It states that *if* there is a cause then there must be an effect, leaving open the possibility that there could be no causes and consequently no effects. So again, as Jacobi and Schelling saw, if there is only nothing, only nothing can follow.

If a thing exists, then it must have a reason for its existence, and if a thing does not exist there must also be a reason for its nonexistence. In *E*Ia5, Spinoza states that "things which have nothing in common with each other cannot be understood through each other." For Spinoza, this Axiom is not making a simple epistemic claim. Because being conceived through another thing is also to be caused by another thing, *E*Ia5 can be restated as "things that have nothing in common with one another cannot be the cause of one another," which is essentially *E*Ip3. With this in mind let us first take the case of nonexistence. If nothing exists, there must be a reason, a discernible and articulable cause, for this nonexistence. In the second proof to *E*Ip11, Spinoza uses the example of a triangle to reinforce this point: "If a triangle exists, there must be a reason, or cause, for its existence. If it does not exist, there must be a reason or cause which prevents it from existing, or which annuls its existence." Now, if we assume the PSR as well as *E*Ia5, then the possibility of absolute nonexistence, pure nothingness, is not a viable option because not to exist is to be *caused* not to exist, and this is a limitation. For anything to be limited, it must be affected by something else with which it has something in common. As a result of this, we can see that for Spinoza, the possibility of absolute nonexistence is absurd insofar as one would have to presuppose the existence of something that causes the inexistence of everything. From the reverse side of this argument, it follows that the existence of (at least one) substance is necessary because the inexistence of all possible substances would imply the existence of some cause of that inexistence. Thus, Spinoza concludes in EIp7 "existence belongs to the nature of substance."

So, if the PSR is to hold in all cases, at least one thing must exist, because nonexistence is a limitation that must have a cause. However, it does not immediately follow that only one, infinite thing exists. Spinoza's proof for substance monism also relies upon a version of the Principle of the Identity of Indiscernibles. The general idea here is that two things with the exact same properties cannot be thought of as two discernibly distinct things. If object A and object B have all the same properties and characteristics there would be no feature to which we could appeal to in order to differentiate A from B. This principle, it must be noted, is not a commitment separate from the PSR but instead follows from it. If one thing is to be considered as distinct from some other thing, there must be a *reason* for this difference. And again, the reverse holds true as well. If there is no property that differentiates one thing from another, then these things cannot be understood to be distinct individuals. As EIp4 makes clear, a substance can be differentiated by either its attributes ("that which the intellect perceives of substance as constituting its essence")[22] or by its modes ("the affections of substance").[23] Because a mode is an affection of substance, substance must precede all modes (EIp1). Modes are dependent upon substance for their existence while substance is dependent only upon itself. Were there no substance there would be nothing to modify or affect. Further, if any two substances were to share an attribute, there would be no possible way to determine them as separate substances. This is because an attribute is not a partial view or aspect of substance. An attribute is what the intellect perceives as constituting the *essence* of substance, and this essence is never partial. So, substances can neither be distinguished by their modes (because substance is necessarily prior to all modes) nor can they be distinguished by their attributes (because each attribute expresses the *full* and not partial essence of substance). Consequently, one substance cannot be the cause of another. If this were possible, the two substances would have to share an attribute, but if they did, they would be the same substance. Further, since according to *E*Ip8 ("every substance is infinite"),

> There cannot be more than one substance having the same attribute (Pr.5), and existence belongs to the nature of substance (Pr.7). It must therefore exist either as finite or as infinite. But it cannot exist as finite, for (Def. 2) it would have to be limited by another substance of the same nature, and that substance also would have to exist (Pr. 7). And so there would exist two substances of the same attribute, which is absurd (Pr. 5).

Because attributes are conceptually distinct, and causal entailment is dependent upon conceptual entailment for Spinoza, no one attribute can limit another.[24] Attributes are necessarily parallel and by extension can have no causal interaction. There can be no blurring between the attributes, in part because if there was, the argument for existence monism would fail. Though we only know two attributes (that of thought and that of extension) this does not imply that there are only two attributes. Because one attribute can never be limited by another, there is no limit to the number of possible attributes. Consequently, substance is infinite "internally" and "externally"—internally because an infinite number of attributes constitute its essence, and externally because there can be no thing "outside" of substance that could act as a limitation.

Take note that the law of identity plays no role in any of this proof. That substance is selfsame and simple *follows from* the PSR, as well as the definitions and the axioms that open Book I of the *Ethics*; it is *not* presupposed in advance. This is perhaps what led Spinoza to say, "I do not say that I have found the best philosophy, only the true one."[25] Thus, the two fundamental commitments of Spinoza's philosophy are inextricably linked. Spinoza's brand of naturalism follows directly from his commitment to rationalism. What Della Rocca refers to as Spinoza's "rationalism on steroids"[26] entails Spinoza's commitment to naturalism understood as the "thesis that everything in the world plays by the same rules; there are no things that are somehow connected with each other but that are not governed by the same principles."[27] Relatedly, Della Rocca claims that "Spinoza's naturalism . . . is the view that there are no illegitimate bifurcations in reality."[28] The general idea here is that if any two things are connected or related in anyway, they must abide by the same overarching set of rules and regularities. Further, any division between things or principles must be accounted for as intelligible and necessary. It is not the case that Spinoza forecloses the existence of dualism; he is instead committed to the idea that any dualism must have a reason for its existence. If the PSR is to hold, it must be the case that there are no arbitrary exceptions. This allows us to better understand how Spinoza complicates what Schelling had earlier referred to as the fundamental problem of philosophy (the transitional relationship between the infinite and the finite). If there is to be a transition from the infinite to the finite, one would first have to justify the bifurcation between the infinite and the finite, and it is precisely this that Spinoza's argument for the necessity of substance monism denies.

Following Della Rocca, we can see that the strongest reading of Spinoza's monism is best represented by the existence monist position. As noted above, if we are to truly understand the overlap between Spinoza's monist metaphysics and Schelling's notion of the Absolute in the identity philosophy, we must outline the identity of the Absolute in its most extreme articulation. Further, if we follow Schelling's explicit isolation of the PSR as the core of Spinoza's philosophy, then it follows that he could only have viewed Spinoza as an existence monist.[29] Existence monism is the idea that "there is only one object, and any multiplicity of objects, such as tables as distinct from chairs, is at best illusory."[30] For the existence monist, only one thing exists and this ought to be taken in a very literal sense. There is one object, and all multiplicity is a distorted understanding of existence largely produced by an insufficient understanding of the relationship between causes and effects. Existence monism can be contrasted with "priority monism." Priority monism is "weaker than existence monism in that priority monism allows that tables as distinct from chairs may exist. Priority monism simply requires that this multiplicity of things is dependent on the cosmos or the one fundamental object."[31] So, for the priority monist, a multiplicity of discrete objects exist, but their existence is dependent on something singular. Schaffer, for example, distinguishes between priority monism and existence monism, and claims that "the world has parts, but the parts are dependent fragments of an integrated whole."[32] Individual things exist, but their existence is dependent upon the existence of a whole that precedes its individual parts. Schaffer identifies this whole that is prior to the parts as the cosmos. Thus, for the priority monist, though they maintain relative autonomy from each other, all things are all connected through the whole by which they are preceded and upon which they are individually dependent.

We may perceive things and the relations between things as the priority monist would claim, but this perception tells us little to nothing about the reality of either relations or things (I will return to this in section 3.1). Importantly, the stronger version of existence monism is more consistent with Spinoza's own position insofar as he explicitly denies the existence of finite particulars. Further, we previously saw that the only way Spinoza can mount a challenge to Kant's antinomies is through the notion of a *totum analyticum,* or a totality given independent of the existence of any parts. We must take seriously Spinoza's dramatic claim that "it is nonsense, bordering on madness, to hold that extended Substance is composed of parts or bodies really distinct from one another."[33] This conclusion that seems so absurd and phenomenologically counterintuitive in fact follows directly from a steadfast commitment to the PSR. So, if a commitment to the PSR and a drive for universal explicability are at the core of Spinoza's metaphysical system, as Jacobi and Schelling both maintain, then existence monism necessarily follows.

Finally, I want to note that existence monism is not some relic of past metaphysics, and though it claims only one thing exists, this does not imply that existence monist metaphysics is a simple affair. Recently, Hogan and Potrč have argued for a form of existence monism they call "blobjectivism," which "asserts that the right ontology is not only free of the kinds of proper part-entities that Schaffer would count as objects, but also is free of regions or points that are proper parts of the whole."[34] The general idea is that priority monism relies on an overly complex ontology that it is incapable of defending. Instead of claiming that parts exist but there is a whole that is prior to the existence of these parts, Hogan and Potrč's austere realism eschews the existence of parts all together. Now, though it is free of "proper" parts or regions, "the blobject has enormous spatiotemporal structural complexity and enormous local variability,"[35] Blobjectivism "incorporates an ontological analysis of spatiotemporal complexity that eschews genuine **parts** in favor of spatiotemporally local **manners of instantiation**."[36] Though the blobject is ontologically simple, this does not mean that it is without complex variability. Like any existence monism, blobjectivism encounters the problem of accounting for the finite particulars we meet with in experience. Accordingly, the other side of blobjectivism is a complex contextualist theory of indirect semantic correspondence. Hogan and Potrč explain of their austere realism that "semantically, it claims that numerous statements that are normally considered true, and that initially appear to have ontological commitments incompatible with an austere ontology, are indeed true but do not really incur such ontological commitments."[37] So basically, when we talk about how *things* are, we are not really making direct correspondence claims about those things as parts of a larger whole. Instead, when properly understood, we are making claims about the structural complexity of a single object, what they call "the world." I bring this up not to suggest that the existence monism of Spinoza's *Ethics* or Schelling's *Presentation* is a version of austere realism insofar as further analysis of the semantics implied by both projects would be needed in order to make such a claim. Instead, blobjectivism highlights that the prima facia absurdity of the counterintuitive claim that the things singled out in experience and language do not exist does not invalidate the claim that only one thing truly exists. In fact, something like the blobject is an immensely helpful guide in discussions of monism due to both its global ontological simplicity and its localized structural complexity.

2.2. IDENTITY: SCHELLING

Though Schelling shares Spinoza's conclusion that only one thing can be said to properly exist, he arrives at this conclusion by way of this distinct methodological commitment. Schelling's departure from Spinoza is expressed well in the following proposition from the *Presentation*: "The ultimate law for the being of reason, and, since there is nothing outside of reason (§2), for all being . . . is the law of identity, which with respect to all being is expressed by $A = A$," he writes.[38] For Spinoza, the PSR constitutes the essence of rational explicability. Alternatively, for Schelling, the law of identity makes possible the identity of being and reason. Though, as Harris notes, this proposition closely mirrors *E*Id6 in which Spinoza defines God, the difference between the law of identity and the PSR must be kept in mind.[39] Let us begin with some of the similarities between Spinoza's monism and Schelling's 1801 articulation of identity in the identity philosophy. Schelling begins the demonstration of the *Presentation* by defining reason: "I call *reason* absolute reason, or reason insofar as it is conceived as the total indifference of the subjective and objective," Schelling writes.[40] He then continues, "Outside reason is nothing, and everything is in it."[41] Vater notes the similarity between these starting propositions and *E*Ip15, namely that "whatever is, is in God, and nothing can be or be conceived without God."[42] Without God, nothing can be conceived. If there is any autonomy from God, it is only relative insofar as anything, if it is to exist, depends upon God for its existence. Schelling concludes §1 of the presentation with the following description, worth quoting at length:

> The standpoint of philosophy is the standpoint of reason, its kind of knowing is a knowing of things as they are in themselves, i.e., as they are in reason. It is the nature of philosophy to completely suspend all succession and externality, all difference of time and everything which mere imagination mingles with thought, in a word, to see in things only that aspect by which they express absolute reason, not insofar as they are objects of reflection, which is subject to the laws of mechanism and has duration in time.[43]

Schelling's claim here operates on multiple different levels. First, it is a claim about philosophy; the standpoint of philosophy is the standpoint of reason. That is, philosophical thought is not reducible to reflection alone. Further, the standpoint of philosophy must *generate* identity through the suspension of differentiation and duration. Second, Schelling is making a more general epistemological claim. Anything that exists can be known in and through reason. Anything not within reason is nothing. Consequently, not only can it not be known, but it also cannot be said to exist. Thus, in the identity philosophy, reason is without external limitation. Like Spinoza's substance, there is nothing external to reason that could be said to limit it, and by extension it is unlimited and universal in its scope. Finally, there is a metaphysical claim here. Because reason is not exhaustively determined by reflection, the things that exist in reason (that is, everything that exists) cannot be taken as divided, finite objects that are confined by the laws of mechanistic causality and duration in time. So, Schelling's above claim is not just a claim about philosophy, or intelligibility. It entails a broader metaphysical claim about existence.

§2 of the *Presentation* clearly restates the conclusion of the previous section; "Nothing is outside reason, and everything is in it," writes Schelling.[44] In §3, Schelling moves from the simultaneity of reason as the indifference point between subjective and objective toward the notion of identity. He explains, "Reason is simply one and simply self-identical."[45] Like Spinoza's substance, which is simple and singular (though not necessarily in the sense of being numerically "one"), reason for Schelling is not some kind of all-encompassing whole of composite parts. It is, to again quote Spinoza, "in itself and conceived through itself."[46] As we saw previously, with this thought, Spinoza articulates the complexity of the fundamental question of philosophy, that is, the transition from the infinite to the finite. If substance (or reason in Schelling's case) is one and simple, anything that exists must be conceived only through it. Schelling then concludes this section with the claim that "*reason is therefore one in an absolute sense.*"[47] This moment succinctly captures the difference that will make a difference between Spinoza's and Schelling's notions of identity. Though both think of God or reason as the simple unity of everything that exists, Schelling endeavors to render this simple unity *absolute,* that is, as neither subject nor object but instead as a hyphenated unity from which subject and object emerge. However, Schelling is not able to fully render identity absolute in this first formal presentation of the identity philosophy. In his attempt to formulate identity as the sole and absolute principle of all philosophy, Schelling initially privileges unity at the expense of difference. The identity of identity alone is formal condition for the existence of identity as Absolute. As he claims in the second corollary to §16, "*Absolute identity **IS** only under the form of an identity of identity.*"[48] What we see emphasized quite clearly is the doubling of identity in this formulation. Through this doubling, the overwhelming simplicity and simultaneity of the Absolute will give way to a fuller account of the Absolute. In short, the doubling of identity inscribes within it a minimal, but as of yet unstated, difference.

Though the conclusions of the *Presentation* fall largely in line with the conclusions of the *Ethics*, Schelling's subsequent articulations of the identity philosophy begin to distance his version of monism from Spinoza's. Following the initial characterization of what we might call "simple identity," Schelling comes to emphasize the role that the unity of opposition and difference plays in the constitution of absolute identity. In doing so, he moves from the characterization of the Absolute as the "identity of identity" to the characterization of the Absolute as the "identity of identity and difference." Berger and Whistler describe this as a movement from an "indifference" model of identity to a "dialectical" model of identity. However, they maintain that "while the indifference-model worked out in early 1801 excludes antithetical difference, it nonetheless allows for a minimal form of difference—a non-antithetical difference that can be explained from the category of identity alone."[49] This means that Schelling is not necessarily breaking from his earlier position but is instead making its content more explicit. In the 1802 dialogue *Bruno, or On the Natural and the Divine Principle of Things* [hereafter *Bruno*] Schelling recasts this initially simple identity of the Absolute as follows:

> Since we make the identity of all opposites our first principle, "identity" itself alongside with "opposition" will form the highest pair of opposites. To make identity the supreme principle, we must think of it as comprehending even this highest pair of opposites, and the {abstract} identity that is its opposite as well, and we must define this identity as the identity of identity and opposition, or the identity of the self-identical and the nonidentical.[50]

It is here that we find the more familiar characterization of absolute identity summarized by Hegel as follows: "The Absolute itself is the identity of identity and non-identity; being opposed and being one are both together in it."[51] The exact details of this confluence are debated. Frank suggests that this was Hegel's attempt to "sum up the central thought of Schelling's philosophy" and that "Schelling himself not only accepted this characterization of his Absolute System of Identity without demurral, but enthusiastically endorsed it."[52] However, this convergence does not imply that Hegel and Schelling saw completely eye to eye on the question of the Absolute, as Frank argues. Alternatively, Vater suggests that the "most probable origin, however, for the paradoxical assertion that self-identity is self-opposition, is Schelling's own prior reflections on the nature of the judgment."[53] It might even be the case, as Nassar argues, that Schelling is responding to Fichte when incorporating opposition and nonidentity into his definition of the Absolute.[54] What interests me in the shift is how this explicit formulation of Absolute identity as not indifferent to difference and not opposed to opposition distances Schelling's monism from Spinoza's. This in turn elucidates the limits of a certain form of discursive rationality. We can see that for Schelling, reason is not reducible to what we now call "rationality." In short, if reason is everything, this includes both the rational and the irrational, much like Schelling will describe the eternal as encompassing both the finite and the infinite.

Lucian challenges Bruno following his articulation of the Absolute in terms of identity and nonidentity. "But how can you acknowledge the reality of opposition in the latter context {viz. the contrast of identity and opposition} and not be forced, for that very reason, to posit it within the former context too, {or within identity itself}? Thus, it seems there is no way you can reach a pure identity, no way you can attain the sort of identity that is not distorted by difference," he states.[55] This objection is by no means trivial, especially when it comes to Schelling's critique of Spinoza. Spinozism, Schelling maintains, is constitutionally devoid of a living God and a living nature precisely because it denies the reality of opposition. Bruno responds to Lucian's objection as follows:

> If you maintain that identity and difference are opposites with respect to the supreme identity, and that the supreme identity is thus distorted by some opposition, I deny it; specifically, I deny your premise, that in the context of the supreme identity, identity and difference are opposed to each other. Hence you would be able to predicate being distorted by difference only of the kind of identity that is opposed to difference, the one that is "identity" only insofar as it is the opposite of "difference."[56]

Bruno is accusing Lucian of being unable to accept that there is a notion of difference that is not premised upon being the mere opposition of identity. "Lucian commits the fallacy of misplaced concreteness," Vater explains, "conceiving identity and difference as if they were opposite things, capable of altering one another."[57] Lucian has presupposed that the unity of identity and nonidentity can only exist under the logical rubric of opposition. Identity is distorted by difference only if identity is negatively determined as the exclusion of difference.

Again, it is not necessarily the case that Schelling has changed his overall understanding of the Absolute despite the explicit introduction of nonidentity into the definition of Absolute identity, and Schelling maintains his commitment to the primacy of the law of identity throughout the identity philosophy. The formula A = A remains the same even if Schelling deepens his understanding of the content of this principle. In the 1804 *System of Philosophy in General*, he writes, "The fundamental law of reason and all knowledge, to the extent that it is rational knowledge, is the law of identity or the proposition A = A."[58] However, in these 1804 lectures, Schelling follows a different path to this conclusion, which is worth briefly presenting. The *Presentation* began with the above discussed definition of reason as the "total indifference of the subjective and objective." Reason is neither subjective nor objective. It is instead the indifference of the two. Alternatively, in the *System of Philosophy in General*, Schelling begins by noting that "the first presupposition of all knowledge is that the knower and that which is known are the same."[59] Instead of beginning with indifference, Schelling asserts an identity. Further, we can see him returning to a problem he sought to address in *Of the I*: "He who wants to know something, wants to know at the same time that what he knows is real," writes Schelling. "Knowledge without reality is not knowledge."[60] Though Schelling was not often preoccupied with strictly epistemological concerns, we can see that he was nevertheless engaged in elaborating an ontology of knowing. *Of the I* foreshadows the project of the *System of Philosophy in General* in the following lines: "If there is any genuine knowledge at all, there must be knowledge which I do not reach by way of some other knowledge, but through which alone all other knowledge is knowledge."[61] Insofar as this concern is filtered through the *Presentation*, we can see Schelling taking a more explicitly Spinozist approach to the question of the reality of knowledge. One cannot begin with the dualism of knowing subject and known object and subsequently arrive at the unity of knower and known. Instead, there is a need for a prior and unacquired identity between knower and known.

Now, in the opening of the *System of Philosophy in General*, it might at first appear as if Schelling is claiming that the knowing subject and the known objects are one, but this is not the case. Schelling clarifies the relation between knowing subject and known object as follows: "There exists neither a subject *as* subject nor an object *as* object, but that what knows and what is known are one and the same, and consequently no more subjective than objective."[62] To assume that subjects and objects are fundamental generates numerous epistemic problems regarding the relation between the knowing subject and the known object. Minimally, to assume the primacy of the subject and object dualism opens a gap between the two that must somehow be bridged. For knowledge to be both possible and actual, there must be an intelligible relation between subject and object. This relation, Schelling explains, can be either unilateral or bilateral. Schelling focuses on the unilateral relation in which either subject or object is taken as entirely determinative. Were, for example, the subject completely responsible for the determination of the object of knowledge, "the latter would not be known as it is in itself but strictly *by virtue of its effects*."[63] From this would arise the problem of correlationism. Alternatively, if the object determines the knowing subject entirely, then the subject is lost in the object and becomes itself unknowable. From this would arise the problems of reductive naturalism. As a consequence of these intractable epistemological issues, Schelling entices us to "abandon forever that sphere of reflection that discriminates between the subject and the object."[64] It is here that Schelling defines reason as the "knowledge in which the eternal self-identity recognizes itself."[65] From this position, Schelling again arrives at the "fundamental law of all knowledge," namely, the law of identity $A = A$.[66] At this point, Schelling introduces the idea of affirmation in order to describe the dynamic through which eternal self-identity recognizes itself. He explains, "This absolute affirmation, then, finds its expression in the proposition $A = A$, regardless of whether we understand it according to its formal aspect or according to its real meaning."[67] To exist is to be affirmed. Schelling connects the dynamic of self-affirmation to the existence of God. "*God is His own absolute affirmation*," Schelling claims.[68] Because God is nothing but His own eternal, absolute affirmation, He is infinite in an unconditioned way. Schelling connects this unconditioned infinity to Spinoza:

> There exists another infinity, however, altogether different from the former two [the infinite defined negatively as that without limit and that which is infinite by virtue of its cause], that applies to a being by virtue of its definition, as Spinoza puts it, or by virtue of its idea. Such an infinity is that of God. For God is the absolute affirmation of Himself

as the infinite reality. This infinity is altogether nonspacial and nontemporal, not an infinity that *develops,* such as the infinity of causal sequence, but an infinity that exists by virtue of an absolute position, i.e., an actual infinity.[69]

So, in short, the Absolute is precisely the kind of *totum analyticum* discussed in chapter 1. Schelling then concludes the opening discussion of the seminars posthumously published as the *System of Philosophy in General* by denying the independent existence of the finite: "Considered in and of itself, nothing is finite."[70] Much like Spinoza claims, nothing can be the cause of its own finitude.`

There is a kind of simplicity to the PSR itself even though following through with the consequences of this principle leads one in complex and sometimes frightening directions. The same is not true for the principle of identity as Schelling understands it. In general, the law of identity is always complex for Schelling, and there are multiple reasons for this. Some regard Schelling's inheritance of certain Kantian themes. Matthews writes:

> Schelling understands the relationship of identity as a disjunctive relation, which . . . is precisely the logical form Kant uses to parse the dynamic of organic life. Only the relational category *of community and reciprocal causation* can articulate the generative opposition of the disjunctive unity Schelling sees in the relationship of identity.[71]

If this is the case, we can see that there is already a kernel of life in Schelling's notion of identity. The logical form of identity is not logical in a reductive sense. In addition to the possible Kantian motivations for the complexity of identity, there are also formal reasons to arrive at this conclusion. Grant explains "'$A = A$' is and operates several formal differentiations: firstly, in the fact of expression; secondly, in the differentiation of subject and predicate; thirdly, in the function of the copula."[72] So, again, the law of identity is itself not a simple unity. It is instead a gathering together of three distinct terms and functions. It indicates not a single thing but instead a complex relation between isolatable elements. Grant explains à la "Schellingean identity" that "when the extensional set of identity is greater than one (= identity *itself*), identity itself is not identical to the factors of which it is posited."[73]

This exact point is nicely (and perhaps more clearly) articulated by Schelling when in the *Freedom* essay he observes of the law of identity that "this principle does not express a unity which, turning itself in the circle of seamless sameness [*Einerleiheit*], would not be progressive and, thus, insensate or lifeless."[74] He continues on to claim that "the unity of this law is an immediately creative one. In the relation of subject and predicate we have already shown that of ground and consequence, and the law of the ground [*Gesetz des Grundes*] is for that reason just as original as the law of identity."[75] Frank illustrates a similar point in a more general semantic way. To speak about identity in any meaningful sense, one must necessarily include some minimal inscription of difference in the articulation of an identity between two terms. To pick up on just one of Frank's examples, the identification of "Mount Everest" and "Chomolungma" asserts an identity between the two nominations but can only meaningfully do so in a nontautological fashion by asserting this identity in light of a minimal difference.[76] Drawing upon Frege, Frank explains, "Frege did not understand identity as a sterile self-relation of a relation (a thing, 'only' on itself), but as a real relation between different names or signs of a thing."[77] The difference inscribed in the linguistic formulation above signals a real difference. The differential relation is not apparent but real. So, in a sense, it is difference that makes identity intelligible. Further, as Frank discusses, when speaking of identity, Schelling is picking up two distinct yet interrelated conversations. The first, following Leibniz, regards the logical status of identity as a kind of consistency. The second, incorporating Hume, regards the ontological status of identity as it relates to difference.[78] As a result of this dual approach, Frank concludes that "identity (as opposed to logical consistency) seems to include a kind of difference; and there lies the problem that Schelling's identity philosophy confronts."[79] Unlike the existence monism that follows from the PSR, the existence monism that takes the law of identity as its guiding principle has inscribed within it a difference from which a dynamic self-relation can emerge.

3.0. Thinking through the Most Monstrous Thought

If there is to be no arbitrary limit to rational explicability, then reason demands the existence of the Absolute as simple, indivisible, and total. Alternatively, experience seems to demand some account of the existence of finite particulars. In the tumultuous history of the reception of Spinoza's *Ethics*, his denial of the existence of finite particulars struck many as acutely absurd. This is what Bayle calls "the most monstrous hypothesis that could be imagined, the most absurd, and the most diametrically opposed to the most evident notions of our mind."[80] The denial of finite particulars renders Spinozism a doctrine so contrary to everyday experience that it is difficult for anyone to even grasp. If we embrace the existence monist reading of Spinoza, then this thought becomes all the more monstrous. There is no way of softening the blow to common sense of Spinoza's monism through the more palatable priority monist reading. Further, Spinoza's atheism is, for Bayle and others, a product of this denial of the independent existence of finite particulars in the name of the Absolute. That is to say, Spinoza did not set out to articulate an atheistic doctrine that denied the kind of transcendence desired by Jacobi and others. Instead, in his quest to expand rationalism to its outmost limits, Spinoza had to conclude that only one thing exists.

The existence of finite particulars also appears as a problem in Schelling's early works. The principles outlined in the *Presentation* seem not simply to fail in their attempt to account for finitude. Instead, they seem to foreclose the possibility of giving any such account at all. Alderwick claims that Schelling's identity philosophy "ultimately fails because it is unable to secure a coherent conception of the finite independent individual."[81] Now, as previously noted most commentaries on the role of Spinoza in the identity philosophy focus primarily on the *Presentation*, and with good reason. First, and most obviously, Schelling himself invites this interpretive strategy with his comments in the introduction. Second, Schelling would later insist that the *Presentation* was the only version of the identity philosophy "certifiably acknowledged by the author as authentic."[82] His desire to distance himself from the other articulations of the system of identity stems in large part from his desire to bypass criticisms of his use of intellectual intuition, which, he insists, "is not found in the *first* presentation of the philosophy of identity."[83] If we take Schelling at his word here, we can see that the role of Spinoza in the *Presentation* is largely metaphysical instead of epistemological. After detailing the role played by experience and maladjusted intellect in Spinoza's account of differentiation, I will turn to the notion of negative expression in Schelling's *System of Phi-*

losophy in General. While presenting this material, Schelling would have been working on his essay *Philosophy and Religion*, which in many ways signals the close of the identity philosophy and a shift in Schelling's philosophical focus back to developing an account of finitude's "falling away" from the Absolute. At the close of this chapter, we will have a fuller picture of what Schelling borrows from Spinoza as well as what he will begin to leave behind.

3.1. Differentiation: Spinoza

Spinoza does not explicitly deny the existence of individuality in the *Ethics* and in fact devotes a good amount of effort to developing an account of individuality and particularity in Book II.[84] What follows is a deflationary account of finitude in the *Ethics*. By *deflationary* I simply mean that it appears to me that Spinoza's attempts to account for the reality of finite modes simply fail insofar as the true lesson of the *Ethics* is found in Book I alone. This means that in opposition to commentators such as Renz, I am more comfortable giving up on Spinoza's account of finitude in favor of his existence monism, even if this means abandoning his ethical and moral philosophy.[85] I think that Spinoza's failure to adequately account for the reality of the finite is part of the larger point of the *Ethics* as a whole, namely, that the demands made in favor of rational explicability necessarily yield phenomenologically counterintuitive claims. In fact, it is precisely this ability of rationalism to "supervene on the spontaneous insights of lived experience" that Peden argues spurred forth the twentieth-century French Spinozism that still dominates much of continental Spinozism today.[86]

Anyway, it is generally accepted (correctly) that for Spinoza, nothing can be the cause of its own finitude, as this would go against EId2. This means that finitude is a product of dependence, limitation, and in some ways negation. Spinoza turns to bodies and ideas to explain the presentation of finite modes conceived under the attributes of extension and thought respectively. "We do not feel or perceive any individual things except bodies and modes of thinking," writes Spinoza in EIIa5. Spinoza begins the second book of the *Ethics* with a definition of bodies. EIId1states, "By 'body' I understand a mode that expresses in a definite and determinate way God's essence insofar as he is considered as an extended thing." Spinoza's definition of an idea takes a slightly different form. "By idea," he writes in EIId3, "I understand a conception of the Mind which the Mind forms because it is a thinking thing." For Spinoza, finite things exist in "a certain and determinate way," but only insofar as they are modifications of an infinite and single substance, the essence of which each mode somehow expresses. Further, according to *E*Id2 finitude is always the product of an external limitation, meaning nothing can be the cause of its own finitude. A body is finite insofar as it is limited by another body, and an idea is finite insofar as it is limited by another idea. If a thing can never be the cause of its own finitude, we must look at the relation between finite modes and infinite substance to understand how (if at all) individual things come to exist as individuated. Further, the final definition of Book II states that "by individual things [*res singulars*] I mean things that are finite and have a determinate existence. If several individual things concur in one act in such a way as to be all together the simultaneous cause of one effect, I consider them all, in that respect, as one individual." Already, we see that there is something fuzzy about Spinoza's treatment of singular things. Though some things may appear to be singular, their singularity reaches beyond what we might loosely call their individuality. There are several different ways of understanding this relation between substance and its modifications, and briefly presenting some of the more well-known versions of interpreting this relation helpfully frames what is so monstrous about Spinoza's existence monism. Further, it provides a rubric for evaluating Schelling's account of differentiation and, by extension, the extent of his Spinozism by the end of the identity philosophy.

We know that modes are dependent upon substance for their existence, but the form this dependence takes is a bit opaque if we follow the *Ethics* alone. Of primary interest is the debate regarding whether the modes are merely caused by substance or if they inhere in substance.[87] This debate connects back to the discussion of the differences between priority monism and existence monism insofar as it concerns the ways that finite things relate to substance as well as the relative autonomy of the existence of finite things from substance. A prominent defender of the causal position is Curley. "Instead of having modes inhere in substance," Melamed summarizes, "Curley suggested that the modes' dependence upon substance should be interpreted in terms of (efficient) causation, that is, as committing Spinoza to nothing over and above the claim that substance is the (efficient) cause of the modes."[88] This reading falls nicely in line with priority monist accounts more generally. If modes are merely caused by substance, then they can maintain a relative autonomy from substance as well as from each other. For example, mode (A) can be caused by substance (1) and have qualities (x) and (y) while mode (B) can also be caused by substance (1) but have qualities (y) and (z). This would allow each mode to have actual differences even if they are both effects of a single substance. This position has been criticized for various reasons, most of which we will not engage with here.[89] I'll simply raise again an objection mentioned above. If modes are independent or finite "things" that merely share a common cause, then this would violate a number of Spinoza's commitments including the aforementioned proclamation that "it is nonsense, bordering on madness, to think that extended Substance is composed of parts or bodies really distinct from one another."[90] The idea that substance could cause something that would then exist in any relative autonomy from it would directly violate the idea of substance as infinite, simple, and without parts. This would be a bifurcation that, if left unaccounted for, is forbidden by the PSR.

On the inherence interpretation, the space of relative autonomy opened by the causal model is not possible. Any mode is not just a mode *of* substance, but a mode "in" substance as well. The usage of "in" here must be carefully qualified. To say that things are "in" God is not to pose a mereological problem regarding the relation of a whole to its composite parts. Partially following Schaffer, the whole must necessarily be prior to its parts. However, the existence of things (in the plural) at all is one that must be accounted for. As Melamed explains, "Finite things are in God, but they are not parts of God," and again, "Particular things are *in* God, but *not parts* of God. They are *modes* of God."[91] Melamed points out that this interpretation is more in line with what Bayle found to be so absurd in Spinoza.[92] If the notion of totality Spinoza is working with is the *totum analyticum* then only the inherence model can be a legitimate interpretive candidate. Further, if the substance-mode relation were anything other than a relation of inherence, the problem of pantheism would never arise. The claim that finite things are caused by the infinite would not have terrified Jacobi so deeply; it would instead fall more or less in line with his own teachings. Jacobi would simply add that there is an infinite difference between the infinite and the finite. Alternatively, it is precisely the model of inherence, insofar as it eliminates the possibility of absolute externality (the infinite difference between the infinite and the finite), that causes the controversial association between Spinozism, pantheism, and atheism.

Lin explains the relation of modes to substance with the image of waves in an ocean, and this image in general has some utility. "When Spinoza says that bodies and minds are modes of God," he writes, "what he means is that they stand to God as waves stand to an ocean. Bodies are waves on the waters of extension and minds are waves on the waters of thought."[93] However, Lin's position commits a similar error to the causal reading outlined above. Lin attempts to account for the reality of finite modes by differentiating between fundamental and nonfundamental things.[94] This falls in line with the idea that modes are dependent upon substance, but substance is not in turn dependent upon modes. However, the problem of bifurcation still arises. Assuming the PSR, we would have to give a reason for the division between fundamental and nonfundamental things. This is a problem that the existence monist can again avoid insofar as existence monism denies the existence of things in general and nonfundamental things by extension. The wave in the ocean to which Lin refers could just as easily represent the localized complexity and variation of Hogan's and Potrč's blobject. So again, if it is simplicity that we are seeking to attain, existence monism remains the best candidate.

For Deleuze, the action of expression provides a unity to substance, its attributes, and its modes. In order to distinguish modes from one another, Deleuze emphasizes the quantitative as opposed to qualitative difference between modes:

> Only a quantitative distinction of beings is consistent with the qualitative identity of the absolute. And this quantitative distinction is no mere appearance, but an internal difference, a difference of intensity. So that each finite being must be said to *express the absolute,* according to the intensive quantity that constitutes its essence, according, that is, to the degree of its power. Individuation is, in Spinoza, neither qualitative nor extrinsic, but quantitative and intrinsic, intensive.[95]

Finite things, if they are to be understood as not separate from the infinite, must be differentiated in terms of their quantity or intensity. In the following section, we will see that Schelling too believes that the only possible form of differentiation is quantitative differentiation.

The Absolute is a qualitative identity that admits of only quantitative differentiation. That is, all quantitative differentiations remain qualitatively identical. This means that the difference between things cannot be understood as a difference between objects with qualitatively distinct properties. Instead, if we are to maintain a commitment to existence monism, distinctions between particulars must result from differentials in activity alone. The emphasis on expression as an activity allows us to understand why Spinoza would claim in EIIp13 Lemma 1, that "bodies are distinguished from one another in respect of motion-and-rest, quickness and slowness, and not in respect of substance." The differentiating characteristics of bodies are never qualitative or substantive. There are only quantitative differences determined by differentials in motion and rest. However, this is a definition of the differentiation *between* bodies. Through differentials in motion and rest, bodies may become a "certain and determinate" expression of God's essence. Motion and rest, speed and slowness are comparative qualities. Consequently, this definition of differentiation seems to presuppose the existence of individual things and consequently fails to give an account of their existence. An emphasis on motion and rest seems to represent an epistemic explanation for differentiation that at best fails to consider the ontological unity of substance and at worst contradicts the ontology of the *Ethics*.

Assuming the existence monist reading of Spinoza, we can see that any differentiation in the *Ethics* cannot be an actual, qualitative determination of substance itself. This would result in a determination that would render things as *more* than or *otherwise* than infinite substance. The rationally supported conclusion that only one thing exists comes into conflict with the fact that in experience, there are finite particulars. I want to close by suggesting that it is experience itself that generates finite particulars, albeit in an illusory, irreal form. This proposal is similar to the perspectivalist reading offered by Mátyási, according to which, "For Spinoza, expressions such as 'x is a part of y' or 'x is a whole composed of some ys' convey abstract judgments from a particular limited perspective."[96] The idea is that when it comes to parts, or finite objects, Spinoza is at bottom an antirealist. Though we may speak of things as if they were distinct individual parts, this way of speaking ultimately has little ontological weight. As Schelling saw, it is the unity of substance from which Spinoza's realism grows. This reading builds upon Spinoza's notion of "things of reason" found in the *Short Treatise* and the appendix to the *Principles of Cartesian Philosophy*. In the *Short Treatise*, Spinoza writes that "'part' and 'whole' are not true or real entities, but only 'things of reason,' and consequently there are in Nature neither whole nor parts."[97] This squares nicely with the existence monist reading of the *Ethics*. Recall Della Rocca explaining that for the existence monist "there is only one object, and any multiplicity of objects, such as tables as distinct from chairs, is at best illusory."[98] In the *Ethics*, Spinoza calls this illusory form of individuation "experience." Much like the things of reason discussed in the *Short Treatise*, in the *Ethics* the objects of experience may be entities of a limited kind, but in the end, they have no reality in nature. Or, like the "Beings of Reason" discussed in the *Principles of Cartesian Philosophy*, they are a kind of shorthand for more easily retaining, explaining, and imagining things that are more fully understood through intuitive knowledge of the whole.[99] Now, I do not mean to suggest that this is how Schelling's account of the genesis of particularity in Spinoza's metaphysics would go. I am simply trying to provide an account of the appearance of individuality that does not contradict the commitment to existence monism.

The support for this deflationary reading of finite modes comes from Spinoza's threefold epistemological distinction drawn in *Ethics* II. In the second scholium of *E*IIp40, Spinoza distinguishes between the three kinds of knowledge ranging from (1) knowledge of symbols, (2) "common notions and adequate ideas of the properties of things," and (3) intuitive knowledge that "proceeds from an adequate idea of the formal essence of certain attributes of God to an adequate knowledge of the essence of things." The third type of knowledge is the most complete form through which we come to know the necessity of the one thing that exists. It is this third type of knowledge that has been likened to Schelling's early usages of the notion of intellectual intuition. The first two forms of knowledge presuppose a relation to individuated things, be it signs, recollections, or ideas. Alternatively, the third type of knowledge is concerned with the essence of all things. However, before Spinoza draws this threefold distinction, he describes a type of perception "[f]rom individual objects presented to us through the senses in a fragmentary [*mutilate*] and confused manner without any intellectual order . . . ; and therefore I call such perceptions 'knowledge from casual experience.'" Experience is not some kind of intuitive or preconceptual access to things as they are. Instead, it is experience itself that individuates, differentiates, and erroneously presents the one thing that exists as finite particulars. What is interesting about this is how

Spinoza essentially agrees with the idea that in experience and perception there are finite particulars. What he adds, though, is that these perceptions are "mutilated" and "confused" precisely insofar as from experience one draws the unwarranted conclusion that the appearance or representation of individual particulars necessarily implies an ontological difference in their existence as thus and so. The experience of the mind that takes itself to be finite is a limited and limiting perspective that carves out a distorted finitude from the infinite. Experience differentiates, and intuitive knowing unifies. Though we experience finite things as thus and so, we would be in error to conclude that individuated things exist. The very notion of independent existence is at best the illusory product of an ill-attuned and poorly directed mind. To return to the blobject, just because there is an incredibly complex semantic system for describing local variations there is no reason to believe that this semantic complexity corresponds to an ontological complexity dependent upon the same kind of discrete entities. Another way of putting this is that complexity in the ideal does not imply a correspondent complexity in the real. Ontological individuation is an error that must be overcome by the supervenience of rationality upon what appears to be given in and through experience. Thus, the failure to account for the reality of finite, individuated things reinforces Spinoza's larger-scale commitment to rationalism and the counterintuitive truths that follow from the PSR.

3.2. Differentiation: Schelling

Schelling motivates his account of the production of finitude in a way Spinoza cannot. Whereas for Spinoza, the immediate self-comprehension of substance is both its essence and its existence, for Schelling the *process* by which the Absolute comes to self-knowledge is an indispensable part of both its essence and its existence. This falls more in line with Deleuze's characterization of expression as the active source of unity in Spinoza, but there remain significant differences discussed below. Schelling writes in §21 of the *Presentation* that "absolute identity cannot cognize itself infinitely without infinitely positing itself as subject and object."[100] In order to come to know itself, the Absolute must double itself. Doing so allows it to egress from its simplicity while paradoxically never exiting from or canceling out its own identity. How is this possible?

The first step in answering this question is to emphasize that for Schelling, differentiation is always quantitative. "Between subject and predicate, none other than quantitative difference is possible," Schelling explains.[101] There is no qualitative difference in kind between subject and predicate, the two are not different in kind. Instead, there are quantitative or intensive differences between subject and object. Schelling continues to elaborate this thought, and in §37 he remarks that "quantitative difference of the subjective and the objective is the ground of all finitude, the quantitative indifference of the two is infinitude."[102] The question that follows from this claim regards the mechanism or dynamic by which quantitative differentiations occur. The mechanism by which the Absolute creates quantitative differences within itself through self-reflective activity Schelling calls "positing" in the *Presentation* and "affirmation" in the *System of Philosophy in General*. Let's focus on the latter account of differentiation by way of affirmation. Therein, Schelling describes differentiation as a kind of erasure of indifference that would be foreign to the schema set up by Spinoza.

There is a will to self-knowledge at the core of Schelling's notion of the Absolute, which Schelling increasingly calls "God" from the *System of Philosophy in General* onward. This will to self-knowledge shows both affinities to and divergences from Spinoza's God. Spinoza famously denies God a will insofar as this would imply that God could choose to act otherwise. Schelling claims that the self-relation of reason is the process through which God thinks Himself, and in doing so He affirms Himself as thinking subject and thought object.[103] Thus, much like Spinoza, it is conception that precedes and determines causation. In fact, to be caused just is to be conceived by God. "God does not know things *because they exist*, but conversely, *they exist because God knows them*," Schelling writes.[104] God comes to be differentiated as subject and object insofar as He thinks Himself. Schelling will explain that God becomes subject insofar as He is actively affirming, and He becomes object insofar as He is "passively" affirmed. Passivity is here in quotes because the God that affirms and the God that is affirmed are one and the same, and therefore God can never be understood as completely passive. Any quantitative differentiation of the Absolute is made possible by a self-relating activity present simultaneously in the affirmation and the affirmed albeit to different degrees. Through this forming activity of affirmation, God becomes quantitatively differentiated without becoming qualitatively divided. Schelling explicitly relates this dynamic of affirming/affirmed to Spinoza's distinction between *natura naturans* (or active nature insofar as it is forming) and *natura naturata* (or passive nature as it is formed). Schelling writes, "We distinguished between *natura naturans,* or God as the absolute position and as the absolute creative force, and *natura naturata,* by which we understand the mere appearance of the absolute universe or the finite world."[105] Though he draws this distinction, we must keep in mind that it is not an ontological distinction insofar as throughout the identity philosophy, only one thing can be said to exist. In other words, forming nature, or God as the absolute position, and formed nature, or the finite world, are different *ways* of being, and not different beings. As Lauer notes, Schelling's goal is precisely to dissolve the steadfast distinction between the two operations of nature central to Spinoza's metaphysics.[106] The dynamic of affirming/affirmed as different ways of God's being also generates the quantitative differentiation without division of the real and the ideal. The Absolute, if it is to contain everything, must be both real and ideal simultaneously. Schelling unpacks this thought as follows:

> To the extent that He is infinitely affirmed as something affirming, God is the *ideal* universe. For . . . the form of being affirmed constitutes a real and that of affirming an ideal form. However, because God, as the affirming, i.e., as ideal, is also infinitely affirmed, He is also = the universe in an ideal sense, that is, *He is the ideal universe (natura naturans idealis).* Everybody will concede, for example, that *knowledge* . . . is not *merely* ideal or mere *thought* but that, as something ideal, it is simultaneously real, i.e., simultaneously affirming and affirmed. Likewise, all activity, to the extent that it can also be subsumed under the ideal world, constitutes an affirmation that, *as such,* is simultaneously also affirmed or *real.*[107]

In this passage, Schelling outlines how thought is not merely ideal or conception without content. Thought, if it is to be thought proper, is likewise and simultaneously real. The being of God as thinking is not some empty, transcendent circulation of thought in relation to only itself. So, in Schelling's schema, as affirming, or more specifically as affirming His own affirmation, God exists as ideal, whereas insofar as He is the affirmed, He is real. The affirmed affirmation is the ideal in the universe, while the affirmed itself is the real. These two are in turn co-dependent insofar as one cannot be produced without also producing the other. In the end, both real and ideal are interdependent *ways* of being and not different realms of being.

The affirmed affirmation is not just ideal but is real-ideal insofar as it is both the affirmed and the act of affirmation. The function of thought as both realizing and idealizing marks a significant difference between Schelling and Spinoza. In the proof to *E*IIp5, Spinoza discusses the expression of God insofar as he is thinking. The infinite essence of God conceived through the attribute of thought is expressed as a thinking thing and *not* as an extended thing. In Spinoza's words, "Our conclusion that God can form the idea of his own essence and of everything that necessarily follows therefrom was inferred solely from God's being a thinking thing, and not from his being the object of his own idea." When God thinks Himself, He thinks Himself as a thing that thinks and does *not* take Himself as object. Or, more precisely, God does not objectify Himself through thinking Himself. As subject, God does not *become* object by way of this self-relation. To translate back into Schelling's diction, Spinoza's God is only an abstract affirmation and not the full triad of affirmed—affirmed affirmation—affirmed. Additionally, though Schelling employs the language of the "ideal universe" and the "real universe," it must be emphasized that this does not create two separate realms or sides of the Absolute, which is necessarily One and simple: "To each mode of being affirmed in the real universe there corresponds an equal mode of the affirming in the ideal universe."[108] This seems to set up a parallelism between real and ideal, but Schelling takes care to reunite the two. Consequently, Schelling concludes, "the real and the ideal universe are but the same universe."[109] This marks an important departure from Spinoza to which we will return in the next chapter. In the *Presentation*, Schelling relates the correspondence of real and ideal to Spinoza's doctrine of the attributes: "Since A is the knowing principle, while B, as we shall discover, is what is intrinsically unlimited or infinite extension, we have here quite precisely both the Spinozistic attributes of absolute substance, thought and extension."[110] It is odd that Schelling posits absolute substance as an attribute, but what is really at stake here is the doctrine of parallelism. In the next chapter, we will see Schelling attempt to distance himself from this kind of parallelism between real and ideal. In fact, Schelling's critique of parallelism lies at the heart of his comments regarding the lifelessness of Spinoza's system.

Schelling shows little direct interest in Spinoza's proclamation in Letter 50 to Jelles, in which one finds Spinoza's relating of determination to negation. Hegel was quite fond of the slogan "*omnis determinatio est negatio,*" or "all determination is negation." Much like Schelling's analysis of the dark feeling intuited and disavowed by Spinoza, Hegel takes up this formulation while marking Spinoza's failure to realize its immanent potential. The context of this claim is important for understanding the scope of Spinoza's proclamation, which, it should be noted, is absent from the *Ethics* itself. "With regard to the statement that figure is a negation and not anything positive," writes Spinoza,

> it is obvious that matter in its totality, considered without limitation, can have no figure, and that figure applies only to finite and determinate bodies. For he who says that he apprehends a figure, thereby means to indicate simply this, that he apprehends a determinate thing and the manner of this determination. This determination therefore does not pertain to the thing in regard to its being; on the other contrary, it is its non-being. So since figure is nothing but determination, and determination is negation, figure can be nothing other than negation.[111]

Though he does not directly pick up on this claim in the same way Hegel does, Schelling does express a somewhat similar view regarding the relation between determinate existence and the Absolute. In reference to the notion of expression in Schelling's *System of Transcendental Idealism*, Dodd observes that

> [e]ach product, in its difference from others as well as in its status as a finite interruption of the infinite, will obviously "express" something of the absolute in emergence, insofar as productivity is something that finds itself in its own products. Yet a product is "expressive" precisely to the extent to which it is *not* the expression of the absolute: its very emergence is grounded in the surplus of the absolute I, which remains reticent in the form of a flight from the stasis of the produced.[112]

What Dodd is calling to our attention here is that for Schelling in the *System of Transcendental Idealism*, the I withholds itself from the "stasis" of the finite particulars it produces. In its surplus, it provides a condition for the being of finite products. But, insofar as these products are particular, the Absolute cannot be said to express its full essence within them. With this in mind, Dodd then turns to the *System of Philosophy in General* and traces further the idea of expression as the flight of the Absolute from stasis. "The eternal self-sameness (*dasselbe Eins*) is still being approached through the subject-object split, though now explicitly in the form of its denial, or better: its *erasure*," Dodd explains, "this is the new figure of the theme of emergence: identity emerges as a pole of recognition in which both subjectivity and objectivity *cease*, a pole that Schelling calls reason."[113] The Absolute in its self-identity is best understood as the point at which the distinction of subjectivity and objectivity disappear. Better still, the Absolute is apprehended precisely as this erasure or suspension. Thus, the emergence of subject and object from the Absolute is an erasure of this erasure. By extension, "Being is here affirmed not in the manner of a synthesis, but above all in the form of an absolute *negation of nothingness*."[114] The affirmation that allows for the being of Being is not a synthetic genesis of a larger unity out of separate parts. Even less so is it the terminus of synthesis as subject or object. Instead, "it is Nothingness itself, affirmed in its nullity, that secures ultimately a role for expression in Schelling's later thought."[115] This analysis of expression places the concept in a new terrain, highlighting the depth of Schelling's insight regarding the relationship between the Absolute and the individual. Expression will "provide a powerful philosophical argument for the necessity of the separation, irrationality, and madness of the constructed being of the individual."[116] Determinate and particular beings are not the product of an addition of properties to some substratum or being in general. Instead, particularization is a becoming less than being. The quantitative amplification of the Absolute's nonidentity is what allows things to be determined as thus and so. Only through their relative inexistence can individual things express themselves as things. By extension, individuated being, insofar as it is only through the negation of nonidentity and the flight from reason, is a madness. Again, beings are the erasure of an erasure. If reason just is the erasure of the division between subject and object, then the existence of subject and object, if this is to be possible at all, must be in a significant sense unreasonable.

We find ample textual evidence for this reading in the *System of Philosophy in General*. Schelling tells us that "the relative Nonbeing [*Nichtseyn*] of the particular with respect to the universe, when understood as a relative Nonbeing, is the concrete and authentic thing."[117] Instead of associating or equivocating the concrete thing with being itself, Schelling argues that concrete particularity is in fact a species of nonbeing. He is articulating a doctrine of finitude that is dependent upon the possibility of degrees of existence. The finite thing is only finite insofar as it is a quantitative expression of the infinite. Additionally, this kind of expression is no longer an expression of the positive being of God. Instead, it is precisely the opposite. "Nothingness allows for the very expression of this imperviousness to expression," Dodd explains.[118] Further, it is in the dissolution of their nonbeing, the negation of their nothingness, that particulars come to inhere in the Idea: "The[y] *do inhere* in [the idea] to the extent that they have dissolved into their own infinity, as a strictly identical and indivisible proposition, and they do *not* inhere in it with regard to their particularity," explains Schelling.[119] Moreover, it is precisely this that Schelling associates with expression. "*The addendum between the universal and the particular*, as it is applied to the concrete contains *nothing positive*," he writes, "but it, too, expresses a mere *negation*."[120] Finally, against the idea that power is the ground of a particular's Being, Schelling reverses this relation: he writes, "The powers [*Potenz*] are not determinations of the thing in itself or of its essence but, rather, of its nonessence [*Nicht-Wesens*]."[121] This claim distances Schelling's understanding of power from Spinoza's *conatus* doctrine insofar as the latter is defined in *E*IIIp7 as the "power or conatus by which it endeavors to persist in its own being." Spinoza's *conatus* characterizes the continuation of the essence of substance whereas for Schelling, power is the determination of a thing's nonessence. Dodd concludes that "what we see, so to speak, in the light of the Idea or in appearance itself is the darkness that has been infused with the pure radiance of the self-affirmation of the divine."[122] Despite all the language of affirmation in the identity philosophy, we can find the equally important dynamic of the negation of nonbeing that renders both particularity and identity possible and intelligible. In fact, things are even more complex. There must be an affirmation of the negation of nonbeing in order for the Absolute to remain active throughout this process of negative expression.

All of this shows that for Schelling things exist as determinate, individuated things precisely *insofar as they do not exist*. For example, the existence of a thing in space and time (as thus and so) occurs through the affirmation of what the Absolute is not, namely, confined within space and time. In this way, the Absolute's affirmation of that which it is not generates the becoming otherwise of finite particulars without entailing the becoming less of the Absolute. In a sense, we must maintain two perspectives regarding the differentiation of the Absolute. On the one hand, from the perspective of the Absolute, the being of any differentiated individual is a quantitative augmentation that is dependent upon the self-affirmation of the Absolute insofar as it comes to think itself. On the other hand, from the perspective of concrete particulars, differentiation is relative nonbeing that becomes Absolute through the erasure of this very Nonbeing; in this way, concrete particularity is a negative expression of the Absolute, or an expression of what the Absolute is not. There are concrete and particular things insofar as they are affirmed in their maddening nullity. Or, to borrow from Žižek, "there are things because they cannot fully exist."[123] It is thus not the case, as Lauer suggests, that the Absolute in the *System of Philosophy in General* "can contain no negation."[124] This would constitute a limitation of the Absolute, rendering it no longer absolute. Though God may be the ground of all Being, Nothingness is a precondition for particularity. Were there no Nothing to affirm precisely in its nullity, God could never become otherwise than He is. God would be merely a static identity instead of a dynamic one. This brings us back to the dynamic character of Schelling's notion of identity. As Pfau suggests, "identity, for Schelling, ultimately designates a controlled and continuous play of differential relations."[125] As a result of this "controlled and continuous play" that which is in God but is not God is *dynamically repulsive*. In His self-affirmation God doubles over and generates sickness and madness. The freedom in nature that passes through finitude is an expression of the nausea of God. Consequently, it is this affirmative negation of Nothingness, or negative expression, that begins to shape Schelling's unique account of emergence. Further, we can see how this account of differentiation is dependent upon Schelling's notion of the Absolute as the identity of identity and nonidentity, and not his initial definition of the Absolute as the identity of identity alone. If the Absolute were not both what it is and what it is not, there would be no nothingness internal to the Absolute that could be affirmed.

4.0. Conclusion

Any divergences between Spinoza and Schelling's 1801 system of identity as articulated in the *Presentation* appear at first to be relatively minor. For both Schelling and Spinoza, only one thing can be said to properly exist, and it is in this sense that Spinoza is indeed the undeniable predecessor of the identity philosophy. Though they take different roads to this conclusion (the PSR for Spinoza and the principle A = A for Schelling), they both agree that no thing can be the cause of its own finitude. Schelling takes Spinoza as a model for the *Presentation*, yet we can see that as the identity philosophy develops, the ontology posed by Schelling therein begins to distance itself from that of Spinoza. For Spinoza, finitude is ultimately an illusion produced by the maladjusted intellect that attributes ontological primacy to the objects given in experience. Spinoza is an antirealist when it comes to the existence of finite things. For Schelling, finite particulars are not, properly speaking, illusions, and they are not entirely unreal. Instead, as argued in the *System of Philosophy in General*, the determination of things as thus and so in space, time, and causal relation is a negation of existence or a quantitative, partial erasure of the Absolute that is indifferent to the spatial, temporal, and causal relations between things. In other words, things exist as determinate things insofar as they do not exist, whereas the infinite exists precisely insofar as it is not a specific, determinate thing. When we follow Schelling's understanding of the law of identity as an expression of the Absolute as the identity of identity and nonidentity as well as his doctrine of determinate particularity as species of nonbeing we open a crack from within Spinoza's notion of simple identity. Only when identity is no longer assumed to be identical at the expense of a particular kind of quantitative difference can we begin to move past Spinoza's monism.

Chapter 4
Realism, Idealism, and Parallelism

1.0. Introduction: Against Abrasive Philosophy

In his writings following the initial publication of the 1801 *Presentation*, Schelling begins to articulate more formally his criticism of Spinoza's monist metaphysics. As outlined in chapter 3, though he found inspiration in Spinoza's monism, Schelling did not strictly adhere to Spinoza's account for the relation between identity and differentiation. This divergence can be traced back to the distinct role played by the PSR in Spinoza's metaphysical argument for existence monism. Further, though the *Presentation* sought to articulate the Absolute as the identity of identity, in the *Bruno* dialogue Schelling believed the logical form of the Absolute was best captured as the identity of identity and nonidentity. With this in mind, Schelling argues that Spinoza's attribute dualism fails to account for the *identity* of identity and difference. Consequently, the duality of attributes vitiates the unity Schelling initially found in Spinoza's existence monism. Schelling's criticism of Spinoza's attribute parallelism helps motivate the more complex relation between realism and idealism Schelling articulates as he moves away from the identity philosophy. Without a unity of unity and duality, the conflict of forces characteristic of what we call life can be only ideal and never real. Thus, though he does not explicitly state it this way in the *Freedom* essay, the lifelessness of Spinozism is, for Schelling, a product of the *Ethics*'s doctrine of attribute dualism. This in turn presupposes a static understanding of the relation between the real and the ideal.

Schelling opens the *Presentation* with a warning to the reader:

> If I should say, however, that this present system is "idealism," or "realism," or even some third combination of them, in each case I might say nothing false, for this system could be any of these, depending on how it is viewed . . . but by doing so I would bring no one to a real understanding of this system, for what idealism or realism might be, or some possible third compounded from the two, is by no means clear or obvious, but something still to be decided.[1]

Our common sense cannot be our guide in understanding precisely how to classify the identity philosophy. Further, Schelling warns us that the categories of realism and idealism elucidate little about the system of identity itself. One may view the system of identity from either the perspective of realism or of idealism, and the full determination of the system is left to a decision. Despite this cautioning, Schelling continually evokes the real and the ideal throughout the identity philosophy, just as he does both before and after. Thus, we must read him as claiming that *reducing* the system of identity to realism, idealism, or "some third combination" says little about the system of identity itself. But again, this does not entail that the system of identity has nothing to say about realism, idealism, and the relation between the two. This brings us to the core of Schelling's critique of Spinoza. This critique comes down to the relation between the real and the ideal as it is conditioned by their co-presence in the Absolute. There must be some kind of identity between realism and idealism (and the real and the ideal by extension), but this identity cannot be structured in such a way that real and ideal fail to maintain their differences. That is, the identity of real and ideal must not erase their simultaneous nonidentity. In brief, Schelling criticizes Spinoza's unwillingness or inability to account for the genesis of the attributes of thought and extension from a shared root. For Schelling, there must be an originary and unquarried unity of the real and the ideal in the Absolute.

In *Philosophy and Religion*, Schelling is quite clear about what the Absolute and the relationship between real and ideal is *not*. He writes of philosophers who believe they are able to "describe the idea of the absolute" as either the simple negation of difference or "as the *product* that brings about the unification of opposites."[2] As a consequence of this perspective, "they think of the philosopher as holding the ideal or subjective in one hand and the real or objective in the other and then have him strike the palms of his hands together so that one abrades the other. The product of this abrasion [*Aufreibung*] is the Absolute."[3] The Absolute is not the product or outcome of the unification of differences; the Absolute is not the end of a process. Further, the Absolute is not equal to the combination of the subjective and the objective; it is not something that could be expressed in the equation (real) + (ideal) = (Absolute). This abrasive equation has two errors. First, as Schelling notes, it takes the Absolute to be the product of the real and the ideal. Second, it assumes that "real" and "ideal" are isolable, discrete elements of a larger whole in the first place. From this, it would follow that realism and idealism exist dualistically, much like Spinoza's attributes of thought and extension. This duality, Schelling will argue, is ultimately unaccounted for in Spinoza's metaphysics, and this in turn ruptures any form of monism one might inherit therefrom.

This chapter is structured to address the following question: If, as Schelling suggests in the *Freedom* essay, idealism is the soul and realism is the body of the system of the world, then what kind of realism and what kind of idealism come together to form a living, philosophical whole? To respond to this question, it must be broken into three parts: one concerning idealism, one concerning realism, and finally one concerning the dynamic interpenetration of the two. Section 2 begins with the theme of unity as it relates to idealism more generally. We have already seen that it is through the unity of substance that Spinozism is able to reach the peak of realism. However, when taken in conjunction with Schelling's critique of Fichte's eliminative idealism, we can see that unity alone is not enough to formulate a realism that can come alive when infused with the spirit of idealism. Section 3 presents the core of Schelling's critique of Spinoza's attribute dualism. Schelling argues that the strict parallelism between the attributes of thought and extension forbids any mutual saturation or dynamic interpenetration of the real and the ideal. Section 3 concludes with a presentation of Schelling's notion of spirit as articulated in the 1797 essay "Treatise Explicatory of the Idealism in the *Science of Knowledge*" [hereafter *Treatise*]. Therein we find a vivid description of the kind of dynamic interpenetration of real and ideal that inherits his discussion of creative reason and will later become characteristic of the self-determining dynamics of the Absolute.

2.0. Idealism, Elimination, and Amplification

"If the doctrine that all things are contained in God is the ground of the whole system," Schelling writes of Spinozism and pantheism in the *Freedom* essay, "then, at the very least, it must first be brought to life and torn from abstraction before it can become the principle of a system of reason."[4] Schelling claims that idealism must be added to realism in order to render philosophy's reach equal to its desire. The question that follows from this regards the kind of idealism that must be added to realism in order to bring the latter to life. To address this question, it is helpful to contrast two forms of idealism. The first is the reductive or eliminative idealism of Fichte. The second is Schelling's own ampliative idealism. Looking at Schelling's criticisms of Spinoza and Fichte in tandem concretely displays why neither realism nor idealism alone is a sufficient philosophical approach for articulating the actual dynamics of the Absolute. Schelling's criticism of Fichte brings him back into contact with the writings of Jacobi and the idea of Fichte's system as an inverted Spinozism. As Schelling claims in his lectures *The Grounding of Positive Philosophy*, "Fichte's true significance is to have been the antithesis of Spinoza, insofar as the absolute substance was, for Spinoza, a merely dead and motionless object."[5] Further, as Schelling himself wrote to Fichte, in order to distinguish his own system (the system of identity at the time) from Fichte's, he must likewise distance himself from Spinoza. Understanding why this is the case highlights what is unique about the idealism Schelling comes to embrace. Section 2.1 presents Schelling's criticism of Fichte's idealism as an inverted Spinozism. Section 2.2 outlines Schelling's ampliative idealism as a realism concerning the Idea. Taken as a whole, these sections illustrate that unity is simply not enough to satisfy Schelling's philosophical aspiration of constructing a living system of the universe.

2.1. Eliminative Idealism as Inverted Spinozism

In his "Letter to Fichte," Jacobi claims that his entry point into what he therein characterizes as Fichte's nihilistic philosophy was through "the representation of an *inverted* Spinozism."[6] The idea that Fichte and Spinoza form an inverted pair is shared by Schelling. Consequently, we must view Schelling's critique of Spinoza's realism as a mirror of his criticism of Fichte's idealism. The most punctual framing of the split between the Fichte and Schelling can be found in a set of letters they exchanged between the years of 1800 and 1802. Further, and perhaps not coincidentally, Spinoza plays an intriguing role in this exchange. Both Fichte and Schelling were greatly concerned with the differences between criticism and dogmatism and the related issue of the interconnection between idealism and realism. The marked difference between the two, however, is that while Fichte saw dogmatism as subservient to and derivative of criticism, Schelling came to believe that the systems of dogmatism and criticism (and the principles of idealism and realism by extension) are not so easily subordinated to one another.[7] The core disagreement of the correspondence is voiced concisely by Fichte in a letter dated November 15, 1800. "I still do not agree with *your opposition between transcendental* philosophy and philosophy of nature," he writes.[8] Fichte believed that there was no opposition between transcendental philosophy and the philosophy of nature. Instead, he concluded that the philosophy of nature was derivative of transcendental philosophy. This means that for Fichte, the philosophy of nature and transcendental philosophy are not opposed insofar as the former is subsumable by the latter. That is, transcendental philosophy alone is the necessary and sufficient condition for the philosophy of nature. Because the not-I is without being and is only determined in relation to the free activity of the I, nature itself cannot be free or active. Therefore, nature is only of philosophical interest inasmuch as it acts as the shadow cast by transcendental philosophy. In short, "philosophy of nature" is itself a misnomer because there is simply nothing philosophical about nature.[9]

The self-constituting activity of nature is perhaps the single most important element of Schelling's naturephilosophy and thus we can quickly see that this would already appear to be an insurmountable conflict between the two philosophers. To deny nature an activity proper to itself is to uncritically accept the mechanistic notions of natural causation emblematic of the modern philosophical worldview Schelling sought to leave behind. In a letter from October 3, 1801, Schelling compares the disagreement between Fichte and himself to a central distinction in the philosophy of Spinoza. Schelling writes,

> Spinoza posits thought and extension as the two attributes of substance. He does not deny that everything that is can also be explained through the mere attribute of thought and through a mere modification of infinite thought. This kind of

explanation would certainly not turn out to be false, though it would not be absolutely true, but it is comprehended in the absolute itself. Something similar holds between us; which might explain to you in one way among others why, despite our initial fundamental difference, I have nonetheless used idealism as a tool [and] thereby was indeed able to produce so much clarity and depth, as you admit.[10]

In this appeal to Spinoza, Schelling is trying to emphasize that one can maintain the importance of idealism without subordinating nature to it, a move he views as analogous to Spinoza's understanding of the attributes of thought and extension. Both attributes are necessary expressions of the essence of substance, but neither is subordinated to or dependent upon the other for its existence. Further, both attributes are equally necessary for comprehending the essence of the Absolute. The invocation of Spinoza here is an offering of peace to Fichte. Schelling appeals to the lens grinder's doctrine of parallelism as a method for alleviating the sharp theoretical divergence at which the friends had arrived. It is also important to note in passing Schelling's appeal to what we might call a strategic idealism that can be contrasted to the essential idealism of Fichte. For Schelling, idealism serves a particular philosophical function and is not just an unquestioned presupposition. Idealism is a tool that does something. Minimally, idealism for Schelling is an explanatory viewpoint that constructs something.

Subsequently, in a letter dated January 15, 1802, Fichte too appeals to Spinoza: "I also wanted to clarify this in an earlier letter when I said that the absolute (obviously the absolute of philosophy) only ever remains a *seeing*."[11] He continues,

> You replied that it cannot be a seeing of something, which is wholly correct, but this is not what was meant; and this is where the matter has to rest.—This is what Spinoza does. The *One* should be *All* (more precisely, the *infinite,* for there is no totality here), and vice versa; which is then entirely correct. But it cannot indicate to us *how* the One *becomes* the All, and the All, the point of transition, the turning point, and the point of their *real* identity; hence, it loses the One if it grasps the All, and the All when it grasps the One. . . . The Absolute *itself,* however, is neither being, nor

cognition, nor identity, nor the indifference of the two: but it is precisely—*the Absolute*—and to say anything else about it is a waste of time.[12]

What is at issue here is twofold. First, there is the critical problem of the possibility of the presentation of the Absolute as knowable by finite thought, that is representable within the confines of the categories and the a priori forms of intuition characteristic of the discursive intellect. Again, this is something strictly forbidden by Kant's first *Critique*. Second, we see that Fichte is here identifying a problem similar to that which Schelling does in the *Letters*. Namely, he is indicating that the possibility of becoming is a problem for Spinoza's system. More specifically, the possibility of the finite emerging from the infinite, or of the All coming to be from the One, seems to be absolutely excluded from the *Ethics*. Spinoza can have either the One (the monistic unity and simplicity of substance) or the All (the sum total of existing things) but never both at the same time.

Interestingly in the final letter dated January 25, 1802 (approximately three months before the publication of the *Bruno* dialogue), Schelling concludes with another reference to Spinoza. "If you make Spinoza your imaginary opponent in [the *New Presentation*]" Schelling pens,

> that does not seem to me to be the right way to proceed, since you manage to refute more than what is contained in Spinoza (presuming that it will not be less), and then I shall have double the work that would otherwise be necessary in having to sharply distinguish what belongs to him and to me, though I in no way think I have to fear that anything of his will be misunderstood under my name, or anything of mine under his.[13]

Thus, for Schelling, distancing himself from both Fichte and what he perceived to be Fichte's criticism of his own work necessarily involves distancing himself from Spinoza, or at least what he views as the problematic content of Spinoza's metaphysics. These exchanges acutely bring to light the complexity of Schelling's relation to Spinoza. On the one hand, he sees in the doctrine of parallelism a possible model for reconciliation between transcendental philosophy and the philosophy of nature. As we will see, however, this appropriation is not reducible to the letter of Spinoza's doctrine. On the other hand, Schelling views his own affinity with Spinoza as a possible stumbling block that might impede his attempts to reach beyond Fichte's antinaturalist idealism. Finally, we should take note of Schelling's claim in the 1802 letter quoted above that "I in no way think I have to fear that anything of his will be misunderstood under my name, or anything of mine under his."[14] So, between 1800 and 1802, Schelling became acutely aware of the need to distance his identity philosophy from both the antinaturalist idealism of Fichte and the lifeless monism of Spinoza. To fail to distance the identity philosophy from Spinozism would result in a corresponding failure to distance it from Fichte's eliminative idealism.

Schelling later criticizes Fichte along similar lines that are worth quoting at length. In reference to Fichte's opposition between the knowing I and the determined not-I, Schelling writes,

> [B]ecause this opposition is not a real one, it can happen that between systems that arise from only one or the other side, no real contradiction takes place, and the one could immediately dissolve itself in the other. Realism, were it to genuinely arise from the true, that is, absolute being, would also of itself arrive at absolute knowledge, that is, self-affirmation. This is the case with Spinoza's realism. Idealism, if it genuinely considers absolute knowledge, that is, self-affirmation, penetrates through to the indifference thereof with being, and dissolves itself into its opposite. We interpreted the Fichtean doctrine as an idealism of this type, in that we considered the absolute I as absolute self-affirmation and consequently as the eternal form in the eternal essence. The extensive psychological explanations of this idealism by its author as well as his repeatedly demonstrated inability to see self-affirmation in being, and the restrictions of true life and being to the I of consciousness or the subject, which have followed from that convinced us that we have only loaned this standpoint to him, and that the idea of it, if indeed he was ever aware of it, has completely been lost and had therefore never clearly been understood.[15]

The rhetoric here is a bit complex. Schelling is chastising himself for at one point being more generous to Fichte than he in fact deserved. Recall that for Fichte, active knowing develops in relation to passive being. The I that gives existence conquers the not-I that is ultimately an ephemeral residue of the I's positing. *Both* being and knowing are only on the side of the I. According to Schelling, Fichte fails to see that there is self-affirmation on both sides of this equation, and it is through this shared dynamic that knowledge and being are qualitatively identical and only quantitatively distinguishable. Further, insofar as he denies active self-affirmation to being, Fichte fails to maintain the real, *living* opposition between the real and the ideal.

Again, Fichte's major error is that he only *inverts* Spinozism. He takes Spinozism, the only viable form of transcendental realism as well as the most sublime realism and turns it as a whole into idealism, or more precisely into the kind of criticism Schelling attacked in the *Letters*, in which everything is subsumed by the subjective. One consequence voiced by Schelling echoes the criticism of Fichte penned by Jacobi discussed in chapter 1. Schelling writes,

> That nature is an objective world, says Fichte, has occurred to no one to doubt, and that remains well established as ever and can generally be assumed. However, what is essential to philosophy is not to see nature as an objective world, indeed to hold the objective world *as* objective in general for a mere creature of reflection. *This* objective world that Fichte has in mind, is therefore not even dead; it is nothing at all, an empty phantom. Fichte would be happy to destroy it, yet at the same time preserves it for the sake of its moral usefulness. It only needs to be dead in order to be affected; that it disappear altogether was not at all the intention.[16]

We see Schelling and Jacobi here in direct agreement.[17] Because the I alone determines the not-I as objective in its passivity, it is unable to affirm the objectivity (the actuality) of the object. Further, this problematic repeats Kant's worry taken up in his Refutation of Idealism. Kant knew that self-consciousness depended upon the actual and independent existence of the objects of consciousness persisting through time. By grounding the actuality of objects upon the oppositional positing of the I's relation to the not-I, Fichte forecloses this solution to the problem of idealism as framed by Kant. Finally, Fichte's phantoms exist "beyond death." That is, the objects that constitute Fichte's world were never alive at all insofar as their determinate actuality lies solely and completely on the side of consciousness.

138 | Schelling and Spinoza

The case of Fichte allows us to see that Schelling is *not* advocating for a mere inversion of Spinozism. He holds true to his commitment in the *Letters* that realism and idealism both have a mutual need for each other. Again, the notion of life elucidates this codependency. It must be emphasized that for Schelling life is not locatable exclusively on one side of the opposition between realism and idealism. That is, life is neither *just* real nor *just* ideal. Instead, the dynamic of life expresses itself as the dynamic unity of the real opposition between actually existing contraries. Life is only possible in an actual unity of (real) identity and (ideal) difference. When Fichte wraps nature into the I, he effectively destroys it by reducing its being to nothing apart from what it can do for the mind. In "On the True Concept," Schelling explains, "For this consciousness [the objective world] becomes object and vice versa. With this concept [something originally and simultaneously subjective and objective] we have reached back further than Spinoza managed with his concepts of *natura naturans* and *natura naturata*, which are merely relatively opposed, and *both* are only subject-object regarded from different points of view."[18] Schelling now distances himself from Spinoza precisely regarding the possibility of real, living opposition. Recall again Schelling's final letter to Fichte in which he sets for himself the task of "sharply distinguish[ing] what belongs to him [Spinoza] and to me," in an attempt to more clearly demarcate his own philosophy from Fichte's.[19] What we can conclude at this point is that what was initially the most sublime and perfect realism becomes the most sublime and perfect corpse. Further, and perhaps more tragically, unlike Fichte whom Schelling labels the murderous harbinger of death to nature, in Spinoza's hands the demise of nature is suicidal; the *Ethics* become nature's suicide note.

2.2. IDEALISM AS AMPLIFICATION

Now that I have outlined Fichte's reductive idealism, which Schelling finds unacceptable insofar as it is simply inverted Spinozism, let us turn to Schelling's own ampliative idealism. To better understand the usage of idealism in the *Presentation*, Schelling refers the reader to his *System of Transcendental Idealism*. This ought to strike us as odd, due in part to the fact that in the *System of Transcendental Idealism* Schelling further refers the reader directly to Fichte's *Science of Knowledge*. This at least seems to indicate that Schelling initially understood his idealism as explicable by way of Fichte's method. By contrast (and in a seemingly contradictory way), the preface of the *Presentation* takes care to differentiate Schelling's own use of idealism from Fichte's: "Fichte, e.g., might have conceived idealism in a completely subjective sense while I, on the other hand, conceived it in an objective one," Schelling explains.[20] More specifically, Schelling describes Fichte's subjective idealism as maintaining the standpoint of reflection and contrasts this to his own objective idealism, which is concerned with production.[21] More precisely still, Schelling attributes to Fichte's reflective, subjective idealism the formula "the I is everything," while by contrast his own productive, objective idealism is encapsulated by the schema "everything = I."[22] In placing the I before the All, subjective idealism is a reductive idealism. It begins with the unity of the I and then excludes all that is not the I from the realm of philosophical importance. This move is of course exemplified in the debate between Fichte and Schelling regarding the status of the philosophy of nature in relation to transcendental philosophy. When the All is placed before the I, as it is for Schelling, the task of philosophy is ampliative. Instead of seeking to understand how everything is subsumable under the activity of the I, one must discover how everything in its totality is equal to the I. That is, the unity of the All in the I can only be produced whereas the I's precedence over the All can only be reduced.

For Schelling, idealism always *does* something, and in this acting it fundamentally changes that within or on which it operates. This was an essential aspect of what he had called creative reason in the *Letters*. Idealism properly understood is not a reduction of all things to the mental or to ideas narrowly construed. It is instead a practice of making all things more than what they once were. The ampliative nature of idealism is perhaps more clearly stated in the *System of Transcendental Idealism* when Schelling explains,

> Just as natural science brings forth idealism out of realism, in that it spiritualizes natural laws into laws of mind, or appends the formal to the material . . . so transcendental philosophy brings forth realism out of idealism, *in that it materializes the laws of mind into laws of nature*, or annexes the material to the formal.[23]

It is not the exhaustive task of idealism to list first principles and then subsume everything under them. Just as realism for Schelling is never a reductive realism in which subjectivity is subsumed by objectivity, the same is true of idealism. To reduce either realism or idealism to the other would be to commit the mistake of the abrasive philosopher who attempts to haphazardly slap idealism and realism together. Instead, it is idealism's task to make realism manifest out of itself, and again, this is a task it shares with realism. Each seeks to "bring forth" the one out of the other, to actualize what is only nascent in the other. This mechanism recalls Schelling's claim that the ideal must be prior to the real in order to give it the form that renders it real. As he explains in "On the True Concept":

> Through the gradual but *complete* becoming objective of the pure subject-object, the (intuiting) activity, which in *principle* is limitlessly ideal, raises itself to the I, i.e., to the subject for which that subject-object (that ideal-real) is itself object. From the standpoint of consciousness, nature appears to me as objective and the I as subjective; from this standpoint I cannot otherwise express the problem of the philosophy of nature than as it is expressed in the Introduction to my System of Idealism—that is, *to let the subjective emerge from the objective*.[24]

As we will see, just as spirit, the primordial unity of real and ideal, must come to know itself as finite first by opposing itself to the finite *by producing this very finitude,* the "pure" subject-object must *become* objective by producing itself *as* objective. Further, just as spirit comes to know itself as infinite when it becomes self-conscious of what is productive in its product (i.e., itself), the subjective must subsequently *emerge* from the objective. This complex dynamic of ideal-realization allows us to better understand Grant's claim that

> Schelling's project is the morphology or topology of the sheerly but not merely ideal insofar as this consists in the self-augmentation of the real, rather than as a suppression, suspension, replacement, or merely epistemic elimination, a "rising up" into something higher than it, of nature. This is

why, I would suggest, naturalistic idealism outflanks eliminative realism of the side of the real, and why it outflanks the reducibly conceptual part of the ideal.[25]

Schelling's ideal-realism grounds the possibility of his antireductionist account of nature as well as his non-eliminitivist perspective on the Idea. This relation allows us to understand further the genetic priority of the idealism of nature over the idealism of the I in Schelling's claim that "there is an idealism of nature and an idealism of the I. For me the former is original, *the latter* is derived."[26] Just as there is a "real universe" and an "ideal universe," there is an idealism of nature and an idealism of the I. Further, it is the idealism *in* nature that conditions the possibility for the emergence of the subjective from the objective. Though there is a primacy granted to the ideal, this is the ideal *in nature*, or the ideal articulated on the side of the real. Consequently, the emergent production of the subjective from the objective must have genetic primacy over idealist questions regarding the subjective structures of cognition. Idealism retains genetic primacy over realism only insofar as this idealism is an idealism of nature. However, the idealism capable of augmentation is not the one-sided idealism of Fichte, but a real-idealism that captures the larger unity of unity and duality neglected by both Spinoza and Fichte.

In his February letter of 1795 in which he enthusiastically proclaimed his Spinozism to Hegel, Schelling explained, "For Spinoza, the world (the absolute object opposed to the subject) was everything; for me it is the I."[27] Though *Of the I* makes good on this claim, we have already seen how it became necessary for Schelling to leave this position behind— even as early as the *Letters*. Spinozist realism was only one part of the solution Schelling sought to outline in that essay. In the transition out of the identity philosophy, Spinozism was no longer a sufficient historical model for the unification Schelling believed was necessary to recuperate his philosophy of nature in light of Fichte's criticisms. Were he to remain a Spinozist in the aforementioned sense, a systematic reconciliation of realism and idealism would be just as impossible as finding a common root for thinking and being in Spinoza's metaphysics. Thus, a different historical model was necessary. The model for unification most fruitful for accomplishing this can be found in what Kant and the subsequent German Idealists, following Plato, called the Idea.

In the *System of Philosophy in General*, Schelling emphasizes to his readers that it is the Idea that is the difference that truly makes a difference between himself and Spinoza:[28]

> [B]y idea, here and subsequently, I do not understand the mere mode of *thinking*, as the term is generally understood (even in Spinoza); instead, I understand the idea (following its original meaning) as the archetype [*Urgestalt*], as the essence or heart of things, so to speak: it is that [aspect] of things which is neither merely subjective, like the concept, the mode of thinking, nor merely objective, like the thing purely in itself; instead [it is] the absolute identity of these two aspects.[29]

This we can starkly contrast to Spinoza's definition of ideas in *E*IId3: "By idea I understand a conception of the Mind which the Mind forms because it is a thinking thing," he writes. Spinoza, it must be said, does not explicitly limit the idea to the human mind. *E*IIp4 states that "the idea of God, from which infinite things follow in infinite ways, must be one and only one." He then continues in *E*IIp5, "The formal being of ideas recognizes God as its cause only insofar as he is considered a thinking thing, and not insofar as he is explicated by any other attribute." So even in the case of God, ideas are causes only insofar as they are expressions of God as thinking. Regardless of certain interpretive debates, we can see that for Spinoza, the primary function of ideas is contained in the attribute of thought. As Della Rocca explains, "For Spinoza, ideas enter into causal relations only with other ideas, just as modes of extension enter into causal relations only with other modes of extension."[30] By extension, a parallelism holds between the causal order of ideas and the causal order of extended things. Spinoza provides an epistemology of the Idea by focusing exclusively on the causal relations between ideas in thought. Without the mind, either human or Divine, there can be no idea. Likewise, without thinking, there can be nothing for Ideas to do. Against this reductive approach to the function of the idea, which presupposes both mindedness and thought, Schelling expands the function of ideas beyond the epistemic realm. The Idea, for Schelling, is not reducible to a component of thought. It is, as he says, not "merely" subjective. For Schelling, the Idea is never "my idea" nor is it reducible to an element of my thinking. However, this does not mean that the Idea is objective in some metaphysical or ontological sense. Instead, the Idea is "the unity" between what come to be called "concepts" and "things"; it is the organizational archetype in which subjective and objective (ideal and real) are united.

The *Bruno* dialogue further elucidates what is unique about the Idea in Schelling's work around the time of the identity system. Bruno asks Lucian rhetorically, "Are we not forced to say, for example, that unity and multiplicity, or boundary and unbounded {reality} are absolutely identified in one and the same absolute, wherein the ideal and the real are indivisibly one?"[31] Unlike the concept, the Idea is equally real and ideal not because it is "merely" real or "mere" finitude in the same way that the concept is "mere" infinitude. Instead, the Idea is real because it expresses at once the unity and the difference of unity and differentiation. Bruno again explains to Lucian that "everything that subsists in the domain of the absolute, inasmuch as it is ideal it is immediately also real, and inasmuch as it is real it is directly also ideal."[32] Further, and this is of prime importance for Bruno to differentiate himself from Lucian's Fichteanism, the unity of real and ideal in the Idea is not a simple unity of two opposites in some third thing. Instead,

> if the real detaches itself from absolute identity and subsists within the ideal, so too the ideal detaches itself by reason of its connection to the real. The upshot, viewed from the perspective of absolute identity, is this general rule: *Absolute identity must necessarily appear as two distinct though correlated points, one of which actualizes the ideal through the real {and this is nature}, the other which actualizes the real as such by means of the ideal {and this is the domain of consciousness}.*[33]

The function of the Idea is internal to the relation between the real and the ideal; it is not a transcendent third that stands over and above the two distinct orders. Real and ideal detach themselves from absolute identity and constitute the ordered domains of nature and consciousness. The becoming of nature is the actualization of the ideal within the real, whereas the becoming of consciousness is the real's actualization by way of the ideal. "The identity of the dynamic and the transcendental" Grant explains in relation to this twofold process, "therefore lies not in any procedural similarities, nor in any essential 'likeness' of the two sciences, but in identity itself, that is, in self-fracturing identity at the base, at the level of the forces."[34] It is this fracture that is the "distinct yet correlated point" of real and ideal. These two processes of actualization are points that mirror one another while remaining fully distinct. This is not because of a preexisting harmony between the actual unfolding of real and ideal. Instead, in a way that recalls Schelling's 1797 discussion of spirit, to which we will turn shortly, there is a common *logic* to this actualization that derives from the self-fracturing of identity.

3.0. Realism *sive Natura*

I want to go back to the association of realism and Spinozism in the earlier version of the identity philosophy in order to frame the kind of realism Schelling thought he had located in Spinoza's *Ethics*. Doing so allows us to contextualize the importance of Schelling's critique of Spinoza's attribute dualism. Schelling's characterization of realism in the *Presentation* begins in the following key quotation:

> The situation may be no different for what used to be called "realism" than it is for idealism, and it seems to me, as I hope the following presentation proves, that until now realism in its most sublime and perfect form (in Spinozism, I mean) has been thoroughly misconstrued and misunderstood in all the slanted opinions of it that have become public knowledge.[35]

Here, we find Schelling's parenthetical assertion that the most sublime and perfect realism is Spinozism. Just as idealism has varied and often misunderstood meanings, so too does realism. However, to our dismay, Schelling does not follow this observation with references or suggestions to his reader. Instead, he begs our generosity in interpreting his earlier works on the philosophy of nature and transcendental philosophy as comprising a larger, unified whole. We find no hints other than the replacing of "realism" with "Spinozism" in the following: "All further clarifications of the relation of our system to any other, especially to Spinozism and to idealism, are to be sought in the following presentation itself."[36] Schelling appears to think that a general definition of realism can be drawn from Spinoza seemingly without any needed modification. The most straightforward way of reading this would be to rely on Spinoza's formulation of substance as "Deus *sive* natura." As is frequently remarked, Spinoza's *sive* here is inclusive, and not exclusive. God and nature act as interchangeable names for the one thing that exists. Insofar as God/nature is the one thing that exists, it remains real regardless of its expression as thinking, being, or any other attribute. In fact, in the 1797 Introduction to the *Ideas for a Philosophy of Nature*, Schelling says essentially this:

> The, *first* who, with complete clarity, saw mind and matter as one, thought and extension simply as modifications of the same principle, was *Spinoza*. His system was the first bold outline of a creative imagination, which conceived the finite immediately in the idea of the infinite, purely as such, and recognized the former only in the later.[37]

Regardless of some terminological slippage here between mind-matter and thought-extension, we can see Schelling emphasizing that the parallel attributes are of the same ontological status. They are distinct, but they are also equally real. This thought is made possible by Spinoza because of the inherence of attributes and finite modes within infinite substance that he describes in the *Ethics*. Consequently, Spinoza's analysis of mindedness and thinking is equally "real" as his analysis of extended bodies insofar as only one thing truly exists. However, thought and extension are not real in themselves, because each is dependent upon substance. Any attribute exists only insofar as it is immediately in and conceived through the infinite. Because of this dependence, the attributes of thought and extension are real only insofar as they express the infinite essence of substance. It is the infinite unity of substance from which Spinoza's realism arises. Schelling subsequently interrogates whether this this unity of substance can hold in light of the duality of the attributes.

3.1. SCHELLING'S CRITIQUE OF ATTRIBUTE DUALISM

The second edition of Schelling's *Ideas for a Philosophy of Nature*, published in 1803, contains extensive amendments to each chapter of the original edition. This amended text is particularly interesting and challenging in part because it attempts to fold the 1797 work on the philosophy of nature into the larger system of identity Schelling began developing after initial publication of the *Ideas for a Philosophy of Nature*. In the revised introduction to that work, Schelling presents his criticism regarding the irreducible duality of the attributes in Spinoza's philosophy. He describes the shortcoming of Spinoza's *Ethics* as follows:

> There is still a want of any scientifically observable transition from the first definition of substance to the great first principle of his doctrine [EIIp7]. . . . The scientific knowledge of this identity, whose absence in Spinoza subjected his teaching to the misunderstandings of a former day, was bound to be the beginning of a reawakening of philosophy itself.[38]

What is absent from Spinoza's *Ethics* is a scientific knowledge of the unity of the duality of thought and extension. Interestingly, at this point Schelling suggests that it was for want of this scientific knowledge of the genesis of duality from unity that triggered the many misunderstandings of Spinoza's philosophy. Schelling remains committed to this critique in the writings that follow the identity philosophy, and he explicitly connects it to the reality of conflict, which again is the condition of possibility for any kind of life. In the 1815 *Ages of the World*, Schelling writes,

> Instead of the living conflict between the unity and duality of both the so-called attributes and substance being the main object, Spinoza only occupies himself with them as both opposed, indeed, with each for itself, without their unity coming to language as the active, living copula of both substance and attribute. Hence the lack of life and progression in his system.[39]

Here, we see the explicit connection between Schelling's critique of Spinoza's dualism as well as his claim that Spinozism is lifeless.

EIIp7, the proposition to which Schelling refers in the 1803 addition to the *Ideas for a Philosophy of Nature*, reads, "The order and connection of ideas is the same as the order and connection of things." This is the wellspring of what is now referred to as the doctrine of attribute parallelism. In the corollary to this proposition, Spinoza continues, "It follows that God's power of thinking is on par with his power of acting." So, in general, God acts in two ways: as thinking and as extending. Each of these attributes is self-contained, and consequently, there must be some kind of relation within and not between the two attributes that allows them to be intelligible. This equality of the attributes is not intended to be merely formal. Instead, "thinking substance and extended substance are one and the same substance, comprehended now under this attribute, now under that." Spinoza's hope is that the unity of substance can overcome the apparent duality of the attributes. Further, he needs this to be the case if his monism is to live up to Schelling's standards and meet the latter's need for identity. If it fails to establish some fundamental unity from which all attributes spring, Spinoza's system lacks a transition from divine existence to the divine intellect through which knowledge (God's self-knowing as well as the knowing of finite beings) becomes possible.

The most sublime realism of Spinoza is grounded in his insistence on the simple unity of substance, the one thing that exists. Duality is subsequently introduced into the *Ethics* with the doctrine of the attributes. This aspect of the *Ethics* gives rise to just as many, if not more, hermeneutic and interpretive challenges as his argument for existence monism. And, like everything else in the *Ethics*, the doctrine of attribute parallelism cannot be considered in isolation from the doctrine of substance monism. Recall that the argument for existence monism depended upon the impossibility of two distinct substances sharing an attribute that could properly express the infinite essence of each substance while allowing these substances to remain distinct. This followed from the necessary conceptual independence of the attributes outlined in the Axioms of Book I. For anything to be limited, it had to be limited by a thing with which it shared some feature. Though the attributes were one candidate for this shared characteristic that would make mutual limitation possible, we saw how if an attribute expresses the very essence of substance, then two substances that shared an attribute could not be distinguishable as two substances because their essence would be the same. The existence of two substances, each with at least one shared attribute (that would make mutual limitation possible) as well as one unshared attribute (that would make each substance distinguishable *as* a distinct substance), was shown to be strictly impossible. Finally, substance's infinite essence is also proved by way of the conceptual and causal independence of the attributes. Again, though we only know the essence of substance through the attributes of thought and extension, this does not entail that these are the only attributes of substance. "Each attribute of one substance must be conceived through itself," writes Spinoza in *E*Ip10. This follows from *E*Ia2: "That which cannot be conceived through another thing must be conceived through itself." Attributes are necessarily dependent upon substance and necessarily independent of each other. Because attributes cannot limit each other (as a result of their conceptual independence), there can be no nonarbitrary way to demarcate precisely how many attributes there are. *E*Id6 states that "by God I mean an absolutely infinite being, that is, substance consisting of infinite attributes, each of which expresses eternal and infinite essence." Because, by *E*Ip9, "the more reality or being a thing has, the more attributes it has," we can see that the attributes are infinite internally insofar as each expresses the complete essence of substance, as well as externally insofar as no attribute can exclude the existence of another. This means that both thought and extension are equally infinite expressions of substance, and by extension, they share an ontological status. Neither is more real than the other. Further, they are real in the same way, their being is said in one voice, as Deleuze might put it.[40] Despite this ontological equality and univocity, a general problem regarding the relation of the attributes remains. If, as *E*Ia6 claims, "a true idea must agree with that of which it is the idea [*ideatum*]" but ideality and reality are strictly parallel, then what is the nature of this agreement that makes any true idea possible?

Book I of the *Ethics* deploys the attributes in large part to demonstrate the necessary existence of one infinite thing. Book II then turns to the problem of minds and bodies as they relate to God as their immanent cause. To recap, a body is a mode that "expresses in a definite and determinate way God's essence insofar as he is considered as an extended thing" (*E*IId1), and an idea is "a conception of the Mind which the Mind forms because it is a thinking thing" (*E*IId3). So, the problem of production in Book II involves both the production of extended things, as well as the production of the intelligible order of those things. As Deleuze claims, the attributes are introduced in this context in order to account for God's production of a "modal universe."[41] Minimally, Spinoza turns to the attributes in Book II in an attempt to explain the existence of and the intelligibility of substance insofar as it is productive. The first propositions of Book II bring us back to the attributes to which we have access. *E*IIp1 states, "Thought is an attribute of God; i.e., God is a thinking thing." *E*IIp2 says the same of the attribute of extension: "Extension is an attribute of God; i.e., God is an extended thing." God is a thinking thing, and God is an extended thing. What now comes to light is the question of how God can be singular, on the one hand, as well as constituted by conceptually independent attributes, on the other. Substance is necessarily indivisible, yet God is both extended and thinking.

This brings us to the idea of parallelism. The doctrine of parallelism is drawn from *E*IIp7, in which Spinoza claims, "The order and connection of ideas is the same as the order and connection of things." We know from the demonstration of existence monism that there can be no intersection or interpenetration of attributes. Yet, at the same time, the order and connection of things is fully explicable and must therefore have some formal relation to the order and connection of ideas. There are several interpretations of the parallelism between ideas and things, and briefly outlining two prominent ones allows us to better understand what Schelling will appropriate from Spinoza's doctrine of attribute parallelism, as well as what he will leave behind. Let us begin with a minimalist interpretation of this parallelism, often referred to as the subjectivist interpretation. According to this position, the best way to understand the attributes is as points of view. If we approach the attributes from this subjective perspective, we can posit an epistemological isomorphism between the explanatory order and connection of ideas and the explanatory order and connection of things. This is because the order and connection of ideas is not an expression of one thing while the order and connection of things is an expression of some other thing. Both are "views" on the single thing that exists. In other words, each attribute expresses the essence of substance in a distinct descriptive regime. This interpretation seems to follow from Spinoza's definition of an attribute as "what the intellect perceives of a substance." A common example used to elucidate this is in the debates surrounding the status of mental events. Let us take a memory as a particular mode. From a Spinozist perspective, one might argue for the irreducibility of "mental" descriptions (my experience of happiness when reflecting upon a trip I have recently taken) and physical descriptions of mental states (an account of the physical states underlying mental phenomena, such as the mechanisms of memory inscription, recollection, the emissions/uptake of dopamine and serotonin, etc.). Now, though these descriptive regimes are distinct, they remain descriptions of one and the same event or object. There is consequently a duality of description but an identity of the mental event itself. As Della Rocca explains, "The dualism here is not, for Spinoza, a dualism of extended things and thinking things. Rather the dualism is a dualism of ways of *conceiving* or *explaining* the same thing."[42] So, in the case of my memory, one and the same experience is accounted for from two distinct explanatory perspectives. One of the primary attractions of this perspective is the way it allays reductionist attacks from physicalists or idealists of a certain type.[43] Thought and extension are necessary and irreducible aspects of description, and their conceptual independence means that consistent explanation cannot blur the borders between the two discursive regimes. However, because each attribute must be conceived through itself and through itself alone, one can never appeal to extension in order to explain thought, and vice versa.

This minimalist reading of the parallelism of the attributes would seem to avoid the vitiation of substance's unity. However, it is not clear that Spinoza would be comfortable with an interpretation of the attributes so dependent upon the structures of finite cognition. This is where the objectivist reading of the attributes comes into play. As Lin summarizes, on the objectivist view, "the attributes constitute real metaphysical diversity in a substance."[44] If the attributes constitute real metaphysical diversity in substance, then Schelling's criticism begins to take hold. If we follow an objectivist interpretation of the attributes, then they are not just epistemologically distinguishable views upon substance. Shein explains that "objectivists, therefore, take the definition as stating that attributes are what the *infinite* intellect perceives of substance *as in fact* constituting its essence."[45] In this case, the attributes are, in some way, ontological expressions of the essence of substance. This interpretation seems to square well with the proof to *E*Ip16, in which Spinoza comments, "Since divine nature possesses absolutely infinite attributes (Def. 6), of which each one also expresses infinite essence in its own kind, then there must necessarily follow from the necessity of the divine nature an infinity of things in infinite ways." Thought and extension are equally real for Spinoza insofar as they are immanent articulations of the infinite essence of substance, and this is their unity. However, the parallelism that follows from the conceptual independence between the attributes of thought and extension generates a division that cannot not be stitched back together. If the objectivist reading is correct, then Spinoza lacks an account of the *genesis* of the parallel duplicity of these attributes.

In the previously discussed letters exchanged between Fichte and Schelling, the references to Spinoza seem to imply that both Fichte and Schelling held a minimalist interpretation of the attributes in the *Ethics*. In the *Further Presentation from the System of Philosophy* of 1802, Schelling even seems to explicitly endorse this subjectivist reading.[46] Further, Schelling's critique of Spinoza's concept of the Idea also seems to imply a subjectivist understanding of the attributes. In the correspondence between Fichte and Schelling, it was suggested that transcendental philosophy and naturephilosophy were not irreconcilable because both were complementary views upon a single existence. It was this existence that unified the distinct perspectives of transcendental philosophy and naturephilosophy. Schelling himself even suggested that the real and the ideal in the identity philosophy are to be understood in relation to Spinoza's attributes of extension and thought respectively. However, Schelling does not embrace this minimalist or subjectivist interpretation of the real and the ideal in his philosophy of identity. Real and ideal are actual self-determinations of the Absolute. Though there must be a real distinction between the real and ideal, this distinction must somehow have its origin in a preexisting unacquired unity existing in the Absolute. To posit the relation otherwise would be to fall prey to the abrasive construction of the Absolute after the fact, which Schelling explicitly rejects in *Philosophy and Religion*. Further, if reason is eternal then it necessarily incorporates both the rational and the irrational into a higher unity that expresses their identity without erasing their nonidentity. This would mean that the specific form of discursive rationality that forbids unaccounted-for bifurcations would not hold globally in relation to the Absolute as a whole. Because the Absolute is formally bound to the complex logic of the principle of identity and not to the strictures of the PSR, reason can relate to itself in such a way that it bifurcates in what might be called illogical ways. Now if, coming back to the suggestion made by Melamed's reading of Schelling's *Presentation*, reason is no longer reducible to the finite intellect but is instead one and the same as substance, we can intertwine the subjectivist and the objectivist understanding of the attributes. Lin suggests of the single essence of substance that "this essence is presented to our intellect under a diversity of guises, with the result that a distinction of reason obtains between the various attributes."[47] If it is the case that in Schelling's *Presentation* reason becomes another name for substance then the division between real and ideal would be one drawn by substance and for substance. But again, by "reason" here we cannot understand anything that can be reducible to the intellect, perception, or discursive forms of rationality. Following Schelling's opening definition of the *Presentation*, we must understand reason as "the total indifference of the subjective and the objective,"[48] as well as that which is *"one in an absolute sense."*[49] Substance would have to divide itself in order to account for the bifurcation of the attributes.

Coming back to Schelling's critique of Spinoza, we can see that the question is the following: If there is necessarily an irreducibility of the attributes to each other how could one then reintroduce the unity of substance in light of this? Candidates such as univocity or ontological unity may at first seem to allay this worry, but doing so renders any duality of attributes as merely formal or apparent. This would in turn violate the conceptual and causal independence of the attributes that played such a crucial role in the argument for existence monism. Perhaps the attributes can be considered as emergent from the unity of substance. If this were the case, the duality of the attributes would not be absolute, because the emergence of this duality would be grounded in the unity of substance. However, if we follow the existence monist reading of Spinoza, this would be a violation of Spinoza's naturalism. As previously noted, in addition to the commitment that "everything plays by the same rules," Della Rocca defines the second characteristic of Spinoza's naturalism as the commitment that there can be "no illegitimate bifurcations in reality." If any division in nature is to exist, there must be an explicable reason for why and how this bifurcation came to be. If this is indeed the case, the duality of the attributes would have to be taken as a legitimate bifurcation that would demand explanation. The question then is: To what would one appeal to account for the bifurcation between the attributes? If the attributes really are conceptually and therefore causally distinct, one could appeal to neither thought nor extension in the attempt to render this bifurcation legitimate. Further, if we were to appeal to some third thing in order to account for this bifurcation, this third thing could not itself be an attribute. This would call into question the very intelligibility of this emergence. In light of this, it seems as if any genetic explanation of the bifurcation of the attributes would force us to reject either Spinoza's rationalism or his naturalism. So, we can now see how the duality of real and ideal in Spinoza's *Ethics* ruptures the model of unity provided therein. Consequently, though his realism might remain sublime it is no longer perfect. Or, put otherwise, perhaps it is simply too perfect to become otherwise.

3.2. Auto-Affective Spirit as Precursor to the Absolute

Now I want to turn to the theme of *Wechseldurchdringung*, understood as absolute synthesis, mutual saturation or dynamic interpenetration. One way of putting Schelling's critique of Spinoza's attribute dualism is that the division between thought and extension is simply too clean. Each attribute can peacefully remain in relation to itself alone. There is no conflict and no interpenetration of thinking and being. By extension, there is no life and no progression. What must be uncovered is a model of the dynamic interpenetration of real and ideal that will come to characterize the self-differentiation of the Absolute. In the 1795 *Letters*, we saw Schelling turn to Spinoza in order to balance out what he took to be the one-sided form of critical philosophy made possible by (but not representative of) the *Critique of Pure Reason*. These forms of criticism were one-sided because they were concerned with the subjective conditions of synthesis that rendered the world intelligible while neglecting the objective synthesis that rendered these subjective syntheses real and not merely ideal. As we have already seen, Schelling initially offered realism as an antidote to this one-sided idealism and thereby provided a supplementary reconciliation of realism and idealism. The problem with this supplementary reconciliation was that it neglected the Absolute. The creative reason that was supposed to act as the common root of subject and object ultimately buttresses the dualism between the two. It established an emergent parallelism that it could not maintain. Though constructing a philosophy from the perspective of the Absolute is a novel methodological commitment in the identity philosophy, the self-relating function of the Absolute is foreshadowed in the 1797 *Treatise*. Spirit is a self-relating unity that, unlike Spinoza's substance, does not lose its unity in light of its duality. The self-differentiating dynamics of what Schelling calls "spirit" in this essay might remind the reader largely of what Schelling calls "nature" in the philosophy of nature. Moreover, and more importantly for my present purposes, this self-differentiating dynamic will later be framed as the dynamics of the Absolute. In other words, we can trace a circuitous yet continuous route from the notion of creative reason to spirit to nature and eventually to the Absolute.

The tone of the *Treatise* shows a marked difference to the *Letters* written two years prior. The *Letters* took the form of a series of invocations to an unidentified recipient. Though its content is polemical, its tone is more conversational. Alternatively, the *Treatise* is an all-out attack on those who have so manipulated the legacy of the first *Critique* as to render it unrecognizable. Schelling begins the *Treatise* by taking aim at two distinct philosophical positions. The first is represented by the "moral atheism" of Karl Heinrich Heydenreich. Schelling quickly dispatches with this line of thought by claiming that it fails to push atheism to its most sublime form, namely "the atheism that believes in immortality while denying *God*."[50] If atheism is to "follow with any necessity from the moral principles of critical philosophy,"[51] it must saddle itself with the burden of immortality while at the same time denying the existence of God as a transcendent third that reconciles the world and human action. Schelling then builds on the infinite force of the soul (or spirit) in order to confront the second philosophical position at which he takes aim. This is the idealist who is unable to figure out the true relation between the fundamental dualisms of the critical project, such as the division between representations and their content, concepts and intuitions, understanding and sensibility, and theoretical and practical philosophy. Schelling says of the dualist idealist that "they fail to recognize that everything within ourselves remains *petty* if it is not effected by nature herself."[52] This is already an early articulation of the claim that idealism must be grounded in realism if philosophy is to be anything other than the petty exchange of phantasmic opinions. Subjective thinking is nothing of importance if it is not somehow grounded in objective reality. Or, as articulated in "On the True Concept," an idealism that fails to recognize the primacy of the I of nature will always remain without an anchor in the real. Schelling's presentation of spirit in 1797 already details how the relation between realism and idealism must be more intimate than the earlier supplementary method of reconciliation can allow. Schelling argues that only by finding a primordial origin in which these dualisms are distinct yet not divided can we overcome the one-sided idealism that views these divisions only from the perspective of consciousness. The task set forth is thus the isolation of the primordial unity of activity and passivity that allows both to remain actually but not absolutely distinct. Again, thought (and the structures of cognition) must in some way be grounded in nature (and the real genesis of the conditions for thinking) if thinking is to be anything other than petty. It is in this context that Schelling turns to the notion of spirit.

Ameriks notes the Spinozist undertones of Schelling's analysis of spirit in the *Treatise*. "Schelling is already here speaking of the quasi-Spinozist absolute that, as Hegel would later say, must be thought of not as a merely inert 'substance,' but as a 'subject' in a complexly dynamic ontological sense," he writes.[53] Ameriks continues, "Schelling's point is that the substance or 'spirit' that is the original essence of the world is not a simple being but is rather something that has an internal necessity to distinguish or 'create' finite components within it that are organized in an 'original conflict.'"[54] In order to explicate this dynamic and conflicted process of self-production, the *Treatise* contains within it the association of active and ideal as well as passive and real. In the previous chapter, we saw the role that the active affirmation in relation to a passive being affirmed played in Schelling's account of the quantitative differentiation of the Absolute's simple identity. The Absolute was said to be ideal insofar as it was affirming and real insofar as it was affirmed. "An action in view of which we feel *free* we shall call *ideal*, whereas one in view of which we feel *restricted* [we shall call] *real*," Schelling explains in the *Treatise* foreshadowing the dynamics described in the identity philosophy.[55] However, just as in the identity philosophy where there is no absolute division between activity and passivity, here too this strict division does not do justice to the larger interrelation, or the common root, of the real and the ideal:

> The concept appears to us as *ideal* and the intuition as real; yet each [can be designated] in this manner only in reciprocity with the other; for neither are we *conscious* of the concept without intuition, nor can we be conscious of intuition without a concept. Anyone maintaining the standpoint of mere consciousness must necessarily claim [that] our knowledge is *partly* ideal, *partly* real; such claims are likely to lead to a phantasmic system that can never explain how the ideal could have become real and vice versa. Anyone who has attained a superior perspective will find that *originally* there is *no* difference between ideality and reality, and that

consequently our knowledge is not *partly* but *completely* and *thoroughly* ideal and real *at once*.⁵⁶

Knowledge is completely ideal and real at the same time. This alone disrupts any straightforward equivocation of the ideal with transcendental philosophy and the real with naturephilosophy. However, just because knowledge is completely real and ideal at the same time, this does not mean that it is real and ideal in the same way. The unity of knowledge is consequently a discordant one due to the subtle functional difference played by the real and the ideal. That is, proper knowing is able to maintain a unity of real and ideal without rendering the two equivalent. Further, it is only from the standpoint of "consciousness" that anything would appear as "partially" real and "partially" ideal. We can see that Schelling's use of "consciousness" here is similar to Hegel's characterization of what *Verstand* or understanding does. Reflective consciousness divides and stagnates its objects in order to construct something to which it could be properly, albeit temporarily, opposed. For Schelling, these divisions made by consciousness are only the temporary divisions *for* consciousness through which it comes to know itself as an organ of the larger unity of subject and object that exists prior to and indifferent to these divisions. In short, to reduce knowing to reflective understanding is to neglect the ways in which the ideal has *become* real just as the real has *become* ideal.

This now brings us explicitly to the notion of spirit in the *Treatise*. Schelling defines spirit as follows:

> As *spirit* I designate that which is only *its own* object. To the extent that the spirit is to be an object *for itself* it is no object in the *original* sense but an absolute *subject* for which *everything* (including itself) is an *object*. Such indeed it will have to be. Any object is something *dead*, static, *incapable* of an activity itself, and only the *object* of an activity. The spirit, however, can be apprehended only *in its activity* . . . ; the spirit, then, exists only in *becoming* or, rather, it is nothing but an *eternal becoming*.⁵⁷

In short, it is spirit's infinite activity of becoming finite through which it comes to know itself as infinite. This process itself is that through which the duality of real and ideal find their unacquired, equiprimordial unity. The unity of ideal and real are found in spirit insofar as "the spirit's *mode of activity* and the *product of this mode of activity* are the same."[58] So, for example, unlike Kant's moral God, spirit is not some third thing that stands external or transcendent to two seemingly irreconcilable orders (in this case, that of active productivity and passive product). Further, unlike Jacobi's notion of divine life, spirit does not have an origin outside of its immanent unfolding. Spirit does not transcendently guarantee a correspondence between the real and the ideal. Instead, spirit is the unity of this mode of differentiating activity determined as nothing other than its function of perpetual production. Consequently, spirit's actuality is indistinguishable from its formative activity.

In addition to being at once its own mode of activity and the product of this very activity, spirit sets for itself the goal of coming to know itself as both the mode and product of its own activity:

> We will conceive of the soul as an activity that continually strives to extract something finite from the infinite. It is as though the soul comprised an infinity that is constrained to present outside itself. This cannot be explained any further, except by referring [again] to the constant striving of the spirit to become *finite* for itself; that is to become conscious of itself. All acts of the spirit thus aim at *presenting the infinite within the finite*. The *goal* of all these acts is self-consciousness, that their history is none other than the *history of self-consciousness*.[59]

The goal of spirit is to come to know itself, and it can only do this through determining itself within finite instantiations of the infinite. Here we can see Schelling setting up the task to be carried out in the *System of Transcendental Idealism*. Further, there is a sense in which this journey Schelling describes is a path back to an earlier state:

> Yet what is absolutely purposive is *in itself complete and perfected*. It contains within itself *the origin and the final purpose* of its existence. Precisely this is the primordial quality of the spirit. Inherently destined to finitude, it constructs itself, produces itself into infinity, and thus constitutes both beginning and end of its own existence.[60]

Spirit is neither the middle point on a path from origin to end, nor is it a traveler on a linear journey. The temporality of spirit's journey is not one that can be captured in simple narrative form. Instead, spirit contains within itself at the same time both its origin and its end. Further, the nonlinear interpenetration of origin and end make possible the unity presented in the dynamic interpenetration of form and matter as well as concept and intuition. Schelling explains, "In purposiveness, form and matter, concept and intuition interpenetrate. Precisely this is the character of spirit in which the Ideal and the Real are absolutely united. Hence, there is something *symbolic* in every organism, and every plant is, so to speak, *an arabesque delineation of the soul*."[61] Again, the unity of spirit is found nowhere but in its very activity of self-directed becoming. Its unity is found precisely in the differentiations that express its purposiveness. In the function of spirit, real and ideal are united throughout the interpenetration of form and matter as well as concept and intuition. Moreover, because this unity of ideal and real is the beginning and end of spirit's journey, the unfolding of the ideal becoming real as the real becomes ideal unites spirit's journey with its origin and end.

In its journey of progressive self-knowing, the function of spirit mirrors the purposive, self-reflective determinateness of life. Schelling claims that "if the [spirit] is to have an intuition of itself as active in the succession of its representations, it will have to inspect itself as an *object* that contains an *inner principle of movement* within itself. Such is what we properly call a *living* being."[62] The idea here is that at first, from the perspective of consciousness, spirit divides itself into production and product. This opposition is posited as irreconcilable insofar as the productive force is unable to find itself in its product. If it is going to know itself, spirit must first know itself as an object; it must take itself to be objective. In other words, the productive process must be posited temporarily in a product in order to come to know itself not just as subjective process but also as objective determination. However, spirit cannot stop here in the opposition between product and productivity, because its ultimate goal and its inner drive are to come to know itself not just as an object (or the product of its own activity), but as an object that contains within it the ability to take itself as an object (its activity as such). In short, spirit must forget and then remember that it itself is the origin of the objects it comes to know.

The *Treatise* concludes with Schelling's attempt to reconcile the theoretical and practical sides of the critical project. He again appeals to a primordial and originary unity of the two. "It is only on account of this *originary identity of the theoretical and the practical in us* that the affective within us becomes thought, that the Real becomes *Ideal,* and vice versa," Schelling writes, continuing on to note that "without making this [identity] the principle of our entire philosophy, we may refer the apprentice to the *primordial* theoretical acts of the spirit, to be sure, yet we can never afford these acts anything but a merely *ideal* significance."[63] Now, here in this second quotation we find a perplexing comment: "Without making this [identity] the principle of our entire philosophy." Without making the principle of originary identity the whole of philosophy, the acts of spirit have "merely" ideal significance. They have yet to become fully real. The *Treatise*'s discussion of the life of spirit paves the way for an understanding of how the Absolute differentiates itself through a practice of self-understanding. In this way, we can distinguish Schelling's approach to the Absolute's ideal-reality from that of the image of the abrasive philosopher with which we began. Ultimately, what is at stake is the original in-division of the real and the ideal in the Absolute in which being maintains primacy over thinking without denying the central functionality of thought in relation to the determinations of being as thus and so. Being is necessary but being alone is not enough. If it were sufficient for the Absolute just to be, then we would have no need to exit from Spinozism. In short, the journey of spirit is a messy one in which no strict division can be drawn between the ideal activity of spirit and the expression of this activity in reality.

4.0. Conclusion

Despite Spinoza's best efforts and his most sublime insight into the dark past that Schelling himself attempts to know and narrate, Spinoza was unable to reach the seemingly contradictory notion of a living Absolute. Due to his position regarding the universal applicability of the PSR, Spinoza concluded that only one thing exists and the two ways we can conceive of the essence of this one thing that exists are conceptually and causally distinct. That is, our knowledge of the

Absolute is irreducibly dualistic. This dualism, as Schelling interprets it, applies not just to the ways we know the Absolute. Spinoza's Absolute itself is constitutively dualistic. Against the abrasive tendency discussed in the *Philosophy of Religion* that arises directly from the duality of real and ideal, Schelling's identity philosophy articulates both how one can and why one must become an organ of the Absolute instead of just an external observer. As Schelling explains in the *System of Philosophy in General*, "In *reason* all subjectivity ceases, and this is precisely what our proposition argues. In reason, that eternal identity itself is at once the knower and the known—it is not *me* who recognizes this identity, but it recognizes itself, and I am merely its organ."[64] In the identity philosophy, Schelling articulates the way in which reason is necessarily irreducible to the subjective. The subjective recognition of the identity constitutive of reason is but an organ or local articulation of the larger unity of knower and known that is *grounded "outside" of or irreducible to the subject alone*. In this way, the hyphenated unity of realism and idealism in the identity philosophy dispels earlier threats of subjectivism present in Schelling's notion of creative reason. When he turns to identity as both a logical and ontological condition for the unity of real and ideal, he no longer needs to appeal to the more Kantian and Fichtean notion of synthesis. Further, the simultaneous unity and duality expressed by the hyphen allows Schelling to move past Spinoza's static monism and into what Schelling will later call a "living realism."[65] Because in the end, "the lack of life and progression in [Spinoza's] system"[66] is a result of this privileging of duality at the expense of unity, Schelling reinscribes duality within unity while privileging neither at the expense of the other. This in turn has profound implications for the possibility of any philosophical monism. Now, given the praise voiced for Spinoza at the opening of the *Presentation*, it ought to strike us as odd that the failure of the philosophy of identity comes precisely from the fact that it was unable to sufficiently differentiate itself from that which it explicitly took as a model in both form and content.

I have suggested that this mutual saturation of realism and idealism is best captured by the mark of the hyphen, which simultaneously binds and separates. Ultimately, it is the erasure of the hyphen that disallows realism from functioning as it should. For Schelling, the solution to this problem so precisely embodied by Spinoza's dead realism and its inversion in Fichte's eliminative idealism can only be solved by the activities of intuition and life (both of which find their ground in the hyphenated indifference between subject and object). In the 1806 essay *Statement on the True Relationship of the Philosophy of Nature to the Revised Fichtean Doctrine*, Schelling writes in reference to Fichte that

> the cause of spiritual spitefulness of all kinds is the lack of that intuition by means of which nature appears to us as living; indeed this lack leads sooner or later to complete spiritual death, which cannot be concealed by any art. There is something incurable in it (we are happy to acknowledge) since the entire power of healing lies in nature. This alone is the true antidote to abstraction.[67]

These lines written in 1806 further testify to the depth of the split (both philosophical and personal) between Fichte and Schelling. Fichte is not merely in error. As a consequence of turning nature into phantasmic nothingness he has become sick, his spirit has become spiteful. This quotation is revelatory in that it further emphasizes Schelling's conviction that the task of philosophy as a whole is not just to think nature. Instead, the more ambitious task of philosophy is to think the life and history of nature through a series of intuitions. The antidote to "abstraction" as well as the path to philosophy and art is found in nature *intuited as living* alone. Further, this intuition of the life of nature Schelling calls "divine life." However, unlike the life invoked by Jacobi, this divine life is not transcendent to the life of nature: "This presentation of the divine life, not outside or above but rather in nature, as a truly real and present life is doubtless the final synthesis of the ideal with the real, knowledge with being, and therefore also the final synthesis of science itself," Schelling writes.[68] The actuality of divine life as the final synthesis of ideal and real is not outside or above nature but is instead nested within nature. That is, the final synthesis of real and ideal occurs within the real. However, this real in which the final synthesis of real and ideal occurs is not a homogenous ontological unity. Once again, the proper place of this synthesis is the hyphen. Neither Spinoza nor Fichte grasp that it is the *hyphen itself* that makes possible any expression of the Absolute because it is the hyphen that is able to hold together disparate elements in a disjunctive unity. It is the hyphen that binds subject and object, real and ideal, without collapsing or reducing one into the other.

With this picture of Schelling's critique of Spinoza's parallelism in mind, we can better grasp the philosophical history behind the analysis of Spinoza and pantheism more generally in the *Freedom* essay.

Death arises within both realism and idealism as a result of the erasure of the hyphen and the unique spacing it makes possible. The hyphen simultaneously binds and separates, allowing duality to stand in real opposition without erasing the co-determinate unity of the two terms. It is nothing short of life that this actual opposition makes possible:

> Reason is just as original and true as the unity, and it is only through grasping both in the same way that the living unity is known. The contradiction has to exist, because a life must exist; the contradiction itself is life and movement in unity; but the true identity subjects it to itself, that is, it posits it as contradiction and unity at the same time, and thus arises the unity that in itself moves, originates, and creates.[69]

It is in its hyphenated unity presented in reason that the "organic" or living unity of reason as such comes to be known. It is posited simultaneously and somewhat paradoxically as both contradiction and unity. Without the identity of identity and difference, the unity of reason ceases to be alive. The hyphen maintains the minimal difference between real and ideal necessary for the living unity of the two.

In the *Freedom* essay we find Schelling formalizing the necessity of the hyphen as it relates to what he calls life. Therein Schelling writes of Spinozism that "it is a one-sidedly realist system, which expression indeed sounds less damning than pantheism, yet indicates what is characteristic of the system far more correctly and is also not employed here for the first time."[70] As Schelling discussed previously in the text, pantheism as a system was poorly defined and poorly understood since Spinoza and up until Schelling's time (and, arguably, until ours as well). Against this commonsense trend and consistent with his earlier positions, Schelling finds realism to be a far more accurate classification for Spinoza's system. However, to repeat Schelling's punctual formulation of his "once and for all" opinion of Spinozism,

> A mutual saturation of realism and idealism in each other was the declared intent of his efforts. Spinoza's basic concept [*Grundbegriff*], when infused by spirit (and, in one essential point, changed) by the principle of idealism, received a living basis in the higher forms of investigation of nature and

the recognized unity of the dynamic with the emotional and spiritual.[71]

It is idealism that must be added to Spinozism in order for it to come to life. Developing upon this claim Schelling then gives a genealogy of the emergence of naturephilosophy from Spinozism. "Out of this grew the philosophy of nature, which as pure physics was indeed able to stand for itself," Schelling claims, "yet anytime in regard to the whole of philosophy was only considered as a part, namely the real part that would be capable of rising up into the genuine system of reason only through completion by the ideal part in which freedom rules."[72] When *infused* with spirit and the principle of idealism, Spinozism becomes a realism capable of thinking nature as something other than a mere machine or other than as a dead thing. Finally, it is through idealism that the living realism expressed as the philosophy of nature finds its completion. This genealogy then leads to one of the core claims of the *Freedom* essay: "In the final and highest judgment" writes Schelling, "there is no other Being than will. Will is primal Being [*Ur-sein*] to which alone all predicates of Being apply: groundlessness, eternity, independence from time, self-affirmation."[73] It is through ampliative idealism that realism is changed and then completed in the system of philosophy. This system of philosophy, if it is in fact *both* systematic *and* philosophical comes to know itself as the very expression of primal Being.

PART III

Chapter 5

Divine Indigestion

1.0. Introduction: Identity Crisis

As Schelling approaches the close of the identity philosophy in *Philosophy and Religion*, directly following a reference to Spinoza Schelling reminds us that "aside from the teachings on the Absolute, the true mysteries of philosophy have as their most noble and indeed their sole content the eternal birth of all things and their relationship to God."[1] From this claim, we can isolate two distinct issues. The first concerns the things that emerge from the Absolute. What is the nature of the things that are eternally born from the Absolute, and in what ways are they things? That is, how are things determinable both logically and ontologically as finite particulars? The second issue returns us to the problem of the relation between the infinite and the finite. What relation do these things maintain to the Absolute from which they emerge or from which they are eternally born? In what way is the birth of finite things eternal? As we have previously seen, Spinoza stands as an exemplar in the history of the "teachings on the Absolute." However, Spinozism has been found wanting in its contribution to the "true mysteries of philosophy" insofar as it denied any transition from the infinite to the finite.

The transition away from the system of identity is of particular interest for the question regarding the systematic unity of Schelling's philosophy. Basically, the problem is this: Does the identity philosophy represent a breach or break in Schelling's philosophical trajectory?

Or is the identity philosophy an expression of Schelling's underlying philosophical commitments and preoccupations? Žižek, for example, characterizes the shift in Schelling's philosophy around the time of the *Weltalter* project as "abandoning his earlier project of the so-called philosophy of identity."[2] Alderwick does not see the identity philosophy as a complete break in Schelling's philosophical development, but she does suggest that it was worries regarding Spinoza's conception of freedom that "led Schelling to move away from the *Identitätssystem* and which define his goals in the *Freedom* essay."[3] She concludes that the identity philosophy was in fact a failure and that the Schelling's post-1804 writings on freedom more closely fall in line with the powers-based ontology articulated in the naturephilosophy. Alternatively, Whistler has argued that to take the identity philosophy as solely a transitional period of Schelling's work overlooks the role it plays in the overall construction of Schelling's philosophical system and his understanding of symbolic language.[4] In their co-written commentary on the exchange between Schelling and Eschenmayer, Whistler and Berger have endorsed the idea that the identity philosophy is continuous with naturephilosophy by turning to "On the True Concept."[5] Grant and Woodard also endorse this thesis on the back of Grant's proclamation that "Schellingianism *is* naturephilosophy throughout."[6] Whatever the case may be, it is clear that Schelling himself did not initially believe he was going back to the drawing board while developing the identity philosophy. Instead, he viewed it as providing the larger metaphysical framework in which his previous philosophical endeavors could be reconciled.

Schelling himself came to view the identity philosophy as a failed project, but for reasons quite different than worries about philosophical continuity. "*The philosophy of identity* had the ambition to be *that pure science of reason*," claims Schelling in the 1841–42 lectures on the Philosophy of Revelation, "At the same time, it will need to be shown how the philosophy of identity *failed* in this ambition."[7] The philosophy of identity desired to be a pure science of reason and at this it failed. Schelling continues, "The philosophy of identity was the purest, entirely free flight of the activity of thinking. It could only fall away from itself by wanting to be something more."[8] Because of its freedom without constraint, the identity philosophy's failure gives way to something other. It opens, but onto what?

After relating the identity philosophy to Fichte's system, Schelling notes that this philosophy "did not acknowledge a non-being object as such."[9] As the purest, entirely free activity of thinking, the identity philosophy is a prime example of what Schelling came to call negative philosophy. Schelling continues his self-criticism of the philosophy of identity by claiming that the "philosophy of identity could call itself absolute idealism since there can be no talk at all about existence. (Relative idealism *denies* the existence of things independent from us.)"[10] Though he at first describes the identity philosophy as the "determined opposite of Spinozism," insofar as Spinoza begins with God and the identity philosophy ends with God, he ultimately concludes that "the philosophy of identity let itself be turned into Spinozism."[11] So according to Schelling, the identity philosophy did in fact fail insofar as it lapsed back into Spinozism. This then brings us directly to the problem of emerging from Spinozism, which is in turn not far removed from the question of emergence as such. Schelling's worries revolve around the relationship between logical determination and ontological determination. "Spinoza continued to have a powerful influence," Schelling explains in the Berlin Lectures on Positive Philosophy from around 1842, "for he first brought this confusion of the positive and the negative into philosophy in that he made that which necessarily *exists* into his *principle* (beginning), but from which he then just *logically* derived *real* things."[12] The problem here is the assumption that one can derive reality logically from first principles even if this first principle is free Being itself. "For Spinoza," Schelling explains, "all things are *logical emanations* of the divine nature."[13] Were this the case, it would presuppose the reality of the logical over and above actuality, and this is precisely what Schelling hopes to avoid in drawing his distinction between positive and negative philosophy.[14]

This brings us to the problem of emergence and creation more generally. In contemporary philosophical discourse, the problem of emergence typically refers to a cluster of debates surrounding the relation between immaterial mindedness and material nature. Though Schelling is not indifferent to this specific emergent relationship, his discussions of emergence cannot be reduced to this contemporary framing. Consequently, to tackle this problem we must first formulate it in terms proper to Schelling's own project. To do so, let us turn to Schelling's descriptions of the becoming of God, a conversation initiated in *Philosophy and Religion*, continued in the *Freedom* essay as well as the 1810 "Stuttgart Seminars" and the subsequent drafts of the *Ages of the World*. Gabriel suggests that, with Schelling, "instead of finding a place for mind in *nature,* we locate a place for both in a domain that is neutral with respect to both of them."[15] This common domain, Gabriel claims, is what Schelling calls God. On this deflationary reading of Schelling's theology, God is neither mind nor nature, but is instead the space in which both mind and nature take place. So, in short, the question of the egress from the Absolute is once again a question of the relation between qualitative identity and the differentiated quantitative determinacy of both the natural and the normative.

Spinozist monism, as we have seen Schelling repeatedly argue, remains only in the One as a consequence of its dualism. Because there is no living interpenetration between thinking and being for Spinoza, he remains trapped in the past. More precisely, Spinoza's monism is a One that remains trapped within itself. This dualism of the attributes, like the argument for existence monism, is dependent upon the universal scope of the PSR insofar as it demands that *everything* plays by the same rules and denies the possibility of illegitimate (that is inexplicable) bifurcation. Hegel too believed that Spinoza remains stuck. Spinoza, he argues, failed to capitalize on both of his key insights. On the one hand, Spinoza embraced the essential nature of the *causa sui*. Yet, on the other hand, though he acknowledged that all determination was the result of a negation of the infinite substance, according to Hegel Spinoza was unable to transform this doctrine of negativity into a determinate form of self-relating negativity such that substance could become subject. Though this in part echoes Schelling's claim that Spinoza's God is without life and personality, it relies upon the primacy of a kind of self-relating dialectical negativity that Schelling rejects. Beach differentiates Schelling's methodology from Hegel's through the notion of *Erzeugungsdialektik*. This is a dialectic that focuses on production and reproduction, as opposed to the centrality of negativity in Hegel's *Aufhebungsdialektik*.[16] This general methodological difference also appears in each philosopher's respective engagement with Spinoza. Beach directly connects this *Erzeugungsdialektik* to the notion of doubling. He writes in reference to the passage from the "Stuttgart Seminars" that "Schelling's notion of a 'doubling' (*Doublierung*) of the essence—a clear instance of his *Erzeugungsdialektik* at work—led to the conception of a generative order which must be prior even to dialectical logic itself."[17] To turn to the doubling of essence that makes possible the transition from identity to difference returns us to the problem of beginning.

Thus, in this analysis, we find both a deep continuity as well as a significant difference between Hegel and Schelling.[18]

As Schelling is discussing the coming to be of difference from identity in the "Stuttgart Seminars," he makes the following claim: "This transition from identity to difference has often been understood as a *cancelation of identity* [*Aufheben der Identität*], yet that is not at all the case, as I intend to demonstrate without delay. Much rather it is a doubling [*Doublirung*] of the essence, and thus an intensification of the unity."[19] Difference is not the product of less identity, of a negating or sublating of identity. Instead, difference is the product of more identity, an expression of the doubling of the essence of identity.[20] Creation by way of a doubling of identity is primary for Schelling, and determination by way of dialectical negativity is only secondary. The purpose of this chapter is twofold. First, I outline the strictures of beginning that Schelling inherits from both Kant and Spinoza in order to contextualize the place and novelty of Schelling's account of doubling. Second, I investigate how the notion of doubling outlines an exit from Spinozism distinct from the Hegelian approach that relies upon dialectical negativity alone. My focus on Schelling's characterization of the Absolute as a unity of unity and difference, or of identity and nonidentity, already belies that I believe there to be less difference between Schelling and Hegel than some suppose. However, the primacy of doubling as a response to the prohibitions that Kant's Antinomies place on any metaphysical account of emergence highlights what is distinct about Schelling's mobilization of the Absolute.

2.0. The Strictures of Beginning

As Wittgenstein notes, "It is difficult to find the beginning. Or, better: it is difficult to begin at the beginning. And not try to go further back."[21] To fail to begin at the beginning precludes the possibility of beginnings giving way to what is supposed to come after. In other words, to begin before the beginning results in the failure to begin. This is an issue with which Schelling and the German Idealists more generally were keenly aware. In fact, it is precisely the problem of the beginning that Kant's Antinomies highlight. From Kant and Spinoza, one inherits two strictures on any account of emergence. The first of these strictures of beginning brings us to the topic of emergence ex nihilo. The second regards the rejection of transcendent causation. The Absolute creates, it becomes otherwise, without exiting or leaving itself behind. Both of these strictures are generated by the PSR, used by Spinoza to argue for the existence of only one thing and subsequently used by Kant to rupture the very possibility of a totality of all possible objects of experience given in existence, what we colloquially refer to as "the world." Demarcating the space opened up by this rupture allows us to more precisely formulate Schelling's question of emergence, as well as the conditions through which he articulates his response.

2.1. Antinomies and Impossibilities

In chapter 2, we saw Schelling attempt to triangulate Kantian idealism, Spinozist realism, and the common root (what he called creative reason) from which both emerged. Schelling presented a twofold problem. On the one hand, there was the need to account for the logical structures of cognition, and on the other hand there was a need to account for the actual existence of the objects of cognition. By extension, we find therein the common problem of establishing a relation between the subjective and the objective such that we lapse neither into one-sided subjectivism nor into a kind of naturalism that erases the subjective. Simultaneously, in accordance with his critique of Spinoza, Schelling eschews transcendence while avoiding any kind of strict parallelism.

With this in mind, let us outline the relation between Kant's Antinomies of Pure Reason and the problem of emergence. In the thesis of the First Antinomy, Kant presents an argument for the finitude of the world. The thesis seeks to show that the world is limited in space and (more significantly for our purposes) it has a beginning in time. Kant asks us to assume the opposite, that there is no beginning in time. If this were to be the case, "then up to any given moment an eternity has elapsed, and there has passed away in the world an infinite series of successive states of things."[22] If there is no beginning then there is only eternity. Yet, if this eternity is truly infinite, it "consists in the fact that it can never be completed through successive synthesis."[23] Thus, the antithesis position (that the world is infinite in space and time) is self-refuting. Because a completed infinite series is impossible, there must have been a beginning of the world in time. Alternatively, if the world is to have a beginning in time, as the thesis argument would seem to prove, then there must be "empty time" preceding the existence of the world. Now, assuming the PSR, there is no possible way for an empty time to have any causal relation to the world that comes to be within it. Kant explains, "No coming to be of a thing is possible in an empty time, because no part of such a time possesses, as compared with any other, a distinguishing condition of existence rather than of non-existence."[24] In an empty time in which there is nothing, there are no distinguishing conditions that could act as the cause for the emergence of existence from nonexistence. There can be no reason for there to be something rather than nothing; from nothing only nothing can come.

So, according to the PSR, an absolute beginning of the world is impossible while the infinite existence of the world is equally impossible. The Third Antinomy's arguments also hinge on the possibility of a beginning: "If, therefore, everything takes place solely in accordance with laws of nature, there will always be only a relative and never a first beginning, and consequently no completeness of the series on the side of the causes that arise the one from the other," Kant explains in order to show the absurdity inherent in the antithesis position, namely, that there is a single form of causality that eliminates the possibility of freedom.[25] In order for the PSR to hold, the determinative relations between causes and effects must be intelligible and there can be no arbitrary first cause. However, once again, if this were the case, there would need to be an infinite series of causes and effects, which is equally unintelligible. Consequently,

> [w]e must, then, assume a causality through which something takes place, the cause of which is not itself determined, in accordance with necessary laws, by another cause antecedent to it, that is to say, an *absolute spontaneity* of the cause, whereby the series of appearances, which proceeds in accordance with the laws of nature, begins *of itself*.[26]

We can see that the thesis position occupies a perspective similar to Schelling's as articulated in *Letters*. If there is to be a system of appearances that is subject to causal regularities, there must be an uncaused cause (an independent ego untouched by external causality) that makes these regularities possible and binding. Much like in the First Antinomy, this position unravels itself due to the unintelligibility of a spontaneous first cause without antecedent. The denaturalization of freedom (the assumption that freedom must be either un- or extra-natural) generates a total opposition between transcendental freedom and the laws of causality. Consequently, the former cannot be the cause of the latter. "If freedom were determined in accordance with laws," Kant writes, "it would not be freedom; it would simply be nature under another name. Nature and transcendental freedom differ as do conformity to law and lawlessness."[27] The absolute opposition between freedom and nature renders the position offered in the thesis impossible. We find that freedom is both necessary to ground causal regularities yet this grounding relation is itself impossible insofar as freedom and nature have nothing in common through which they might be related.[28]

This then brings us to the Fourth and final Antinomy. Here, Kant engages with the possibility or impossibility of an absolutely necessary being that stands either external to the world as its cause or exists internal to the world as its unconditioned totality. The thesis argument begins by positing that the "sensible world, as the sum total of all appearances, contains a series of alterations."[29] These alterations generate a problem similar to the one in the thesis of the Third Antinomy. If there is to be any alteration of anything, there must be something by which that thing is altered. Or, as Kant puts it, "Every alteration stands under its condition, which precedes it in time and renders it necessary."[30] This then implies that alteration as such exists "as a consequence of the absolutely necessary, the existence of something absolutely necessary must be granted."[31] Kant then characterizes this absolutely necessary something as "contained in the world itself, whether this something be the whole series of alterations in the world or a part of the series."[32] Much like the situation in the Third Antinomy, the absolutely necessary being must exist as a part of the world because if it did not, there would be no way for it to relate to and condition any series of alterations. Kant's ambivalence here ought to be highlighted; it does not matter if the absolutely necessary being is the cause of the world or the sum total of the world itself. It does not matter if the unconditioned is some Jacobian transcendence upon which each condition depends, or if the Spinozist immanent totality of conditioneds when taken as a whole is itself the unconditioned. Consequently, the thesis position allows for both a form of pantheism, in which the absolutely necessary being and the world are one, or a more traditional theism in which the absolutely necessary being is a part of the causal chain of being but relatively independent of it.

The antithesis position of the Fourth Antinomy denies the identification of the absolutely necessary being with the world, as well as the idea that the absolutely necessary being is a part of the world or external to it. The articulation of this position begins with the First Antinomy:

> If we assume that the world itself is necessary, or that a necessary being exists in it, there are then two alternatives. Either there is a beginning in the series of alterations [the world is finite in space and time—BN] which is absolutely necessary, and therefore without a cause, or the series itself is without any beginning [the world is infinite in space and time—BN], and although contingent and conditioned in all its parts, none the less, as a whole, is absolutely necessary and unconditioned.[33]

Kant claims both options are untenable. The first because it "conflicts with the dynamical law of the determination of all appearances in time"; and the second because "the existence of a series cannot be necessary if no single member of it is necessary."[34] Next, Kant denies that an absolutely necessary being can exist outside of the world "as its cause," because "this cause itself must begin to act, and its causality would therefore be in time, and so would belong to the sum of appearances, that is, to the world."[35] So, just as the world does not exist and a causality distinct from that of nature is both necessary and impossible, a necessary being both must and cannot exist.

These three antinomies present a series of negative conditions for any account of emergence. First, the world cannot be infinite or finite in time. If the PSR holds, then there can be no absolute beginning of determinate existence. However, it is equally impossible for the world to be infinite in space and time, as the PSR would seem to demand. Second, a free cause either of or in the world is both necessary and impossible. Finally, there must be an absolutely necessary being that is either above the world or equivalent to the world as an unconditioned totality. Yet this absolutely necessary being is just as impossible as it is necessary. Kant's negative conditions seemingly fail to provide any path forward, and for this reason it is not unreasonable that one may draw certain quietist conclusions from Kant. Yet, as Negarestani explains, "the point is not to be quietest when it comes to metaphysics. For it is precisely once we presume that we have purged ourselves of metaphysical assumptions, that we become susceptible to the most dogmatic and veiled forms of metaphysics."[36] What, then, are the positive lessons we can learn from the above antinomies?

2.2. The PSR and the Destruction of the World

When Schelling asks, "Why is there something?" he is not simply asking, "Why is there something rather than nothing?" Such a question would vitiate the role played by the Absolute in Schelling's thought. As Schelling moved into what some call the middle period of his work, he came to frame the genetic root of the relation between the real and the ideal in different terms. When considering the problem of emergence in Schelling's *Freedom* essay as well as his "Stuttgart Seminars" and the *Weltalter* project, the following idea, captured nicely by Žižek, cannot be overemphasized:

> Schelling inverts the standard perspective: the problem is not how, in a universe regulated by inexorable natural laws, freedom is possible—that is, where, in the determinate universe, there is a place for freedom which would not be a mere illusion based on our ignorance of true causes—but, rather, how the world as a rational totality of causal interconnections made its appearance in the first place.[37]

The real issue at hand for Schelling following the exit from the identity system is not, (1) Given nature as a complex network of interrelated causes and effects, how can an act that is not determined in advance by this nexus be possible? But instead, (2) How is the determinate regularity of the causal nexus possible at all? Put otherwise, from where did the very logical space of action and intelligibility come to be? In relation to Spinoza, we can formulate this as follows. Again, Spinoza's prohibition of unaccounted for bifurcations *follows* from the PSR; there must be an intelligible reason or cause for any bifurcation, and there must be a justification for any inconsistent application of rules to nature. Consequently, if freedom (understood as a spontaneous, unpredetermined act) is to be anything other than an illusion (and Spinoza will essentially argue that it cannot), one would have to give a reason or cause for freedom, which would in turn erase the very freedom one is attempting to account for. Now, in distinction to this approach, Schelling takes a step back and ask a transcendental question: *What are the conditions of possibility for the PSR itself?* How can one account for the contingent emergence of necessity from contingency? Oddly, perhaps, the problem is not that of the existence of freedom alone, but instead the existence of nature as well (at first narrowly construed as the domain of universally applicable and unchanging laws and regularities). When Schelling muses upon the creation of the world, the problem is not of being itself. Instead, the question is how does being, which itself cannot be thought in advance, become entrapped within the web of inferential relations that allow for its intelligibility?

We can frame the importance of the difference between Kant, Spinoza, and Schelling with a reference to contemporary literature. The significance of this divergence between Kant (and Spinoza) on the one hand, and Schelling on the other when it comes to the question of emergence is succinctly captured in the following passage from Cixin Liu's novel *Death's End*. Liu writes,

> Once, Yang Dong had held a basic belief: Life and the world were perhaps ugly, but at the limits of the micro and macro scales, everything was harmonious and beautiful. The world of our everyday life was only froth floating on the perfect ocean of deep reality. But now, it appeared that the everyday world was a beautiful shell: The micro realities it enclosed and the macro realities that enclosed it were far more ugly and chaotic than the shell itself.[38]

Kant and Spinoza are representatives of the belief that Yang Dong once held: The interrelation of finite particulars may appear as muddled, messy, and chaotic, but at a more fundamental level, there is a harmonious realm of universal laws and regularities. Beneath the chaos of appearances, there are universally applicable laws that can be discovered and known. Schelling, on the contrary, theorizes the ugly chaos from which finite regularities themselves emerge. It is necessity and regularity itself that is illusory. The logical and natural laws that coordinate various objective domains are not themselves underlying scaffolds not at risk from the creation and decay to which appearances are subject. Schelling makes the case that it is only insofar as there is this chaos, this dark ground within God, that the emergence of regularity itself is possible. Necessity can become necessary only if it is preceded by an unbearable contingency. As Tritten explains, "To ask the first-order question of why there is logical space or reason at all, instead of chaos or unreason, is to have departed from a merely logical and epistemic domain in order to ask an ontological question."[39] What kind of ontology, then, is capable of responding to this question regarding the existence of logical space and rationality?

In his lectures on the history of modern philosophy, Schelling himself asks the above question. He ponders "the whole world lies, so to speak, in the nets of understanding or reason, but the question is *how* exactly it got into those nets, since there is obviously something other and something *more* than mere reason in the world, indeed there is something which strives beyond these barriers."[40] Notice that it is not the case that the world exists prior to this entanglement in the nets of understanding and reason. The world *as* world requires some form of structuration in order to be taken as such. Being must come into the net of reasons before it can be taken as a world. Schelling therefore begins with being and not reason or meaning itself. Though this might seem strange at first given the extreme emphasis of reason in the *System of Philosophy in General*, it is largely consistent with the articulation of the Absolute therein. Here, Schelling is not speaking of reason as such; he is instead speaking of reason taken as a net of inferential relations (what is referred to as a space of reasons) through which what exists comes to be intelligible and meaningful. This net distinguishes itself from the simplicity of reason taken as Absolute insofar as the Absolute is given in its simplicity and totality (like Spinoza's substance understood as a *totum analyticum*). In this simplicity, there are no inferential relations. In fact, there can be no relations insofar as there are no finite particulars. Consequently, logical space broadly understood is not a given for Schelling. There is no guarantee that finite particulars accord to necessary and intelligible laws. As Žižek notes, "The problem is . . . how this Nothing of the abyss of primordial freedom becomes entangled in the causal chains of Reason."[41] As a further consequence of this unique framing, we must note the double-edged methodological sword Schelling has grasped: on the one hand, he cannot appeal to the PSR or logical space in order to account for the emergence of order out of chaos, yet, on the other hand, he is not bound by the strictures generated by the PSR and the confines of logical space systematically outlined by Kant's Antinomies of Pure Reason.

So, in short, Schelling's account of emergence cannot be confined to the emergence of the logical from the ontological, the emergence the normative from the natural, or the emergence of spirit from nature. Both the logical and the ontological must emerge from the prelogical and protological Absolute. In other words, God is neither natural or normative, but by falling into Himself, He becomes divided into the natural and normative. The Absolute is neither natural nor spiritual until its abundance forces it to give way. To better understand what is at stake in this twofold formulation of the problem of emergence, we can look to the way Brandom takes up what he sees as the fundamental Kantian problematic. He explains,

> Kant's big idea is that what distinguishes judgment and action from the responses of merely natural creatures is neither their relation to some special stuff nor their peculiar transparency, but rather that they are what we are in a distinctive way *responsible* for. They express *commitments* of ours: commitments that we are answerable for in the sense that our *entitlement* to them is always potentially at issue; commitments that are *rational* in the sense that vindicating the corresponding entitlements is a matter of offering *reasons* for them.[42]

We human beings are natural beings, but we are not reductively natural beings. We can participate in the distinctively rational practice of producing and consuming reasons in accordance with which we freely take responsibility. Brandom continues, "The overall idea is that the rationality that qualifies us as *sapients* (and not merely sentients) can be identified with being a player in the social, implicitly normative game of offering and assessing, producing and consuming, reasons."[43] Brandom draws much of this vocabulary from Sellars, of whom Gabriel makes the following assessment: "Sellars extends the difference between *causes* and *reasons* to a dualism of nature and mind." We can note that the drawing of a distinction between causes and reasons already forces us to leave Spinoza behind insofar as the *Ethics* depends upon the strict identification of conception and causation. As a consequence of the dualism between causes and reasons, Sellars must "explain how we can *know* about a nature that presents a purely natural order, a realm of 'is' rather than 'ought,' even though our knowledge of this order qua knowledge already brings normatively into play and so presupposes its own fallibility."[44] Here, we find the broader distinction between is and ought put into the context of the causal and the normative orders. What this indicates is that understanding the unique place of the human in nature necessitates an understanding of ourselves as both natural and normative beings. Further, there is a distinct logic to the way we act when engaging in the game of producing and consuming reasons that must itself be accounted for as emergent from a pre-logical reality. Consequently, when addressing the problem of emergence, one must account for the determinacy proper to the cognitive/conceptual realm as well as determinacy in the objective or natural realm. Further, to recall Schelling's words quoted above, the eternal birth of *all* things remains in relation to the Absolute. It is not just the emergence of the normative order from the natural order that must be accounted for. This is but one side of the problem. In addition to the normative order of oughts, the very emergence of nature itself from the Absolute must be addressed.

This returns us to the role Spinoza plays in the above discussed antinomies. Recall that it was the Spinozist notion of a *totum analyticum* that was able to sidestep the bind placed upon rational cosmology by Kant's strictures. We can see how Spinozism offers a strategy for wrestling with the strictures of Kant's antinomies from the inside. However, Spinoza's *totum analyticum* brings with it its own set of metaphysical strictures, particularly those of the problems of emanation and the possibility of a transition from the infinite to the finite. We saw that the identity philosophy disallows emanation as a coherent model of emergence insofar as only God is real and anything existing "outside" of God is only real insofar as it is affirmed in its nonbeing. This simple unity of substance at first drew Schelling to Spinoza, though he would eventually render this simple unity Absolute by introducing a kind of nonidentity into identity. However, just because Schelling breaks from Spinoza's specific account of the relation between identity and differentiation by focusing on the qualitative identity of the Absolute and the quantitative differentiation of finite particulars, this does not mean that Schelling abandons Spinoza's arguments for the elimination of transcendent causation and emergence through emanation. Tritten explains, "Schelling's is not a system of emanation or procession, but a theory of novel production and elevation." This is because "Schelling denies that reality has descended from superior originals to inferior copies, instead arguing that reality moves from inferior matter, a principle with its own discordant motion(s), to higher and more superior levels of order and organization."[45]

Now, we have already seen that for Schelling, any kind of radical "beyond" or "above" the Absolute is strictly inconceivable. If philosophy begins with the Absolute, and the Absolute allows of no externality, then any relation of finite to infinite could not lie outside of the Absolute. This brings us back to the problem of immanence. In the case of immanent causation, production remains "in itself" insofar as its products do not, properly speaking, "exit" from what produces them. Were one to assert otherwise, they would be committing what Schelling calls the "most basic mistake of philosophy": namely, the assumption that

> absolute identity has actually stepped outside itself and to attempt to make intelligible how this emergence occurs. . . . True philosophy consists in the demonstration that absolute identity (the infinite) has not stepped outside itself and that everything that is, insofar as it is, is infinity itself—a proposition that Spinoza alone of all previous philosophers acknowledged, even if he did not fully carry out its demonstration, nor express it clearly enough to avoid being misunderstood ever after.[46]

It seems to follow from the rejection of emanation that one would be committed to the immanence of all things in God or nature, even if we do not go as far as accepting existence monism. That is, it seems as if the denial of emanation entails the existence of a monistic ontological field. However, when we restrict the PSR's domain of applicability, we must in turn question the very possibility of a monistic ontological register. The Antinomies identified a set of necessary impossibilities, and in light of this impossible bind in which reason finds itself entwined, Kant concludes that "since the world does not exist in itself, independently of the regressive series of my representations, it exists *in itself* neither as an *infinite* whole nor as a *finite* whole."[47] As a result of the

Transcendental Dialectic (and the First Antinomy in particular), the notion of a monistic ontological field must be rejected as a transcendental illusion that results from the illegitimate constitutive application of the PSR. That is, the conflation of reasons and causes results in the illusion of a self-consistent, self-identical immanence.

Reason's self-examination in the Antinomies yields the positive conclusion that the world is a broken whole, a fractured unity. As Johnston explains, "In the hands of the post-Kantians Schelling and Hegel, this Kantian revival of dialectics ends up, as it were, destroying the world itself qua image of being a monolithic, unified One, a harmonious, coherent All."[48] Johnston details how the destruction of the world image as a monolithic, unified whole forces us to redefine naturalism. The rejection of a monolithic unified whole also forces us to reconsider any oppositional definition of realism, antirealism, and idealism. This is because the inexistence of a unified whole calls into question any definition of either realism or idealism that would rely on the categories of immanence or externality. Both realists and idealists appeal to the idea of immanence in order to justify the coherence and desirability of either position. The realist or idealist invoked the idea of the All. They argue that all is mental, or everything is real. Even the naturalist more generally places everything in a monistic register according to which everything plays by the same rules. Yet if it is the case that the existence of a monistic ontological register is itself incoherent, then realism, idealism, and naturalism traditionally understood fall as well.

Instead of limiting reason, the inexistence of the world demonstrated in the *Critique of Pure Reason*'s Antinomies opens new possibilities for understanding emergence. It is the very fracture in the register of the real that renders possible the emergence of subject from substance. It is the gap that yawns forth into something other than itself. Yet, since the real on this reading is not itself a unified, consistent whole, its opening forth to produce something "other" than itself does not imply and exit from the real. Instead, the Absolute falls into itself. In doing so, it carves itself up by hollowing itself out. This seemingly odd conclusion that the world in the sense of a self-enclosed totality of all objects of possible experience does not exist "in itself," and further, that it is *neither* finite *nor* infinite has gained traction in recent years. Žižek, Johnston, and Gabriel have moved beyond Kant's conclusion that the inexistence of the world is supplemented by the world as a transcendental Idea that guides the regulative employment of reason. Following Hegel, they draw an ontological conclusion from Kant's epistemological insight: reason's demonstration of the inexistence of the world is not an epistemological shortcoming of finite subjects, though it first appears as precisely this. Instead, the world is ontologically incomplete. Further, this ontological incompleteness is an assertible fact about the world itself. Žižek goes so far as to argue that the very ontological incompleteness of the world acts as the condition of possibility for self-consciousness itself. He writes, "The only way to account effectively for the status of (self-)consciousness is to assert *the ontological incompleteness of 'reality' itself*: there is 'reality' only insofar as there is an ontological gap, a crack at its very heart—that is, a traumatic excess, a foreign body that cannot be integrated into it."[49] The inexistence of a whole in itself (of a monistic self-contained totality) opens up the space for transcendence arising from within the fracture that renders immanence impossible. It is not that self-consciousness and the world it comes to know arise out of some gap or nothingness. Instead, the real as such (and not just the reality self-consciousness comes to know) is ontologically incomplete. And again, the incompleteness of reality is not a product of the finitude of subjective understanding and the tragic fate of reason; it is instead a byproduct of a deeper incompleteness at the very center of the real itself.

The commitment to a unified ontological register undergirds a notion of nature shared by seemingly disparate and otherwise conflicting schools of thought. Johnston elaborates as follows:

> For example, Spinozism, Newtonian mechanical physics, eighteenth-century French materialism, nineteenth-century psycho-physicalism, social Darwinism, eliminative materialism, genetic determinisms, evolutionary psychology, epiphenomenalisms, and myriad related orientations both past and present—despite whatever differences there are between them—all implicitly or explicitly subscribe to the belief in something along the lines of what Laplace's demon represents. They all share a common article of faith anchored in an image of Nature as a single, self-contained sovereign power, a unified causal nexus that eternally governs everything in existence with the unwavering iron fist of inviolable laws.[50]

Johnston's point here is that just as there is no single, self-contained world that exists, so too is there no single logical register of overarching rules and regularities under which all things and events are governed. In a sense, Johnston's naturalism is the opposite of the naturalism Della Rocca locates in Spinoza. Not only does everything not play by the same rules; there is no single set of rules in accordance with which everything could play. "*Natur* is doubly weak," Johnston explains.

> It is stripped of its purported God-like attributes and powers by disenchanting de-divinization, and it is also exposed to manipulations of its blindness, fragility, and plasticity by minded and like-minded agents with their different aims, ends, and goals. What is more, the ultimate ontological condition of possibility for natural, material substance morphing into denaturalized, more-than-material subjectivity is nature's own impotence/weakness (*Ohnmacht*).[51]

Nature is incomplete from both the bottom up and the top down. However, the ontological incompleteness of the world is not a failure but is instead an opportunity. Following Hegel, Johnston and Žižek incorporate a dynamic negativity into this ontological incompleteness. Determination arises by way of this self-relating negativity present within nature itself. Schelling's Absolute also entails the incompleteness of the world and the rejection of a monistic ontological register. However, as quoted in the introduction to this chapter, the emergence of difference from identity is not the product of an *aufhebung* of identity into difference. Instead, it is made possible by the doubling of identity.

3.0. The Doubling of Absolute Identity

Strict adherence to the PSR renders the problem of emergence inert. The bifurcation of the finite from the infinite is precisely an illegitimate division forbidden by the PSR. It creates more explanatory problems than it resolves. Alternatively, the rejection of the PSR seems to back one into explanations of emergence dependent upon the ex nihilo. If we no longer maintain that nothing can come from nothing, then creation out of nothing would seem to become a live possibility once again. However, there is a deep problem concerning the intelligibility and explicability of this kind of emergence of something from nothing. We have seen how the doctrine of existence monism dissolves a number of these issues yet remains unsatisfactory due to its inability to capture the true mystery of the Absolute, namely, the eternal birth of things from it. Now that we have outlined the problem of beginnings as framed by Kant's antinomies and Spinoza's *totum analyticum* we can return to the theme of negativity. Moder writes of Hegel and Spinoza that "Hegel's question about Spinoza's philosophy could therefore be understood as a question of movement, specifically of movement or contradiction of the beginning, of the primordial."[52] More precisely, the problem Moder is pointing to is how to begin in such a way that one does not remain trapped in this beginning. Moder's observation recalls Schelling's claim that Spinozism is a kind of vortex "around which everything moves, or rather the impoverishment of thought, from which thought has sought to emancipate itself by the succeeding systems without yet being able to do so."[53] How, then, is one to exit from this vortex of Spinozism? Moder suggests that for Hegel, "the principle of becoming is therefore the principle of self-referential negativity."[54] However, we have already seen that Schelling denies that self-referential, dialectical negativity can be the primary mechanism by which the Absolute differentiates itself. To further unravel this mystery, we can turn to the theme of divine pain.

Jacobi's God is not pained by His creation. His divine life of love is made possible by the safety afforded to Him by his transcendence. It is through good will and divine curiosity that Jacobi's God begets a world of finite beings epistemically available to creatures created in His own image. This is definitively not the case for the God of Schelling. Schelling's God is a God in pain, a suffering God that must endure the impossible task of containing both more and less than what it is. Schelling's God is not natural, but He is most definitely real. The pain of God is not merely a psychic pain as described by Krell[55] and McGrath.[56] It is instead a physical pain. Recall that for Schelling, difference is not the product of less unity or less identity. Instead, it is a doubling of essence that results in an intensification of identity. The notion of doubling is therefore central to Schelling's speculative account of the Absolute as unity and difference. By extension, the dynamic of doubling is a necessary component for moving beyond Spinozism while simultaneously avoiding the Hegelian solution of a primordial, self-relating negativity (or cancellation of identity). However, just because the doubling of the Divine is not primarily an expression of negativity, this does not mean it is an act without conflict or pain. The doubling of the essence of identity carries with it a unique kind of pain that forces God to become otherwise. It is a pain that forces Being into the web of reasons through which it becomes the intertwining worlds of nature and spirit. To further complicate the issue, we must keep in mind Schelling's rejection of the possibility of existence external to the Absolute. Real and ideal intertwine within the Absolute and consequently cannot be accounted for by a doctrine of transcendence, even if this transcendence is only relative. The Absolute falls into itself, and this contraction provides an internal engine for the genesis of the relative nonbeing that is characteristic of particulars. In other words, the doubling of identity causes a contraction of nonidentity, and this contraction in turn accounts for the dependent existence of the relative finitude.

3.1. The Nature of Intussusception

Berger and Whistler suggest that the notion of doubling and self-doubling as found in the "Stuttgart Seminars" and the 1811 *Ages of the World* "can be traced back to the conception of identity first worked out in *On the True Concept* and the *Presentation* of 1801."[57] For Berger and Whistler, the concept of identity explicitly articulated in the *Presentation* (what I have referred to as "simple identity") does not represent a blip or failure in Schelling's work. In other words, Hegel does not correct the *Presentation* when he offers the more complex formulation of "identity of identity and difference" to Schelling. By making this argument, Berger and Whistler seek to open an avenue for avoiding any conflation between Schelling's and Hegel's conceptions of the Absolute. That is, they seek to demonstrate the self-sufficiency of identity and nothing but identity in relation to the genesis of finite particulars. "More precisely: identity is posited, through identity, as identity. Nothing else is required to understand the production of being," they explain.[58] In other words, Berger and Whistler argue that it is not necessary to incorporate nonidentity into identity, what they call "dialectical identity" and I have called "Absolute identity," in order to account for the emergence of finite, order particulars from the Absolute. Difference does not need to be smuggled into identity in order to account for the self-differentiation of identity. Now, I believe it is the case that Schelling's notion of identity is not strictly dialectical in the Hegelian sense, as we can clearly see from his comments on the doubling of identity that makes dialectical differentiation possible. This motivates my choice of the term *Absolute identity* instead of dialectical identity. However, we must also take care to mark the difference between Schelling's notion of identity, Hegel's notion of identity, and Spinoza's account of the simplicity of substance. Consequently, even if Schelling's discussions of doubling shift him away from a more Hegelian notion of dialectical identity, we must still take care to differentiate this productive identity from the simple identity of Spinozism. I want to turn to the concept of intussusception in order to elaborate on the role of doubling in Schelling's work.

Schelling's earlier discussions of intussusception and his discussion of the self-developing system of the world in the "Stuttgart Seminars" both depend upon the reality of conflict and the coexistence of unity and duality. Kant briefly deploys the notion of intussusception as designating the logical function of the internal growth of a system.[59] "The whole is thus an organized unity (*articulatio*), and not an aggregate (*coacervatio*)," he writes. "It may grow from within (*per intussusceptionem*), but not by external addition (*per appositionem*)."[60] Kant's comment here is located in the opening of the Transcendental Doctrine of Method in which he begins to discuss the Architectonic of Pure Reason. He is speaking specifically of the ways systematic understanding can build upon itself in order to construct a complete system of knowing. Because the system is an organized whole and not an aggregate of disparate parts, it can only grow internally. Otherwise, it risks its own systematicity. In the "Stuttgart Seminars," Schelling implicitly picks up on exactly this theme. He claims that any system (if it is to be truly systematic) contains three fundamental aspects. The first is that it must "intrinsically rest on a principle that supports itself, a principle that consists in and through itself and that is reproduced in each part of the whole."[61] This, of course, rings our Spinoza alarm quite loudly. The first element of the system must be a principle that is conceived only through itself and relies on nothing else for its existence. However, Schelling includes in this characterization the relation of parts to whole. The whole (the self-grounding principle) must necessarily be reproduced (*not* represented) in every part of that whole. Schelling refers to this part-whole unity as the "organic unity of all things."[62] The parts of the whole maintain a relative autonomy from the whole (my stomach is not me) just as the whole maintains a relative autonomy from the parts (I am not my stomach). However, this relative autonomy does not equal complete independence. The systematic unity of the whole depends upon the reality of the parts as well as the reality of the holistic relation between these parts. Schelling continues his description of the self-supporting principle of his system with a second familiar characterization. "This principle," Schelling writes, "found its more specific expressing as the absolute identity of the *Real* and the *Ideal*."[63] Here we can find an important shift away from the first principle of the identity philosophy. There, Schelling emphasized of A = A that "the unique being posited through this proposition is that of *identity itself*, which accordingly is posited in complete independence from A as subject and from A as predicate."[64] In 1810, Schelling has moved away from the language of subject and predicate to explain absolute identity. The most specific articulation of the fundamental principle of Schelling's system as presented in Stuttgart unfolds from the absolute identity of real and ideal. This is an unacquired unity of real and ideal that does not need to be posited at all. Further, in the "Stuttgart Seminars," Schelling maintains that identity is a complex relation of unity and difference. He claims, "The primordial essence is in and of itself always unity; namely the *unity of the opposition and of the bifurcation* [*Entzweiung*]."[65] Identity and nothing but identity (without further explication) is no longer sufficient.

In addition to resting upon a self-supporting principle whose essence is the unity of opposition and bifurcation, a system must "not exclude anything (e.g., nature), nor must it unilaterally subordinate or suppress anything."[66] The example chosen here by Schelling is by no means coincidental. Schelling is clearly referring the reader to the root of his condemnation of Fichte's system. As we have discussed at length, according to Schelling, in Fichte's hands nature became a phantom because the division between real and ideal was posited only within consciousness, that is, only in the ideal. Further, it is essential that the construction of the system always be a product of intensification, of a doubling over, and never of elimination or subordination. The third necessary element of the system is "a method of development and progression to ensure that no essential link has been omitted."[67] The method of the system's development is just as important as the system itself, and this idea of a productive method ought to recall my earlier discussions of creative reason and spirit in which subject and object, real and ideal, are self-positing as well as primordially entwined and mutually elucidating. At this point in 1810, Schelling grounds this process explicitly within the cosmos itself. Responding to the question of the very possibility of the system, Schelling writes, "Long before man decided to create a system, there already existed one, that of the cosmos [*System der Welt*]. Hence our proper task consists in discovering that system."[68] Any individual construction, intuition, creation, or discovery is a local instantiation of the already operating system of the world. Here we recall Schelling's earlier claim that "it is not *me* who recognizes this identity, but it recognizes itself, and I am merely its organ."[69]

We can see, then, that Schelling is firmly committed to Kant's claim that any system of reason must grow internally and not through external addition. Further, because the system is not something separate from nature, this kind of internal growth must also be found in nature itself and not merely added to it from outside or above. Even the philosopher is embedded within the internal development of this system as an organ of the Absolute. The system of the world is doubled within itself through the act of the philosopher. This means that the act of philosophy is not a product of thought alone that must somehow bridge the gap between thinking and being. Philosophy is itself an intensification of identity. This forces us to reconsider both the traditional notion of intellectual intuition (understood as an immediate, pre- or nonconceptual bridging of being and thinking) as well as the notion of intellectual finitude.

Though he does not speak of intussusception in the context of philosophical systematicity, Schelling had invoked the term many years earlier. In the *First Outline*, Schelling turns to intussusception to describe the relation between the organic and the inorganic as it relates to the various forces or tendencies of natural arrangement. "The tendency that is produced in all parts of the Earth by the influence of the Sun is a tendency toward reciprocal *intussusception*," Schelling writes.[70] This word, a cognate in the German and English, is a combination of the Latin words *intus,* meaning "within," and *susceptio,* meaning "admission" or "taking within." The term simultaneously designates a taking *within,* an *under*taking and a taking *up.* We can tentatively posit intussusception as Schelling's naturephilosophical operation similar to Hegel's *Aufhebung.* This is not to generalize the term beyond Schelling's specific usage, but to suggest that this tendency is itself a kind of mirror. It is a candidate for thinking emergence without privileging negativity. Contrary to the notorious *Aufhebung* and its emphasis on the dynamics of negation, Schelling's intussusception relies upon the operation of intensification and amplification. In botany (the meaning to which Schelling is most likely referring), an intussusception is the growth or alteration of an existing cellular wall through the addition and incorporation of external organic material. It is a process of augmentation through the incorporation of new materials. However, the word also names a medical condition in which an organ (most commonly the intestine) folds over itself or takes itself into itself. Unlike the botanical case in which one substance is added to or incorporated within another, in the medical case a single thing contorts upon itself, undertaking and taking itself up in the process. Symptoms of such a condition include extreme abdominal pain, nausea, and vomiting. It is this condition that most accurately describes the state of Schelling's God and the subsequent emergence of determinate existents and the logical spaces in which these existents are intelligible. This folding over (the redoubling of the Absolute) and the surplus produced when it both takes itself in and takes itself up forces the expulsion of the world we come to know as well as the logical constraints that make this knowledge possible.

Intussusception's role in the philosophy of nature appears in the transition between anorganic nature and the chemical process. Therein, intussusception is described as a tendency toward the dynamic expression of gravitation. "With universal gravitation" Schelling explains, "the *tendency* towards universal intussusception in Nature is founded."[71] In his discussion of intussusception, we find a familiar theme, namely, the relation between duplicity and identity. While discussing the themes of contraction, organic activity, and excitation Schelling writes, "An activity whose condition is duplicity can only be such as proceeds toward *intussusception* (because the condition of *intussusception* is duality)."[72] Further, in addition to duplicity a contraction of homogeneous space is necessary in order for the process of excitation to take place: "No intussusception is possible without a transition toward a common occupation of space, and this transition does not happen without *density* or *shrinking of volume*. That activity will appear externally as an activity of shrinking in volume, and the effect itself as *contraction*" Schelling claims.[73] The common occupation of homogeneous space, a space without any inherent qualitative differentiations, serves as condition for the combining of heterogeneous elements: "Inasmuch as an intussusception between heterogeneous bodies is possible only insofar as the *homogeneous* is itself sundered *in itself,* no homogeneous space can be absolute; rather, it can only be a *state of indifference*."[74] This self-sundering, homogeneous space gives itself over to the process by which homogeneous simplicity becomes more complex through quantitative intensification. In the very process of intussusception we find the intertwining of both unity and duplicity without a clear attribution of primacy to either.

All change in form expresses both a continuity and a discontinuity with previous states. Insofar as this appearance of shrinking and the dynamic intussusception that accompanies it have the effect of contraction, the shrinking of the anorganic in homogeneous space gives way to what Schelling describes as "the most enigmatic phenomenon of organic nature."[75] Intussusception is thus the transition between universal gravitation and contraction. Schelling claims that intussusception "exists only in the chemical process,"[76] yet because the chemical process nevertheless contains both potentiality and actually *all* other dynamic processes, we find both a unique mode of emergence, and the justification for its generalization. Instead of the language of expression, Schelling invokes the idea of metamorphosis when speaking of origination in the *Presentation*. "Nothing that arises in the chemical process is intrinsically an origination," Schelling writes, "but merely a metamorphosis."[77] Just as Kant frequently emphasized in relation to the Idea, this "merely" should not be taken as pejorative because it helps us understand the deep continuities in the processes of emergence in nature. We can see this in Schelling's discussion of the metamorphosis of insects: "All of these phenomenon prove that the metamorphosis of insects does not occur by virtue of the *mere* evolution of already preformed parts, but through actual epigenesis and total transformation," Schelling explains.[78] When speaking of organisms more generally, Schelling maintains that "*all formation occurs through epigenesis*," adding in a footnote that this epigenesis occurs through either metamorphosis or what he calls "dynamical evolution."[79] The invocation here of epigenesis is instructive. Malabou presents a reading of the transcendental by way of Kant's reference to a "system, as it were, of the *epigenesis* of pure reason" in § 27 of the *Critique of Pure Reason*. The proper context of the term is in debates surrounding embryonic development. Epigenesis as a term, she explains, "refers to a mode of embryonic development through the successive affection of parts that are born from one another."[80] This theory, she continues, "is opposed to the preformationist theory that claims that the embryo is a fully constitutive being, a miniature individual whose growth, which is only quantitative, consists solely in the unveiling of organs and already-formed parts."[81] The problem here is of the origin. Does the origin already contain what will come to be at the end? Or is development something that is not given in advance? Is it instead something that must unfold without the guarantee of arriving at its proper destination? What is interesting at the present moment is the association of preformation and quantitative change. In light of Schelling's later claim that all change is merely quantitative, how is he able to advocate for an epigenetic theory of formation in nature? It is important to remember that Schelling is attributing epigenesis to form and not objects. Though a thing may not undergo qualitative changes, this does not mean that its form is static or presupposed. What we see is that although Schelling claims that there is no pure origination in chemical processes, this does not exclude the possibility of natural development other than preformation.

With this context in mind, I'd like to take a speculative leap. Schelling's references to intussusception are limited and specific. Though it plays a crucial role in one of the more important transitions in the philosophy of nature, Schelling does not seem to want to generalize this happening to the whole of nature. What we have seen, however, is that intussusception links together the themes of duplicity, unity, and contraction. In doing so, it acts as a kind of engine for excitation, transformation, and reformation. Let us return to the second definition of intussusception, to which Schelling is not referring, namely, the case of the folded-over organ. It is this image that illuminates the pain unique to Schelling's God, and it is precisely this pain that gives way to the distinct logical and ontological orders constituting what Schelling calls "the present." That there is a conflict residing in God is not a novel observation, but it is a crucial one when differentiating Schelling from his contemporaries. The God of Spinoza and the God of Jacobi are at peace. Spinoza's because it is without conflict, Jacobi's because He is protected by His own transcendence. As noted previously, commentators such as McGrath, Krell, and Žižek have all used psychoanalytic language to describe the state of Schelling's God prior to the act of creation. McGrath turns to the idea of dissociation in which "personality is constitutively split, but the split is not necessarily repressive or pathological." He continues, "Personality is not monolithic but plural, a network of relations among other alternatives centers of cognition and desire."[82] From this, McGrath concludes that "if the absolute were only one, nothing else could exist—individuality, multiplicity, and time itself would be illusory. If multiplicity and relationality are real, if personality exists, the absolute must have divided itself from itself."[83] Now, we have repeatedly seen Schelling characterize Spinoza's substance as precisely this kind of One that allows for the existence of nothing else. To break free from this claustrophobic Oneness, there must be a splitting or doubling internal to God. Krell takes a more traditional psychoanalytic route and suggests that "some as yet nameless trauma or suffering is still causing the past to be *repressed,* covered over or buried."[84] He then suggests that this trauma that leads to the repression of the past is the conflict between the bisexuality of God that stands opposed to God's single divine life. Krell explains this as such: "God will need all the strength (s)he can muster to confront a dual sexuality and a singular mortality."[85] So again, we see that within God there is a conflict playing out between unity and duality. This duality makes God yearn for creation and ultimately the reconciliation of life, sexuality, and death through revelation.

Finally, in line with his general philosophical method, Žižek turns to Lacan in order to interpret Schelling's writings on freedom and God captured in the *Freedom* essay and the 1813 *Ages of the World* in particular. He focuses on the antagonism of drives within the Absolute as the act through which the Absolute ruptures its own past in order to make way for the present. Of the 1813 *Ages of the World*, Žižek observes that the "horror of this rotary motion resides in the fact that it is no longer impersonal: God already exists as One, as the Subject who suffers and endures the antagonism of drives."[86] Of the act through which this horrifying antagonism of drives is broken, Žižek explains,

> The primordial act of free decision is not only man's direct contact with the primordial freedom as the abyss out of which all things originate—that is, a kind of short circuit, of direct overlapping, between man and the Absolute; this act of contracting being, of choosing one's eternal nature, *has to be a repetition of the same act of the Absolute itself.*[87]

One important takeaway here is the idea that human freedom is a repetition of the original free act of the Absolute. To act is to instantiate the primordial act of existence in existence. However, it must be noted that human freedom is made intelligible in light of divine freedom and not the other way around. The freedom of the individual is not a model for the freedom of the Divine. Any free act of the individual is instead a localized repetition of this primordial act. Or as Heidegger puts it, "Man is at best the property of freedom."[88] Woodard's characterization of Žižek's claim as "human freedom is a rupture in the absolute or in the ontological fabric of being" seems to miss the mark.[89] Human freedom is not a rupture in the Absolute but is instead an expression of the Absolute's own rupture. It does not tear a hole in the ontological fabric of being. It is a product of this ontological hole. Johnston explains in reference to Žižek's Schelling that "being itself is shot through with antagonisms and tensions, riddled with cracks, fissures and gaps (rather than being something homogeneous and harmonious, an ontological plane placidly consistent with itself)."[90] This space of conflict resembles what Schelling called the "world-soul" in *On the World Soul*. Therein, after detailing the expansive role of the "positive force" and the restricting role of the negative force, Schelling writes, "These two conflicting forces conceived at the same time in conflict and unity, lead to the idea of an *organizing principle*, forming the world into a system. Perhaps the ancients wished to intimate this with the *world-soul*."[91] Here, we can find Schelling rejecting the primacy of any kind of formative drive that necessarily finds its way to a destination given at the origin. Instead, the organizing forces that bring the world into an intelligible system are the product of the prior unity and conflict of the positive and negative forces or expansion and contraction.

All of this is to say that Schelling's God is not well. Schelling's God is a mess. There is a deep pain that is essential and not accidental to the Divine. This pain is characterized by an uneasiness with oneself, an inner antagonism between the constitutive duplicity in homogeneity of the Absolute. What the idea of intussusception as the doubling over of a single organ adds to this picture is that it is not necessary to posit some additional aspect of the Absolute in order to account for this inner antagonism. The auto-affection of an organ disrupts the functioning of the organism as a whole. It ceases to work and causes great pain. Though this pain of conflict and contradiction can be captured by a primordial negativity, it can also be accounted for by a doubling over. This pain is secondary; it is an expression of divine doubling. As we all know, pain amplifies our experience of existence.

It augments our experience of identity and nonidentity and generates from within the desire to step outside of ourselves, to flee the enclosure that cannot contain what it envelops. The unity of unity and duality is found within this sickness itself.

3.2. Doubling in God and Philosophy

Though the critique of Spinoza's dualism does not make an appearance in the *Freedom* essay, this does not mean that Schelling abandons it. In fact, in the "Stuttgart Seminars," Schelling draws together the various strands of his critique of Spinoza. We have already seen Schelling explicitly restate his criticism of Spinoza's dualism. To repeat, Schelling explains of Spinoza's attribute dualism that "there obtains between them neither a dynamic opposition nor a living interpenetration."[92] The absence of dynamic opposition and living interpenetration is the precise source of the lifelessness of Spinoza's monism as well what traps Spinozism in a beginning that can never become. Schelling adds that, consequently, Spinoza's philosophy remains too Cartesian. Further, Schelling reminds us that "Spinoza's physics are completely mechanical, a fact that should already suffice to make anyone realize that there remains a fundamental difference between the axioms of the philosophy of nature and those of Spinoza's philosophy."[93] Schelling then returns to the theme of identity and personality in Spinoza's philosophy as it relates to the real and the ideal. He writes,

> To be sure, Spinoza claims that thinking and substance (= the Ideal and the Real) both belong to the same substance and function as its attributes; he altogether fails, however, to think with any precision this very substance of which they are considered attributes, determining it instead through the empty concept of an identity (empty because of the lack of opposition), which is tantamount to ignoring it rather than making *it* the principle object of his philosophy.[94]

We again find a continuity in Schelling's critical engagement with Spinoza. The simple identity of substance does not allow for the kind of dynamic opposition that constitutes the possibility of life and personality. Schelling reinforces the fundamental difference between the notion of identity with which he begins and the kind of simple identity that is erroneously assumed to be the formal model of identity in the identity philosophy. Recall his claim that "the primordial essence [*Urwesen*] is in and of itself always unity; namely, the *unity of the opposition and of the bifurcation* [*Entzweiung*]."[95] The notion of doubling as deployed in the "Stuttgart Seminars" opens a point of entry into the *Ages of the World* project. In the 1811 draft, Schelling makes several comments regarding the dynamic of doubling formulated in the "Stuttgart Seminars." Though Schelling refers to the doubling of identity only once in the "Stuttgart Seminars," the notion plays a more central role in the 1811 draft of the *Ages of the World*. Therein, Schelling speaks of "self-doubling" five times. Taken together, these references forge an intriguing connection between the seminars in Stuttgart and the uncompleted *Ages of the World* project. Further, they justify a generalization of doubling as central to the development of Schelling's philosophical project.

Doubling, it must be emphasized, is a dynamic or a happening, and, as such, it appears in multiple different registers. I have previously suggested that the notion of intussusception in the *First Outline* presents a doubling over in nature. A precondition for this doubling was a contraction of homogeneous space. Through this contraction, a given space grew internally and this growth resulted from a conflicted holding together of unity and duality. When we arrive at the *Ages of the World*, we see that there is the doubling of the Divine not unlike this initial doubling over of nature. Schelling also uses the idea of doubling in reference to what philosophy is:

> This division, this doubling of ourselves, represents a clandestine intercourse in which there are two beings, one that questions and one that answers, one that knows—or is knowledge (*Wissenschaft*) itself—and one that, not knowing, always struggles for clarity. The real secret of the philosopher is this inner art of dialogue. Dialectic, its external correlate, derived its name from it, but is at best only its imitation. Where it becomes a mere form it is no more than a shadow and an empty appearance.[96]

The doubling of oneself is a necessary precondition for any kind of dialectic. The dialectic is an external view upon that which makes the intensification of identity occur. In the notes and fragments to the

1811 draft, Schelling puts this point more forcefully. "This doubling of ourselves," he writes, "this clandestine back-and-forth, this inner art of conversation, is the philosopher's real secret. It has its external correlate in what is called dialectic, which is only the afterimage. Where it becomes mere form, it is no more than empty semblance and shadow."[97] Just as the becoming All of the One is an interplay of the Absolute's self-doubling as known and knowing, so too is philosophy. Dialectic is but the shadow of a more primordial function. This does not mean that the dialectic is without utility within particular domains. It just indicates that the dialectic is not primary in relation to the determinacy of being as a differentiated set of domains.

Schelling does not hesitate to connect this doubling that is operative in the predialectical act of inner dialogue to the larger theme of existence:

> It is therefore easy to understand that all those who do not elevate themselves to an understanding of the divine act of self-doubling will never be able to follow the development further than what we have designated by the term *existence*. If from mere existence they try to go further, they will not be able to bring forth anything but words without meaning.[98]

Once again, philosophy and system coincide. Here, the moment of self-doubling acts as a kind of vantage point. As Schelling wonderfully does so often in the 1811 *Ages of the World*, he transitions seamlessly from a discussion of philosophy and existence to an analysis of the dynamics by which the Divine becomes divine, by which the One becomes the All. He writes, in a passage well worth quoting at length:

> Hitherto there has been nothing outside of the one that exists, not even God. This itself, however, the one that exists, is an indivisible whole, and the way it is, according to our presupposition, is the way it should remain. The god who is entrapped in being is able to posit a second personality, but not by virtue of any division (*Theilung*), or by discharging or separating out from himself one of the principles contained within him. Instead, he acts by remaining true to his own integrity and completeness. To posit a second being outside of oneself, while remaining in one's own wholeness, is to

beget (*Zeugung*). Begetting, self-doubling of the living being that is closed up inside of being (*des im Seyn eingeschloßnen Wesens*), would be the final, the only possible resolution of the highest opposition.[99]

Of primary importance for the present discussion is the final sentence of this quotation. Schelling describes a "living thing" *closed up* inside of being, and this is the duality within homogeneous space. Inside the unified field of absolute simplicity, there is something that cannot be contained. However, without self-doubling and the begetting that follows, the life of this living being is life in name only. It is without the kind of conflict necessary to induce becoming. This again brings us back to the affordances of the Absolute. Recall Schelling's claim that, for Spinoza, God is not yet God. This is because the existence monism of Spinoza is only an identity of identity, and not yet a unity of identity and nonidentity. By extension there is not strife and no struggle internal to substance that could drive it to become otherwise than it is. Schelling connects the doubling of the self to struggle and love:

> The first question we have to ask is whether the original I (*Ich*) acts with or without freedom when it engenders a second I that goes forth from it and overcomes it. In posing the question, we are interested in whether it is free in the way a being is free that acts out of a strong desire for something. Appetite (*Begierde*), hunger for love, becomes sharper and more urgent in every existing being the more severely it gathers itself together. This is what makes it impossible for one fully to contain oneself when struggling with love. It is in turn what drives a living being to that self-doubling through which a first I becomes capable of engendering a second.[100]

If a living being is to become a being capable not just of living but of philosophical and moral activity as well (that is, a being whose activity is embedded in both the natural and the normative), a self-doubling must take place. So, again, just as the Divine must double over in order to bring nature forth from itself, the living individual must repeat this process. Further, this doubling is such that "it is impossible for one to fully contain oneself." The hunger for love presses the original I into a place where it cannot master its overwhelming presence to itself. As it gathers together it becomes all the more difficult to hold itself in this gathering. Thus, it must give way, falling prey to its own weakness and subsequently falling into itself.

Production is a doubling distinguishable from repetition. Frank argues that Schelling's notion of identity draws from Wolff and the "older logic" of "a tradition that reaches back via Leibniz to scholasticism."[101] Most important for Frank is the act of reduplication. Schelling, Frank claims, seeks to understand the relation between mind and nature as a reduplicative relation and by extension, "Here we will not be dealing with a simple identity, but with an identity 'doubled in itself' or with an 'identity of identity.'"[102] This brings Frank to a conclusion that closely resembles the minimalist, subjectivist interpretation of Spinoza's attributes that I have suggested is unappealing to Schelling. "If we deploy *reduplicatio*," Frank writes, "the following compatibilist reading results: Types of psychic and types of neuronal states are not in themselves—or not metaphysically—different (not, namely, insofar as they are considered by X). They are only different from a conceptual (or epistemological) perspective)."[103] This reading, though it does bring out the implicit doubling of even Schelling's 1801 articulation of identity, comes off as overly epistemological and overly semantic. Given Schelling's critique of Spinoza's parallelism as well as Spinoza's unwillingness to reach back beyond the duality of the attributes into their shared ground, it seems Schelling would be unsatisfied with this reductive presentation of his theory of identity and doubling, though it may be more appealing to us contemporaries. Following Matthews's suggestion, Schelling's discussion of doubling ought to be read as drawing in part on Oetinger's engagement with Plato's *Timaeus*, a text of which Schelling was obviously quite fond. Matthews writes, "The soul of man is thus a *typus divines,* the *Ebendild* of God. As a doubling of God, it has the potential to duplicate the divine life; just as the act of creation is freely made by God, so too does man freely choose and create this world."[104] This connects back to Matthews's discussion of Hahn's "theology of life," in which he claims, "This dualism of opposing forces Hahn further characterizes as the *Ebenbild*—the double—of the first personality. This doubling is the producing, the generation of a likeness in the same way as the father generates a son who then becomes his mirror image."[105] The metaphysical interpretation of doubling squares more with this theological lineage picked up early on by Schelling and amplified throughout the *Ages of the World* project.

In the 1815 *Ages of the World*, Schelling makes clear that the self-doubling of the philosopher is in a sense the end of a process that is very much metaphysical. He writes, "Just as in everything living, so already in that which is primordially living, there is a doubling that has come down, through many stages, to that which has determined itself as what appears to us as light and darkness, masculine and feminine, spiritual and corporeal."[106] The history of oppositions is a repetition of the original doubling over made possible by the living, interpenetrating conflict between the forces of real and ideal. "Were the first nature in harmony with itself," writes Schelling, "it would remain so. It would be constantly One and would never become Two. It would be an eternal rigidity without progress."[107] Consequently, doubling is not just an instance of Schelling's *Erzeugungsdialektik*. It is instead its condition of possibility.

4.0. Conclusion

Like Brandom and others influenced by Sellars's distinction between the natural and the normative, as well as Johnston and other similarly inclined Hegelians, Schelling comes to conclude that nature alone is insufficient when trying to account for the essence of human freedom. Relatedly, unlike Jacobi, God alone is not a sufficient condition for the emergence of a form of freedom distinct to human agents. There must be an inconsistency at the heart of the Absolute, a discomfort in the heart of God, able to act as the ungrounding ground of which free acts in a natural world are an expression or property. Commenting on this general idea, Žižek writes, "A deontological tension is inscribed into the very heart of ontology: reality is in itself thwarted, it cannot be what it should be immanently."[108] Because of this inconsistency, this minimal crack at the heart of all that is real, the Absolute falls into itself thereby contorting, twisting, and doubling over. Without this doubling we would remain trapped in the static identity characteristic of Spinoza's monism. Further, this doubling can be found in God, nature, and philosophy itself.

Schelling's depiction of the unfolding of nature and spirit in the 1811 *Ages of the World* captures this complex and seemingly paradoxical relation between nature and spirit:

> The world into which being is unfolded is nature, while the spirit world is the unfolding of being that really is. Nature and the spirit world arise, always uniformly, out of the common middle point of one and the same original unity. Through one act of eternal splitting into two (*Dualisirung*), they arise simultaneously with one another.[109]

Being and what it "really is" (essence) are unfolded in worlds that derive from a fundamental unity. This unity is absolute insofar as it makes possible both the unification of each world as distinct (their difference) as well as the common logic according to which each world is contrastable as a world (their unity). This "common middle point" is precisely the identity of identity and difference best presented in the fractured unity of the Idea. It is this common middle point that is perfectly inscribed by the hyphen that binds and separates, thereby constructing a larger unity of what it is and what it is not. Being unfolds in the world of spirit and the world of nature and this dynamic of unfolding is what is common in both worlds, this is their "dynamic opposition" and "living interpenetration." Their separation, or more precisely their continuous separating, is an *eternal* cision; a beginning that never ceases to begin. They are eternally bound through a function of dualization, of becoming real and becoming ideal. Finally, this unfolding of each is a process that occurs *with* the other. Spirit is not the unfolding of a world through an eternal separation *from* nature, nor is nature the unfolding of a world through an eternal separation *from* spirit. In other words, the intelligibility of spirit is not dependent upon an erasure of the natural (antinaturalism, liberal naturalism, idealist antirealism), nor is the intelligibility of spirit dependent upon a reduction to the natural (reductive naturalism, realist anti-idealism). Instead, the unfolding of the worlds of spirit and nature (understood as coherent organizations of rules, things, and acts) occurs *with* each other, that is, at the same time though not in the same way. Just as nature hollows out God without properly speaking exiting from God, spirit does the same to nature. There is no need here to appeal to any kind of transcendence. We must simply acknowledge that any immanence cannot be what it ought to be, namely a unified ontological register.

Chapter 6

From Freedom to Pantheism

1.0. Introduction: An Unfamiliar Schelling

The "Stuttgart Seminars" are of great importance for understanding the relation between Schelling's earlier philosophical works and the *Freedom* essay. In Stuttgart, Schelling presents many of the ideas found in the *Freedom* essay in a systematic style reminiscent of the primary works of the identity philosophy. In the final part of these posthumously published seminars, Schelling turns to the issue of the particularity of human freedom, as well as the conditions for its historical significance. To do so, he narrates the relation between the individual soul (what he will call the "human spirit," or *Geist*), nature, the state, the church, and, finally, the revelation of God. Schelling describes the human spirit not as a collection of faculties but instead as a play of self-organizing and disorganizing forces that articulate themselves in different domains or potencies.[1] Throughout the account of the human spirit, the real and the ideal appear within each potency but not as two parallel attributes conceived under different perspectives. Instead, the relation between real and ideal is always mediated by a third, and this third is the spacing in which the task of the human spirit plays itself out. This space of connection and separation makes possible the living interpenetration of real and ideal that was strictly excluded by Spinoza's doctrine of attribute parallelism. It is this space that is opened and maintained by the grapheme of the hyphen.

Though any explicit discussion of Spinoza is absent from this final section of the "Stuttgart Seminars," it nevertheless relates back to our guiding thread of the presence of Spinoza in Schelling's project. This subterranean similarity has not gone unnoticed. Zöller refers to these closing remarks as Schelling's "miniature *Tractatus Theologico-Politicus*,"[2] and Chepurin takes up the theme of *Seligkeit* or "bliss" in the final part of these seminars to forge a connection between Spinoza and what he calls Schelling's "pantheism of bliss."[3] In addition to the discussions of the state and the church, Schelling continues to wrestle with the distinctly metaphysical themes of the *Ethics*. In this final part of the 1810 seminars, Schelling applies his doctrine of the potencies as well as his complex thematization of the real and ideal in an attempt to solve a central problem of Spinozism as understood by the post-Kantian German Idealists, namely, the reconciliation of system and freedom. Schelling begins the final part with a distinctly Spinozist idea: "Only that whose nature constitutes its very *being* is also by definition *free*," he claims.[4] This of course echoes the opening definition of the *Ethics*, in which Spinoza explains, "By that which is self-caused I mean that whose essence involves existence." We can, however, mark an important difference between these two definitions. Spinoza's definition does not relate the idea of the *causa sui* to freedom itself. Alternatively, Schelling begins with the freedom of the *causa sui*. Only that which is the cause of itself can be free because its being is not dependent upon anything other than itself. Only that whose nature *is* its very being is free. Here, we can see the paradox Schelling encounters in his discussion of human freedom when framed in this Spinozist light. There is something *necessary* about freedom. Schelling concludes his lectures in Stuttgart with the following claim that again brings us back to Spinoza. In reference to the final potency of God's revelation, he writes, "Then God is in all actuality everything, and pantheism will have become true."[5] Schelling effectively inverts the problem of the *Ethics*. Instead of beginning with pantheism and attempting to arrive at freedom, Schelling begins with freedom and sets out to arrive at pantheism. Reconstructing this path fleshes out the complexity and novelty of what I have called Schelling's ideal-realism. This chapter progresses in three stages. First, I look at the external constraints to the realization of human freedom outlined by Schelling. These are nature, the state, and the church. Second, I turn to the structure of the human spirit and how it prepares itself for a freedom independent of external constraint. Finally, I turn to Schelling's account of life after death, through which the individual is reconciled with the highest potency of the Absolute through the revelation of the Divine.

2.0. Freedom and Flowers

Schelling begins the third and final part of the "Stuttgart Seminars" by reiterating the ontological preconditions for God's freedom and the way this freedom relates to human freedom. The *Freedom* essay reframed this discussion in terms of the relation between nonbeing and being. Human freedom was no longer an abstract, subjective freedom characteristic of a self-constituting I. In other words, human freedom is not understood as an unconditioned condition articulated in the absence of any constraint or condition. Instead, Schelling details the objective and even preobjective conditions for the existence of evil, which is in turn a condition for the reality of a freedom that is distinctly human. Central to the beginning of this account is the self-alienation of nature, understood as the realm of nonbeing, from the world of spirit. This account gives to us a picture of nature somewhat but not entirely distinct from the nature of pure becoming presented in Schelling's early naturephilosophy. Following the quasi-Spinozist claim that "only that whose nature constitutes its very *being*" can be called free, Schelling continues as follows: "All dependency derives only from Being. Yet that which is being [*das Seyende*], both in and of itself and by virtue of its own nature, simply cannot be determined as such by anything else (because all determination is a passivity, i.e., a nonbeing)."[6] We can see a repetition of Schelling's earlier discussions of the unconditioned and its relation to determinacy. The determination of any particular condition as thus and so is dependent upon something else. As discussed in chapter 2, this endless chain of conditioned causes and events presupposed something that is itself unconditioned. Only that which is completely without external conditions, that which is un-conditioned, can be considered as the origin of the sequence of conditions and thereby free from reciprocal, worldly determination. Given all the previous discussions of the relation between the unconditioned, the Absolute, and God, it would seem to follow from this that only God is free. Only God's freedom is absolute, and, relatedly, only God's Being is unconditioned. However, Schelling quickly assures us that this is not the case. "God, as the one who has such absolute *Being* is thus also absolutely free, whereas man, having been raised from nonbeing into being, also attains freedom by virtue of his twofold relation, albeit a most unique freedom," claims Schelling.[7] One way to look at this is that for Schelling, God's freedom is simple. It derives from the fact that God's nature alone constitutes God's Being. Consequently, God never has to struggle to be free. Human freedom, alternatively, is complex, and it is difficult. Because the human is raised from nonbeing and oriented toward Being, human freedom is generated within this dual relation. Further, human freedom is sempiternal. Unlike God's freedom, human freedom must come into being, that is to say, it must emerge. Put simply, human freedom is an achievement and not a given.

Schelling turns to the image of a flower and the sun in order to illustrate the relation between Being and nonbeing in human freedom. He writes of nonbeing that it "relates to God as the flower relates to the sun. Although the flower emanates from the dark earth only through the efficacy of the sun and is transfigured by light, there nevertheless remains always something whose very root exists independently of this [flower]."[8] The freedom of the human is characterized by this tension between a striving for Being, as a flower grows to the sun, as well as its origin in nonbeing, the dark earth without which the roots of the flower would have no place to grow. Schelling explains this as follows:

> Hence, by virtue of occupying the middle-ground between the nonbeing of nature and the absolute Being = God, man is *free* from both. He is free from God by virtue of possessing an independent root in nature and is free from nature by virtue of the fact that the divine has been kindled within him; that is, he is in the midst of, and simultaneously above, nature.[9]

Schelling's point is that the human is not trapped in the middle space between God and nature. Instead, it is this very space in which the human finds its relative independence. Consequently, the freedom of the human is dependent upon the separation of God and nature. That is, it is dependent upon the spacing between God and nature. At first, it seems as if Schelling is describing freedom in a negative sense. Human freedom initially appears as merely the freedom from natural or divine conditions. However, we must consider the "middle-ground" opened by the division of nature from God, or nonbeing from Being, as the space in which freedom takes place. Without the duality of Being and nonbeing, human freedom would be not only impossible but ultimately irrelevant. The meaning of human freedom can only be grounded in the process by which the human *becomes* free. This process takes place in the space between the natural and the Divine, and thus nature must be separated from divinity in order for human freedom to take its proper place. There is a denaturalization of the Divine that serves as a precondition for the quasi-naturalization of human freedom.

2.1. Another Nature

Schelling does indeed claim that nature finds exceptional status in the human, and this claim is central to the overall argument for the movement from freedom to pantheism. Schelling explains that "it is manifest that all material life shows a progression toward man, that a continuous sequence of elevation and intensification leads to man, and that *he* is the epitome of spiritual life."[10] The exceptional status of the human in nature relates back to the drive for unity: "Nature seeks unity and yet does not discover it. Should it ever reach the point of its unity and transfiguration, nature would become fully organic and immersed in the spirit that has been awakened in man."[11] What is interesting about this formulation of a familiar claim is the idea that were nature's quest for unity to succeed, nature as a whole would become "fully organic" in a way distinct from nature in its modern understanding. With this, we can highlight a misconception when it comes to Schelling's understanding of nature. It is important to remember that Schelling does not deny the existence of mechanism in nature. He does not claim that nature as a whole forms some kind of superorganic unity that is analogous to the individual, determinate organisms one encounters in nature. Let us recall Schelling's claim in *On the World Soul* that "not where there is no mechanism, no organism, but rather conversely, where there is no organism, there is no mechanism."[12] Schelling then continues, writing that "the concept of organism does not rule out all succession of causes and effects; rather, this concept indicates only a succession that *enclosed within certain limits*, flows back on itself."[13] Again, the point of Schelling's innovations in the philosophy of nature is not to eliminate entirely any mechanistic understanding of nature. Instead, he seeks restrict the unwarranted generalization of the mechanistic picture of nature to the whole of nature. Schelling's move is not as simple as turning the whole of nature into one organism in order to make room for a more naturalized account of human freedom. It should be noted that this is precisely what he does with the PSR as well. Schelling does not deny that the PSR has a role to play in the constitution of an intelligible order of thoughts and things. He does not reject the possibility of a necessary relation of causes and effects enclosed within certain limits. However, he does deny that the determinative role of the PSR can be generalized to a fundamental law of all reality.

The emergence of nature as something distinct from what Schelling calls the "spiritual world" occurs by way of a decision. Schelling writes,

> As soon as man—rather than subordinating his natural existence to the divine—began to activate the (natural and unique) principle in himself, which is fundamentally destined to be relatively inactive, nature also had to awaken this principle within her because of the now obscure point of transfiguration [*Verklärungspunkt*]; from here on, nature had to become, *nolens volens,* a world independent of the spiritual one.[14]

Schelling's point is that the human makes a choice to relate to something in itself that is not reductively natural, and nature must react to this choice. This division is nothing less than the emergence of nature *as* nature in a particular determinate and intelligible form. The above characterization of nature is not a story we are often told when it comes to Schelling's naturalism.[15] The human is not the accidental product of a contingent play of forces. However, this does not imply that the human spirit in its particular form is a product of preformation. For Schelling, the emergence of the human spirit is necessary. By extension, nature is not blind but instead strives for the unity it can only find through humanity. However, the journey of the human spirit toward divine unity is one fraught with contingency and the constant threat of failure. This history of nature as nature is indeed the history of its alienation from and possible reconciliation with the world of spirit. We can see that there remains a moral teleology internal to nature itself. However, because nature alone cannot attain the unity for which it strives, it becomes but a part of a larger tale of redemption and revelation. Schelling himself acknowledges his instrumental invocation here. "Thus we have also presented a new conception of nature," he claims. "Whereas we previously referred to [nature] as the first power, it now becomes the first *period,* for it does not attain eternity but is absorbed into time."[16] We find here an important indication of Schelling's shift in perspective. The movement from powers to periods indicates that the narrative structure of the account given in part 3 of the "Stuttgart Seminars" must be viewed as a preview to the discussion of times in the *Ages of the World* project. Therein, the periods of time, or "ages," do not exist in a simple narrative structure. The past persists "in" the present through its resistance to being made present just as the present participates in the yearning of the future to become actual.

It must be emphasized that the hierarchical structure of the potencies is explicitly nonlinear. Schelling writes, "Nature in its present state is thus properly speaking only the first period of life, the antechamber of the highest life, though not this life itself. Man remains a spirit, to be sure, though only under the power of *B.*"[17] This, then, brings us to the concept of species. "Man does not exist alone in this world," writes Schelling, "but there is a multiplicity of men, a *human species,* humanity."[18] Our existence as a member of a species draws our individual existence into a temporal horizon broader than ourselves. Through the species, the nonbeing of nature strives to come into Being so that nature can find the unity it seeks but can never find in its own nonbeing alone. This then brings us back to the problem of evil. Schelling succinctly defines evil as "nothing but the usurpation and displacement of being by a relative nonbeing."[19] Schelling points out that the evil of which the human is capable is an analogue and not a pure expression of the evil in nature. Regardless, there is something distinctly postlapsarian about this account. The human must strive for freedom precisely because they are fallen. Schelling concludes this part of his discussion by returning to God. "Nature has lost its true point of unity in the same manner in which *mankind* has lost it," he explains. "For mankind, this [point] consisted of a threshold or a point of indifference, a point where *God Himself* would have been the unity [of mankind], for only God can be the unity of free beings."[20] In the middle-ground between Being and nonbeing, there is a missed opportunity for humanity. By subordinating Being to nonbeing, the unity that could come to humankind from the unity of divine freedom is erased.

2.2. STATE

Habermas's characterization of Schelling as an apolitical thinker has cast a shadow on Schelling's political philosophy. However, the political is by no means absent from Schelling's work. Žižek divides Schelling's politics into three phases, which he associates with the division of Schelling's philosophy into distinct stages. As if often the case with Žižek's proclamations, this division is helpful yet at the same time overly simplistic. Žižek associates the identity philosophy with "a classical bourgeois thinker who conceives the modern State and legal order guaranteed by it as the only possible framework of human freedom."[21] He characterizes the later positive philosophy as "reactionary" insofar as it "is thoroughly *in favour* of the state and of the inviolable, unconditional character of its authority."[22] Finally, Žižek associates his preferred Schelling, the Schelling of the "middle period" that includes the *Freedom* essay and the *Weltalter* project, with a "revolutionary" politics in which "the State is *Evil personified, materialized*, an agency which terrorizes society, a foreign power, a parasite upon the social body."[23] Žižek's characterization falls prey to the contested periodization model, but at the same time effectively highlights what is at stake in Schelling's political philosophy, namely, the accomplishment of freedom through the abolition of the state as well as other mechanisms of external coercion more generally.

Following his discussion of the fall of the human into nature and away from the freedom of God, Schelling turns to the state, the church, and the attempted cultivation of unity in humanity through these institutions. He had previously claimed that it was only through humankind as a species that nature itself could strive for harmony and unity. Humankind fails to find freedom in both God and nature and therefore looks for it elsewhere, namely, in the "modern state." Interestingly, the state is described as a form of second nature. Because the modern state is bound by the same kind of material necessity as the nonbeing that stands opposed to the Being of God, there remains something deeply natural about the state. In other words, the state is not simply the ideal of spirit added to or emerging from the real of nature. Schelling writes,

> The natural unity, this second nature superimposed on the first, to which man must necessarily take recourse, is the

[modern] *state,* and to put it bluntly, the [modern] state is thus a consequence of the curse that has been placed on humanity. Because man no longer has God for his unity, he must submit to material unity.[24]

Already we can see a strong tie between Schelling's theology and his political philosophy. The human is a political being precisely insofar as the human is a fallen being. In this sense, there is always something evil about the political insofar as politics is reduced to statecraft, understood as the artificial construction of external, coercive necessity grounded in finite institutions. To seek unity in the state is to turn one's back on the unity only the Divine can provide. To seek unity in the state is to choose nonbeing over Being once again.

This pessimistic view of the modern state echoes "The Oldest Systematic Program of German Idealism," in which the writers claim, "Only that which is the object of *freedom* is called *idea.* We must therefore go beyond the state!—Because every state must treat free human beings like mechanical works; and it should not do that; therefore it should *cease.*"[25] Now, we do not find this explicitly abolitionist perspective in Schelling's 1810 seminars, but we do find a similar critique of the state. Insofar as humans seek unity through the materiality of the state, they take themselves to be merely natural or merely material beings. Schelling explains, "The idea of the state is marked by an internal contradiction. It is a natural unity, i.e., a unity whose efficacy depends solely on material means. That is, the state, even if it is being governed in a rational manner, knows well that its material power alone cannot effect anything and that it must invoke higher and spiritual motives."[26] The state responds to the conflict created by the division of nature from God, but it cannot resolve this contradiction from within itself. It should be noted that Schelling had previously presented a more optimistic view of what we might call the "ideal state" in the *System of Philosophy in General*. Therein he suggests that the state can serve as the highest institutional unification of science, religion, and art: "That in which science, religion and art become one in a mutually penetrating and living manner and become objective in their unity is the state."[27] Schelling even goes so far as to suggest that it is the state that makes possible the objectivity of "true" science, religion, and art by comparing the state to the earth. "Moreover," claims Schelling, "just as gravity, light and organism are only attributes of the planet, and all things are and can only be upon it, so neither true science, nor true religion, nor true art has another form of objectivity than the state."[28] Further, the subjective mirroring of what is objective in this ideal, living state is ultimately what we call philosophy. Again, from the *System of Philosophy in General*: "What the state is objectively is subjectively . . . philosophy itself as harmonious enjoyment and participation in all the goods and beauties of life."[29]

Against this more optimistic presentation of what the state can do, Schelling comes to believe that there can be no immanent resolution of the state's constitutive antagonism, and there can be no political solution to the fundamental problem of politics and statecraft. Instead, the state must call toward something outside of itself. In this appeal to externality, we can find a marked difference between Schelling's 1810 analysis and that of the "Oldest Systematic Program of German Idealism," wherein the author(s) enthusiastically proclaim, "I want to set forth the principles for a *history of the human race* here and expose the whole miserable human work of state, constitution, government, legislature—down to the skin." The authors continue with reference to the "absolute freedom of all spirits who carry the intellectual world within themselves, and may not seek either God or immortality *outside of themselves*."[30] The dissolution of the state comes through the freedom of the individual that cannot be found outside of individual. Revelation and reconciliation arrive through the very human and material practices of art and mythology (understood as ideas made aesthetic).[31] Additionally, the "Stuttgart Seminars" make note of the external conflict that occurs between states. "The most convoluted situation arises with the collision among various states, and the most blatant phenomenon of the unattained and unattainable unity is that of *war,* which is as necessary as the struggle among the elements of nature," Schelling writes, concluding that "it is here that human beings enter into a relation strictly as natural beings."[32] The state, insofar as it necessarily comes into conflict with other states, drags the human back into a state of natural necessity. So again, even in the practice of statecraft, in this "second nature imposed upon the first," the human remains fallen.

Interestingly, in the lectures translated under the title "Presentation of the Purely Rational Philosophy," given sometime around 1847 as a part of the lectures on the history of mythology, Schelling returns to a more optimistic view of what the state can offer to the human spirit.

In this late lecture, he turns to law and reason in order to present an image of the state that is not doomed to failure in the same way the modern state is. "This external order of reason equipped with coercive power is the *state*," writes Schelling, "which, materially considered, is a sheer fact, and has only factual existence."[33] He continues, "but it is sanctified by the law that lives in it. It is a law neither of this world nor of human invention. Instead, it directly originates and emerges from the intelligent world. The law become actual power is the answer to that act by which human beings posited themselves outside of reason. This is reason in history."[34] Importantly, Schelling is once again not speaking here of a form of rationality reducible to human action. Borrowing from Kant, Schelling suggests that "*it is reason that lives in being itself* that subjects the will to itself."[35] It is insofar as this reason that lives in being itself constitutes the laws of the state that the state can make possible the freedom of the individual.[36]

In the 1847 lectures, Schelling also provides a critique of overtly theocratic political aspirations, commenting of those who attempt to craft a state from "subjective reason" alone that "their goal was to sweep it all aside, especially 'all authority and power,' in order to establish as quickly as possible heaven on earth, without awaiting the lord, with whose arrival Christianity consoles poor and clueless humanity."[37] So again, as in the "Stuttgart Seminars," we see that for Schelling it is Christianity in particular that elevates human life beyond the external confines of the coercive power of the state. However, as we will see, this Christianity is not necessarily of worldly origins. It is a kind of religion developed internal to the individual and not imposed from the outside. "We have recognized as justified and necessary a striving of humanity to overcome the burden of the state," Schelling continues, "but this overcoming must be understood as *internal*."[38] This then brings Schelling to one of his most clearly stated political imperatives: "To exist beyond the state inwardly—not only may I, but I should."[39] The state does not rob the individual of their freedom, but it instead makes possible the transposition from natural individuality to political personhood.[40] However, one must strive to live beyond the state in order to fulfill the state's promise of a lawful order that aligns with the rationality of Being and not just the rationality of the individual. Schelling then cautions us that "when one seeks a perfect state in this world, what comes in the end is (apocalyptic) fanaticism."[41] Against Žižek's characterization of Schelling's political philosophy during this period as purely reactionary, we must acknowledge that Schelling still believes that the actualization of freedom occurs independent of the state. However, we can see Schelling prohibiting the possibility of political redemption in the institutions of this world. Salvation, tentatively, resides in a life beyond this one. So even though Schelling may have relaxed his pessimistic viewpoint on what the state can provide, he retains his view that the elevation of the human spirit can find only partial success in the practice of statecraft.

2.3. CHURCH

With this discussion of the constitutive shortcomings of the modern state behind him, Schelling turns to the possibility of redemption through the institution of the church. Schelling begins his discussion of the redemption of humanity by reintroducing the theme of revelation: "Hence only *God himself* can establish the bond between the spiritual and the corporeal world, namely, by means of a second *revelation*, similar to that in the original act of creation."[42] Schelling first looks to the church to investigate the possibility of human institutions bringing about this second revelation that would return humanity to a state of unity with God. He contrasts the state's external attempt at producing unity to the church's attempt to produce this unity internally. However, by adopting the institutional structures of the state the church fails to accomplish its goal of producing an "inner unity or unity of the mind."[43] The existence of the church is a testament to the first revelation of God in the human, namely the initial resurrection of Christ.[44] According to Schelling, Christ alone succeeded where the rest of humanity has thus far failed. The church initially acted as a monument or archive of this accomplishment. However, the church too is unable to reenact the event that it seeks to memorialize. Schelling explains the reasons for this as follows: "The mistake made by the Church during its earlier, hierarchical period was not that it actively interfered with the state but, rather, that it permitted the state to enter the Church by opening up to the state and by assimilating the [institutional] forms of the state, rather than remaining pure."[45] When infused with the hierarchical, mechanistic, and coercive institutional perspective of the state, the church too fails at achieving the unity necessary for human freedom to become actual. It is still nonbeing that fallaciously paves the road to Being with only broken promises.

Schelling clarifies this position in the late lectures on the Philosophy of Revelation. "**My** view on Christianity," he explains, "is within the totality of its historical development; **my** goal is that a truly universal Church (if Church is still the correct word here), to be built solely in the spirit and only *in a perfect fusion of Christianity with general science and cognition.*"[46] There is something abolitionist about Schelling's theology in a vein similar to that of his political philosophy. Coercive institutional structures must be overcome "internally." This includes the Modern conception of nature, the Modern state, and the church itself.

Schelling concludes his discussion of the two external forces of second nature that attempt to bring unity to the human spirit. He explains that

> [w]hatever the ultimate goal may turn out to be, this much is certain, namely, that true unity can be attained only *via* the path of religion; only the supreme and most diverse culture of religious knowledge will enable humanity, if not to abolish the state outright, then at least to ensure that the state will progressively divest itself of the blind force that governs it, and to transfigure this force into intelligence. It is not that the Church ought to dominate the state or vice versa, but that the state ought to cultivate the religious principles within itself and that the community of all peoples ought to be founded on religious convictions that, themselves, ought to become universal.[47]

The theocratic implications of all of this ought to make us extremely uncomfortable, but they are not my primary focus here.[48] For the earlier Schelling as well as the author(s) of "The Oldest Systematic Program of German Idealism," art played the role of the capstone that was able to reconcile externality and internality in order to actualize freedom in the world. In 1810, Schelling seems to depart from this conviction. He does refer to the transpositions made possible by artistic production, but as we will see, these transpositions are placed in subservience to the pure scientific philosophy of the soul alone. In both nature as well as the second natures of the state and the church, we find only failure and intimations of a false freedom. Consequently, Schelling rejects the institutional hierarchies of state and church and turns to the spirit of the human. Spirit is the site of the internality capable of existing beyond state and church. His goal in focusing here is to formulate the spirit of the human in such a way that the quest for unity (and the accomplishment of freedom by extension) is not doomed to failure from the outset.

3.0. The Tripartite Tripartite Soul

We have now seen that the unification of human and divine freedom cannot be achieved by way of external compulsion or coercion. Schelling thus looks inward to find the source of the reconciliation of humanity and Divinity. The freedom of the human is distinguishable from the freedom of God, but this does not in turn imply that it is divided from divine freedom. After outlining the external constraints of nature, state, and church, Schelling begins his presentation of the human spirit as follows: "In this manner, then, we have been led to the study of the human spirit [*menschlichen Geistes*], not as regards its external fate and ambition but in accordance with its inner essence and with the forces and powers that also inhere in the individual."[49] The human cannot find redemption in any of the previously discussed institutions in which the human is entwined, including nature. Each paves the way for a relative freedom, but each alone is unable to fulfill the promise it whispers into being, or perhaps more precisely each fails to actualize freedom within the space between nonbeing and Being. Here, we return to the themes of the real and ideal in order to differentiate the forces and powers of the human spirit. Schelling immediately introduces us to what will be his strategy in this section. "The human spirit, too, is once again composed of three such powers or aspects," writes Schelling:

> The first one has man face the real world from which he was unable to free himself. This aspect is opposed to the ideal one, the aspect of man's highest transfiguration [*Verklärung*] and of his supreme spirituality. The second, medial aspect lets man place himself in the middle between the Ideal and the Real, thus granting him the freedom either of reestablishing the bond between these two worlds or of penetrating their division.[50]

Though there is a familiarity to Schelling's presentation of the human spirit, it is also far from a basic mind-body dualism. It is important to see that Schelling here outlines a tripartite division of the spirit and not just a simple dualism between real and ideal. Schelling subsequently introduces us to his terminology. "In general," he explains, "these three aspects or powers of the spirit are most appropriately expressed by the German language as temperament [*Gemüth*], spirit and soul."[51] Broadly speaking, temperament is the real that is opposed to the soul understood as the ideal, and at first it seems that real and ideal stand in strict opposition. However, what is crucial to note is that there is a third power between these two that traverses the space opened up by the opposition between real and ideal. It is what Schelling calls spirit or *l'esprit*. Spirit occupies the middle ground in which an individual is free to reconfigure their relation to the real and the ideal of their spirit.

3.1. Temperament

To make matters more complex, "[E]ach one of these is itself composed of three powers which once again relate to one another as temperament, spirit, and soul."[52] The three powers of temperament, spirit, and soul are themselves the products of more fundamental powers or forces.

Schelling begins by discussing the three-part structure of temperament which "constitutes the obscure principles of the spirit . . . it is that whereby the spirit, in a real sense, communicates with nature and by means of which it bears, in an ideal sense, a relation to the higher world, albeit obscure."[53] First off, temperament is not reducible to that which is natural in us. Through temperament, the spirit communicates with both nature and the "higher world," albeit in different ways, one that is real and one that is ideal. Already we can see how Schelling is attempting to avoid a base form of mind-body dualism. Though he claims that, "temperament is the properly Real in man," we can see that temperament is not reductively or exclusively Real. Further, temperament is "that whereby and wherein man is to effect everything."[54] He continues to note that the "greatest spirit will remain barren and incapable of creating or producing without temperament."[55] Without the dark link to the past embodied by temperament, there could be no genuine creation or production by or within the human spirit.

The three powers that compose the properly real, that is, temperament, are nostalgia [*Sehnsucht*], desire, and feeling. We begin with nostalgia. Schelling describes nostalgia as that "which is the inner gravity of temperament."[56] Further, nostalgia "in its most profound manifestation . . . appears as *melancholy*."[57] Without melancholy, Schelling argues, temperament would be completely unmoored from its ground. To return to Schelling's earlier image, without nostalgia, temperament would be a flower floating above the earth that would only wither in the light of the sun. Schelling continues to describe the deep relationship established between temperament and nature through the profound manifestation of melancholy. "It is by means of the latter," he writes of melancholy,

> that man feels a sympathetic relation to nature. What is most profound in nature is also melancholy; for it, too, mourns a lost good, and likewise such an indestructible melancholy inheres in all forms of life because all life is *founded* upon something independent from itself (whereas what is *above* it elevates while that which is *below* pulls it down).[58]

There is a yearning for the past that is present in both the human and in nature. Both mourn in their quest for a unity they are unable to achieve on their own. Further, all life is founded by way of this pull backward into the dark past from which all things at one point came. Thus, on the quest for revelation and redemption, the human relation to nature is one of remembrance and deep sorrow.

Schelling next moves onto desire, which he broadly defines as the power "whereby it corresponds to the spirit, that is, corresponds *in general* to the character of the spirit."[59] If it is nostalgia that binds temperament to nature, it is desire that binds temperament to spirit. However, both powers do not function in the same way. Schelling describes this relation of temperament to spirit by appealing to a flame: "What we call *spirit* exists *by virtue of itself,* a flame that fuels itself. However, because as something existing, it is opposed to Being, the spirit is consequently nothing but an addiction to such Being, just as the flame is addicted to matter."[60] By appealing to a flame here, as opposed to a flower, Schelling separates spirit from the dark ground of the past to which temperament remained bound. By "addiction," here, Schelling is clearly not making a claim about dependence alone.

There is a deep need for Being within the spirit and it is through this need that it is elevated away from nonbeing. This is a kind of internal compulsion through which Schelling explicitly introduces the power of desire. He writes,

> The most base form of spirit is therefore an addiction, a desire, something ethereal. Whoever wishes to grasp the concept of spirit as its most profound roots must therefore become fully acquainted with the nature of *desire*. In desire we witness for the first time something that exists with absolute spontaneity, and desire is something entirely inextinguishable; as far as desire is concerned, innocence can be lost only once, for [desire] is a hunger for Being, and being satiated only gives it renewed strength, i.e., a more vehement hunger.

So, in short, temperament is properly real because its force is grounded in its nostalgia for the past. Alternatively, desire finds its ideality in its hunger for Being. Because desire is not yet Being, it is oriented toward a future. However, this is not a future given *in* time. It is instead a desire for a future fundamentally incompatible with the present, much in the same way that Schelling describes the past as fundamentally incompatible yet coextensive with the present in the *Ages of the World*.

Schelling says very little of feeling, the final power of temperament. He describes this as "a sensibility like that in organic nature, whereas that which precedes it is a certain irritability."[61] Feeling is the receptive part of temperament that responds to external stimuli and irritation. As such, sensibility is dependent upon the present and the given conditions of the world. It is through sensibility that temperament is bound to the actually existing conditions of the world. Despite receiving less attention than the other powers of temperament, Schelling concludes his discussion of this first power of spirit describing feeling as "the supreme dimension of our temperament, the grandest quality of man's temperament, and the one that he should treasure most."[62] There is a temporal conflict constitutive of temperament. In fact, there very intelligibility of temperament is constituted by its complex threefold temporal horizon. Nostalgia pulls it to the past, desire orients it to the future and sensibility leaves it receptive to the present of the world. Temperament would love to lose itself anywhere but here and now, and through sensibility this flight is short-circuited. Sensibility is perhaps the most supreme dimension of temperament precisely insofar as it can balance the backward pull of nonbeing and the forward thrust to Being. It is through feeling, then, that the individual temperament aligns the relation between Being and nonbeing, thereby acting toward good or toward evil.

3.2. L'ESPRIT

After describing feeling as the "highest power" yet "at the lowest level," Schelling moves to the second level of the spirit which he claims is most properly captured by the French "*l'esprit*." He writes that this is "that which is properly man's personality, and [which is] therefore the proper power of being with consciousness [*Bewussheit*]."[63] In this level of the spirit, we find a more common set of distinctions. Whereas the freedom of temperament is largely unconscious, with *l'esprit* we find the introduction of the more familiar volitional and epistemic characteristics attributed to the human spirit by the German Idealists, namely, will and understanding. "In the first power," Schelling writes of temperament, "which is still a preconscious aspect of man, the spirit prevails as *mere* desire and ether, whereas here it [manifests itself] as a conscious desire, in short, as a *will*. Here the will is properly speaking the innermost dimension of spirit."[64] Desire's truth is manifested as will. If desire is where the spirit wants, will is where the spirit begins to act. Will is divided into two aspects, one real and one ideal. Schelling again: "This will contains two aspects, a real one that pertains to the individuality of man, [i.e.,] the *individual will* [*Eigenwille*], and a universal or ideal one, that of the understanding."[65] The will is real insofar as it is contracted into the individual, and it is ideal insofar as it strives for universality. It is important to note that the division between the will as real and the will as ideal (as understanding) occurs internal to the will itself. Understanding is not the ideal added to will. It is instead a particular manifestation originally grounded in the real. As will expands away from individuality and toward universality, it becomes understanding. We can see then that understanding is not, properly speaking, opposed to will. Instead, it is a mirroring of the individual will pulled in a distinct direction (toward universality).

Schelling continues to unpack this complex relation by straightforwardly laying out the three powers of *l'esprit*:

> Hence the spirit (in its more specialized sense) has once again three powers. (a) The first one is that of the individual will [*Eigenwillen*], of egoism, which would be blind without the understanding . . . (b) This power is opposed by the highest one, which is the understanding. The understanding and the individual will together beget the third, middle power, (c) which is the proper will, which here appears at the point of indifference.[66]

So again, here we find a real that stands in opposition to an ideal and a middle ground begat by this separation. Just as with temperament, it is this middle ground in which freedom finds its proper place. The introduction of the proper will that is irreducible to the egoistic, individual will is the introduction of freedom in this second level. Freedom does not reside in the will taken as the real, but instead in the will that navigates the indifference point between individual will and understanding, or real and ideal. Just as feeling operates as an intermediary between the real and ideal powers of temperament, it is through the proper will that the organization of Being and nonbeing occurs in the second level. It is through the will that one would invert the proper relation of Being and nonbeing, thereby enacting evil.

3.3. Soul

Schelling then turns to the final level or power of the spirit. This he calls the "highest good" and claims that it is the "soul."[67] "The soul constitutes what is properly divine in *man*," Schelling explains, "hence it is something *impersonal*, the proper Being, to which personality as an intrinsic nonbeing shall remain subordinate."[68] Schelling carefully distinguishes the impersonal soul from the irreducibly personal levels of the spirit. The individual is permeated by something impersonal, something in me that is not me and that can never be mine. At this point, Schelling's interest in the soul is focused upon what it provides to the intellectual development of the human and the kind of knowing this third and highest power of the spirit makes possible. Schelling writes, "The soul is something impersonal. Meanwhile, the spirit *possesses knowledge* whereas the soul does not know but is science itself."[69] The spirit has knowledge, but the soul is knowledge itself. The reason for this relates back to the reality of evil and the possibility of error. Evil and error arise from an imbalance in the proper relation of Being to nonbeing. Consequently, the "spirit has knowledge because it also contains the possibility of evil; it can only be *good,* i.e., partake of goodness, whereas the soul is not good but is this goodness [*die Güte*] itself."[70]

Instead of breaking down the soul into three composite powers, as he had with the previous levels or powers of spirit, Schelling focuses explicitly on the functions of the soul. Each previous power of the spirit was, like any power, an acting or a doing. At this final level, each function proper to the soul is defined by way of its relation to the other powers of the spirit more generally. Importantly, each previous power was more of a force than a faculty. The soul plays a mediating role between the previously discussed powers. It is captured by its complex and diverse relational function. First, the soul might "relate to the Real in the subordinate powers, that is, to man's nostalgia, to his ego dynamism [*Selbstkraft*], and to the individual will."[71] It is from this relation to the real of human temperament that art arises, the highest form of which "involves the interpenetration of the ideal and the real."[72] Second, the soul "relate[s] to feeling and understanding, the two corresponding powers within the first two powers."[73] The first thing to note here is that the soul can act as an intermediary between different powers or different levels of the spirit more broadly. In this case, it is the soul that establishes a dynamic connection between feeling (on the first level) and understanding (on the second level). From this relation arises nothing less than philosophy itself. Of the interpenetration of feeling and understanding governed by the mediating function of the soul, "science originates in the highest sense, namely that science that is immediately inspired by the soul—philosophy."[74]

At this point, Schelling takes a brief detour in order to redefine reason in light of the tripartite tripartite schema he is setting up. "Ordinarily a distinction is postulated between the understanding and reason," Schelling writes.[75] This is, of course, most clearly found in Kant's division of sensibility from understanding and understanding from reason. Instead of positing reason as a faculty sufficient to itself, Schelling outlines reason as a particular expression of the understanding. He writes that "understanding and reason are the same thing, albeit considered from different perspectives."[76] At first, Schelling turns to the categories of activity and passivity in order to explain these different perspectives through which understanding and reason emerge. "The understanding apparently involves something more *active,* practical, whereas *reason* seems more passive [or] submissive," he claims.[77] What, then, does reason submit to? "Reason is strictly the understanding in its submission to the superior [power] of the soul."[78] The difference between reason and understanding is internal to understanding itself, which was itself a distinction drawn internal to the will. Insofar as understanding stands in disharmony with soul, it is active. Only in submission to soul, the highest power of spirit, can the understanding elevate itself toward the governing principles of soul which are, as Schelling pointed out earlier, nothing short of science and goodness. Reason is the submission of the individual, egoistic will to the impersonal. Schelling draws an analogy to geometry in order to make this clear: "Reason relates to philosophy in the same way in which pure space functions in geometry. Whatever is false in geometry, an erroneous concept, will not be accepted by space but is rejected."[79] We can see the relation between this claim and Schelling's earlier position that anything completely outside of reason cannot be said to properly exist. The nonbeing of the human and natural particularity remain quantitative affirmations of the Absolute's nonidentity. Schelling concludes this discussion of reason and understanding by returning to the power of feeling, which, let us recall, was the most profound and important power of temperament. "All productions require a dark principle," he writes, "a substratum from which the creations of a higher being are derived. In the case of philosophy this dark principle is called *feeling* [*Gefühl*]; without feeling nothing can be attained, to be sure, though this is not to say that feeling itself is the supreme [power]."[80] It is in the interplay of feeling and soul, an interplay of receptivity and absolute form, that theoretical philosophy can be achieved. In short, philosophy is not made possible by a parallelism of real and ideal. It is instead only possible when real and ideal stand in a messy, reciprocally determining relation of mutual saturation and interpenetration.

After this excursus into the relation between feeling, understanding, and reason, Schelling returns to the third function of the soul. This is to "relate to the will and to desire."[81] Schelling connects this function to the problems of moral philosophy largely as laid out by Kant in the Antinomy of Practical Reason. If the coordination of feeling and soul allow the human to know, the coordination of will and desire gives rise to meaningful action. When properly aligned, this third function establishes the highest virtue in the individual. "While the latter are altogether subordinate to (and in continuous rapport with) the soul," writes Schelling of will and desire, "this produces not the individual good act but the moral disposition of the soul, or *virtue*, in the highest sense, namely, as *virtus*, purity, propriety, and fortitude of the will."[82] From this, Schelling derives his moral maximum, which he states as follows: "Permit the soul to act within you, or act as a thoroughly holy man."[83] Now, there is little content to this maximum, but there is an important point that it brings to the fore. To act as a "thoroughly holy man" is to allow the impersonal to act within oneself. To become free, I must harmonize with that which is in me but not mine. Knowledge and moral action take place through a distancing of oneself from oneself or through a letting go of one's finitude.

Unlike the previous powers within temperament and *l'esprit*, soul has a fourth function, and this is the pure relation to itself. "Finally," writes Schelling, "the soul may also act with strict purity, without any particular relation and altogether unconditionally. This unconditional officiating of the soul is called *religion*, not as a science but as the inner, supreme blessedness of [our] temperament and spirit."[84] We can now see why Schelling has taken this digression from the failures of state and church to the complex tripartite tripartite scheme of the human spirit. Though the external institutional strictures of the church foreclose the production of unity in the world, the human spirit is capable of doing so insofar as this unity is a complex balancing of the impersonal (temperament), the personal (*l'esprit*), and the extrapersonal (soul). True religion is within the individual but only insofar as the individual is no longer egoistic or individualistic.

Schelling's conclusion of this discussion returns us to the Absolute. "The soul corresponds to A^3," Schelling explains, "and this A^3 constitutes divine love insofar as it is the bond of creation, that is, the identity of non-being and being, of the finite and the infinite."[85] Let us note Schelling's invocation here of the identity of identity and nonidentity. The soul, in this sense is what is absolute in the individual. That is, the soul is what is eternal within the temporal; it is the impersonal at the heart of the personal. Importantly, the eternal in the individual is an essential aspect of what makes the human spirit human. This means that to be human and to be free is not a case of finitude or infinity in any simple sense. Paradoxically perhaps, it is through the unity of the soul as the identity of Being and nonbeing that the unity once lost can again be reestablished. This reinforces a crucial point about

Schelling's conception of unity, namely, that it is not some empty or static night, but is instead a complex interplay of coordinated, conflicting, and interpenetrating forces.

4.0. Revelation and Reconciliation

Nature, state, and church fail to prepare the individual for the unity made possible by revelation and redemption. Though the human spirit can prepare itself for this reconciliation, it remains incapable of achieving it by itself. The human spirit needs revelation in order to attain the unity that has driven its desire throughout its existence. It is important to briefly clarify Schelling's notion of revelation. McGrath explains that "revelation according to Schelling is not the possession of any institutional form of Christianity; it is not even bound to faith or confession. Rather, revelation disseminates itself freely and universally throughout history."[86] Revelation is not an object or a mode of access to a transcendent truth that exists outside of history. Instead, revelation is more substantive. Further, the substance of revelation is nothing short of the transformation of the Divine. McGrath continues, "God ceases to be *object* in revelation, he becomes exclusively *subject*."[87] Revelation is an intentional unfolding within and through history. It is through this unfolding that God becomes subject, and it is only by becoming subject that God can become "in all actuality everything," thereby eventually rendering pantheism true. Further, revelation is not something that happens *to* the human spirit because, again, it is not something received. Instead, the human spirit is an essential component of revelation. To trace this process, we must look at Schelling's account of the life after life and the moral struggle that remains in this life after life that makes reconciliation with the Divine possible but never guaranteed.

4.1. THE LIFE AFTER LIFE

Though the human spirit is not incompatible with revelation, redemption, and reconciliation with divine freedom, it alone is insufficient to accomplish this grand task. Consequently, to end here with the mortal spirit would result in a failure to render pantheism true at the end. A discordant nonbeing would remain in opposition to the free Being of the Absolute. We might have glimpsed the complex structure in which specifically human freedom plays itself out, but we have not yet arrived at the reconciliation with the Being whose freedom follows from its nature alone. In short, a duality remains where a unity is to become. We have seen how by way of the soul's auto-affective self-relation the human spirit reaches its highest articulation possible under the first potency. "In this manner, then, we have restored man to the highest summit which he is capable of ascending in this life," Schelling writes.[88] The height of this self-relation Schelling compares to an inner religion that is the blessedness produced by the unity of temperament and spirit. This unity also goes by another name. Schelling claims just before this, that "science, too, is in its highest power a work of love and thus bears rightfully the title of philosophy, i.e., love of wisdom."[89] So, the highest summit the mortal can ascend is to philosophize, that is, until the moment of death. But again, this existence, and this philosophy, are only considered under the first potency. The human spirit has found the highest unity of which it is capable, but this unity does not itself coincide with that which the soul corresponds, namely, the "bond of creation" understood as the identity of being and nonbeing. "We can do little more," writes Schelling, "but remark on man's fate in a future life."[90]

Spinoza, Kant, and Schelling all share the view that the soul is immortal. Spinoza's need to posit an immortal soul is largely epistemological. His argument for the immortality of the soul follows from one's capability for what he calls the "third kind of knowledge," namely, intuitive knowledge that "proceeds from an adequate idea of the formal essence of certain attributes of God to an adequate knowledge of the essence of things."[91] *E*Vp23 reads, "The human mind cannot be absolutely destroyed along with the body, but something of it remains, which is eternal." *E*Vp25 states, "The highest conatus of the mind and its highest virtue is to understand things by the third kind of knowledge." This then brings us to the conflict between the existence of the body in time and the possibility of knowing the eternal. Spinoza writes in the proof to *E*Vp29 that "insofar as the mind conceives the present existence of its body, to that extent it conceives a duration that can be determined by time, and only to that extent does it have the power to conceived things in relation to time (Pr. 21, V and Pr. 26, II) But eternity cannot be explicated through duration." This leads Spinoza to claim in the proof of *E*Vp30 that "to conceive things under a form of eternity is to conceive things insofar as they are conceived through God's essence as real entities; that is, insofar as they involve existence through God's essence. Therefore, our mind, insofar as it knows itself and the body under a form of eternity, necessarily has knowledge of God." So, in short, Spinoza argues that there is something immortal about the mind because this needs to be the case if the third kind of knowledge to be possible. In order to know the essence of God, one must have knowledge of their own immortal essence. Were this kind of self-knowledge impossible, then so too would be the *Ethics* itself. Thus, for Spinoza, the immortality of the soul is epistemologically necessary, and it is only through this epistemological necessity that the ethics of the *Ethics* becomes possible.

Kant likewise finds a need for an immortal soul. However, Kant's need is not theoretical but practical. For Kant, the immortality of the soul is a necessary postulate of practical reason. "Complete adequacy of the will to the moral law," he writes, "is *holiness,* a perfection of which no rational being in the world of sense is capable at any point of time in his existence."[92] The rational being existing in the world of sense and time is unequal to the task bequeathed to it by the moral law. Consequently, "the highest good is practically possible only on the presupposition of the immortality of the soul, and hence this immortality, as linked inseparably with the moral law, is a **postulate** of pure practical reason."[93] Now, it is clear that Schelling would reject Kant's argument for the immortality of the soul even if he agreed with its conclusion. In the *Letters*, we saw Schelling dismiss any argument for the existence of the infinite based upon the need of a weakened reason. Such arguments are merely hypothetical and ultimately prove nothing. Though we can imagine Schelling criticizing Spinoza on similar grounds, I think we can ultimately find more similarities between his account of the immortality of the soul and Spinoza's. If the third type of knowledge is to be possible, and by extension the experience of eternal love and blessedness Spinoza discusses in *E*Vp30, then the human mind must exist beyond the body in order to be equal to the order of God's intellect. "The mind's intellectual love toward God is the love of God wherewith God loves himself not insofar as he is infinite, but insofar as he can be explicated through the essence of the human mind considered under a form of eternity," writes Spinoza in *E*Vp36. He continues, "that is, the mind's intellectual love toward God is part of the infinite love by which God loves himself." Spinoza's language remains largely epistemological, particularly the emphasis on the mind's capacity for the explanation of God, but it is significant that it is the rational order itself that renders the mind equal to God's self-directed divine love. Spinoza continues in $EVp38$, "The greater number of things the mind understands by the second and third kinds of knowledge, the less subject it is to emotions that are bad, and the less it fears death." So again, through understanding the internal necessity of God, the mind becomes more powerful because it is affected by what is necessary and not by external passions. In other words, as the mind turns from the infinite and attends to the finite, or to nonbeing, its power is decreased, and it becomes more susceptible to evil. However, Spinoza and Schelling would part ways when it comes to the relation between knowledge, evil, and nature. Spinoza states in $EVp37$ that "there is nothing in Nature which is contrary to this intellectual love, or which can destroy it." For Spinoza, it is impossible to conceive of God (understood as the one thing that exists) as acting contrary to itself. The auto-affective love of the Divine is one of simplicity and of full presence. Alternatively, for Schelling there are multiple expressions of nature (understood as a realm of necessity and nonbeing expelled from the Divine as the result of human choice) that torment the Divine.

If Spinoza and Kant give hypothetical arguments for the immortality of the soul premised upon a need of either theoretical or practical reason, then Schelling's account of the immortality of the soul follows from the first principle of his system as articulated in the "Stuttgart Seminars." Schelling begins this account by contextualizing his previous discussion of the spirit of the human. Though this spirit follows the tripartite structure of the potencies, having internal to itself a first, second, and third potency, as a whole, "[a]ll that has thus far been considered belongs properly only to the first power."[94] The structure of potencies is such that they often nest within each other, meaning that within a single potency of God, for example, the entire sequence of the potencies of the human spirit can play themselves out. In other words, the interplay and tension of powers expresses itself at various levels of organization. Consequently, to elevate oneself from one potency to another does not imply any transcendence. When the human spirit is transposed to the second potency though death, it must itself undergo significant changes. The powers of the human spirit meet with a set of constraints unique to this second potency.

Through this transposition the human spirit enters a new phase of its moral and intellectual development.

Schelling begins the narration of human life after death as follows: "For man the true, second power becomes effective only after his death. Once again, we must set out by considering life; thus we shall initially speak of *man's transition from the first power (i.e., of Life) to the second power,* namely, that of death."[95] Death initiates the transposition of the human spirit from one world into another. "Yet at one point man must attain his true Being [*Esse*] and must be freed from his relative nonbeing," Schelling explains. "This happens when he is transposed entirely into his own A^2, a step that does not separate him from physical life in general but from *this* life, in short, through death or through his transition to the world of spirit."[96] Death frees the individual from a certain relative nonbeing. To attain true freedom, the human must be separated from any dependence upon nonbeing. However, what Schelling is already intimating here is his somewhat odd theory of the materiality of the spirit world. Notice that it is not the physicality of existence that one leaves behind in death. Instead, it is the specificity of *a* life from which we are separated by death. This traces back to Schelling's refusal to formulate the human spirit in strictly dualistic terms. We saw this previously in the ways the real, the ideal, and the complex space in between the two play a role in each of the different levels of the human spirit. In other words, if Schelling held onto a form of Spinozist parallelism, this elevation through dynamic interpenetration would be impossible. Because the individual is not a strictly dualistic amalgamation of body and soul, the transition to the world of spirit does not occur through the shedding of the material from the spiritual, or of the triumph of the ideal over the real. Instead, the materiality *proper* to the spiritual is elevated to the second power. Again, it is not life as such that death extinguishes, but only a particular and personal instantiation of life. Schelling explains this as follows: "Death marks not an absolute separation of the spirit from the body but only a separation from that corporeal element which inherently contradicts the spirit, that is, a separation of good from evil and vice versa."[97] In short, Schelling's claim here isn't as simple as one regarding an immortal soul. What we see is that death is not a moment of absolute division but is instead a path toward establishing a greater unity. This is the unity sought in vain by nature, the state, and the church.

It is only at this point after death that the human spirit is prepared for a possible reconciliation with divine goodness.

With this, Schelling breaks decisively from any common conception of life after death. He writes that "man, after his death is commonly thought as some ethereal being or, rather abstractly, as a pure and angelic thinking. In fact, man is much rather a most authentic, and a much more powerful and actual, being after death than in this world."[98] Instead of taking death to be a moment of division between physical and spiritual, Schelling claims that "death unites the physical (to the extent that it is essential) and the spiritual."[99] Through death, a new unity is established between what is essential in the physical and in the spiritual. Schelling's unique understanding of essence further complicates this transition. As Alderwick argues, essence, for Schelling, is not something that exists prior to form. Consequently, essence as such does not predetermine form. Instead, form and essence are codeterminative. "For Schelling this relationship is one of interdependence," she explains, "rather than essence fully determining form, the relationship of determination is reciprocal; each term has a degree of independence from the other."[100] Significantly, this kind of reciprocal determination and relative interdependence is precluded by any metaphysical parallelism, further emphasizing the importance of Schelling's critique of Spinoza. Parallelism, as we have already discussed, forecloses the possibility of a living mutual saturation of form and essence and of real and ideal. Alderwick continues, "Because a consequent is engaged in a creative and reciprocal relationship with its ground, the way that an agent's essence is actualized is not predetermined, but rather arises through her creative engagements with the world and with her essence."[101] This remains true of life after death. Though the spirit now relates creatively to the spirit world, this does not mean that essence has become something static or immutable. The project of becoming fully human remains.

Though it is only through death that the human moves from A^1 to A^2, Schelling is careful to stipulate that this movement is not necessarily into some transcendent externality. "Upon his death, man is not transposed into the absolute or divine A^2 but into his *own* A^2," Schelling explains. He continues as follows:

> The divine A^2 as the absolute one is necessarily also the absolute good, and to that extent no one but God is good. Outside of God, only that is good which participates in

being as a relative nonbeing; however that which actively opposes this [later] being is the spirit of evil. Hence the good, by being transposed to *its proper* A^2, is naturally also being transposed into the divine A^2; however, the man of evil, when being transposed into his proper A^2, will be expelled for precisely that reason from the divine A^2 in which he was still participating in this world by virtue of the mediating influence of nature.[102]

The task of morality is not abandoned at the moment of death, and the possibility of evil does not disappear when the mechanism of external nature is shed in the moment of death. To be transposed into the divine A^2 requires that the human continue to choose Being over nonbeing. Here, we can see that the quest for redemption is not guaranteed and necessarily continues after death. Though transposition into the human's own A^2 opens up the possibility of reconciliation with the divine A^2, this reconciliation is never guaranteed. One is not necessarily reconciled with divine goodness after death. It is again something that the spirit must actively strive to accomplish. In *Clara or, On Nature's Connection to the Spirit World*, Schelling explains this transposition of the striving of the human spirit when elevated from the first to the second potency as follows: "But just as there are countless intermediate levels between good and bad in this life, so, too, are there between bliss and wretchedness in that life."[103] This example provides insight into the role played by the potencies. In the second potency, entered after death when what is essential of one's physical self is elevated to the spiritual world, what was once the decision between good and bad becomes the decision between bliss and wretchedness. The relation of one's decision between Being and nonbeing remains the same but the coordinates in which this decision plays itself out have shifted. In embracing bliss and Being, the human spirit draws itself closer to the bliss of the Divine. This is in part why Chepurin argues that, for Schelling, "bliss retains its Spinozian—and ultimately Epicurean and stoic—roots."[104] Alternatively, the choice of nonbeing and wretchedness drives an immovable wedge between the spirit and the Divine. It is only through bliss that the spirit is prepared for revelation and reconciliation with divine freedom.

Schelling offers two proofs for this claim regarding the dynamics at play when the spirit is elevated to its own A^2. The first has to do with the role of temperament in the human spirit. We saw previously how temperament presented a threefold tension between past, present, and future. Nostalgia bound the human to the past, desire propelled it to the future, and feeling stood between the two as a faculty or power of receptivity. Consequently, "all weakness originates in the inner division of temperament," Schelling explains.[105] In being elevated to its own A^2, humanity sheds the conflict inherent in temperament and thereby moves beyond a particular instantiation of evil. Second, "because in this life something accidental has been mixed in, that which is the essential is weakened. Hence the spirit that has been freed from the accidental element is pure life and force, and both evil and good are more intense."[106] In short, the quest to live well is not abandoned after death. "Being transposed into his own A^2, man is thus placed in the world of spirit," continues Schelling. "It is here, then, that the construction of the world of spirit takes place. Just as there exists a philosophy of nature there also exists a philosophy of the spirit world."[107] Now, interestingly, despite the fact that the analysis of spirit and revelation relies on the notion of forces and powers that precede any beings, Schelling is suggesting here that the philosophy of nature is inadequate for fully understanding construction in the spirit world. This in turn seems to suggest that (at least in these seminars) the philosophy of nature plays a localized role. In other words, nature too has its proper place, and if this is indeed the case, we can see why it is difficult to generalize Schelling's naturalism to the entirety of his philosophy, and particularly to his discussions of redemption and revelation.

4.2. At the End

After this provocative suggestion that death is an event of unification and not division, Schelling goes on to describe the spirit world further. While the 1810 dialogue *Clara* offers a more literary exposition of the spirit world, the "Stuttgart Seminars" utilizes philosophical categories in order to focus primarily on the structural relation of the spirit world to the natural world and the Divine. It may at first appear as if the relation between the natural and the spirit world could be easily mapped onto the relation of real to ideal. However, consistent with his earlier analyses, this is not the case, as it would imply a static dualism vulnerable to the critique of lifelessness. "Already in the very beginning," Schelling writes,

> when God discriminated between the Real and the Ideal, he also had to posit the Ideal as a world of its own. Hence, just as there obtained, within the Real, the Real, the Ideal, and their indifference, all of these also obtained in the Ideal, only this time posited under the power of the Ideal.[108]

The significance of this passage is immense. We cannot simply equate the spirit world with the ideal. Instead within this world, there remains a real, an ideal, and the indifference between the two that makes both unity and conflict possible. That is, even in the ideal world of spirit we still find the preconditions that are necessary for life and freedom. Consequently, there is a life proper to the spirit world that remains emergent from yet irreducible to natural life. Schelling continues this discussion by evoking the temperament of God. He writes:

> Hence there is, in the Ideal [form] of God, once again something that corresponds to nature, the only difference being that here this something is itself entirely ideal. As we were able to discern in our examination of man's faculties, the Real that inheres in the Ideal is [man's] temperament. God, too, has a temperament, and in the spirituality of God the latter is again the Real [element]; it relates to the *spirit* in God, to the absolute being, once again as the first power, as the foundation, or as the dark principle.[109]

What is important to take away from this passage is the internal complexity of God. As discussed previously, this is one, if not the, major differentiating factor between Schelling's and Spinoza's conceptions of God. For Spinoza, God's unity is simple, whereas for Schelling God's unity is complex and conflicted. It is through this complexity of God that the spirit world finds its materiality. "The temperament in God is thus the material for the world of spirit," Schelling claims, "as indeed the properly Real proved to be the material from which the physical world and man were created."[110] Again, there is a reality and even a materiality to the world of spirit. Schelling helpfully provides us an image to capture the relation he is describing between the world of materiality and the world of spirit. He writes that a "certain sympathy still remains between them as it exists between the strings of different instruments, where, when a tone is produced by one of them, the corresponding string of the other instrument will resonate in a sympathetic manner."[111] At first, it appears as if Schelling is describing two parallel instruments analogous with Spinoza's parallel attributes, but this is not the case. The tones themselves are Schelling's focus here. The sympathy between strings is the emergent result of the excitation of the strings. Though they are dependent upon the instrument's strings for their material support they are not reducible to these strings.

Schelling, of course, cannot end here. He primarily focused on the distinction between the world of nature and the world of spirit. To continue with the image evoked above, Schelling has described the tune played by the individual instruments but has yet to articulate the harmony of the full symphony. This harmonic reconciliation occurs in the highest potency A^3.

> Thus far we have only two periods: (a) the present one which comprises all the powers, to be sure, though in subordination to the Real; (b) the life of the spirit, which [period] also comprises all the powers, though in subordination to the Ideal. Hence there will be a third period, (c) where all [powers] will be subordinate to the absolute Identity—that is, [a period] where the spiritual or the Ideal no longer excludes the physical or the Real, but where both are subordinate to the higher [Being] together and as equals.[112]

Thus far, the life of the human spirit has taken place in the present. Even the life after death described by Schelling remains in the present. It is not an after-life but instead just an other-life. The forces that constitute the space of the spirit world are not exclusively ideal. Consistent with his claims throughout the identity philosophy, just as there is an ideal within the real, there is a reality of the ideal. The differentiation between coexistent potencies in the present occurs by way of the subordination of powers to a particular set of rules and regularities. Schelling concludes that ultimately we are not of this world. The human has natural being, but it is not a natural being. This does not mean that the human spirit is transcendent to the world, existing in full both prior and posterior to the body's worldly existence. The human spirit is instead a hollowing out of the world. It is an expression of the Absolute's fall into itself. Schelling elucidates this discussion of the place of the human between the natural and the spiritual world with a reference to theater. "Hence history," writes Schelling, "is most appropriately understood as a tragedy that is staged on a stage of mourning for which the world provides merely the floor, whereas the agents, i.e., the actors, come from an entirely different world."[113] The performance must be grounded, yet the performers must maintain a relative autonomy from this ground. They are on the stage but not of the stage. In *Clara*, we again find Schelling lucidly describing this final state as follows: "And that invisible kingdom is not as simple as many think it is; rather, if the saying holds true that each will be done by according to how he thought and acted in his corporeal life, that kingdom must look quite wonderfully diverse."[114] We can see the reciprocal relation between form and essence playing itself out here as well. The infinite and even the eternal are in some way affected by the decisions made by the individual in their physical life. There is a codetermination and a living interpenetration between the finite and temporal form of the living human and the infinite and atemporal essence of their afterlife. Further, because this afterlife is a shared one, changed in accordance with each individual essence, the ultimate unity of the potencies in A^3 is one of an identity of identity and nonidentity. It is, once again, not simple but irreducibly complex. It is, so to speak, a perfect mess.

5.0. Conclusion

What we see in Schelling's presentation of the complex structure of the human spirit and its place in the natural and spiritual worlds is that there is no simple relation between real and ideal. Each level of the human spirit consists of three powers, including the real and the ideal as well as a third that traverses the space between the two. This means that there is a conflict inscribed within each level of the soul. The active traversing is presented in the perpetual realigning of the various powers of the spirit. The spirit is therefore active at each level, and though some parts may be fuller expressions of the unity sought by the soul, each is equally important in terms of the fulfillment of this unity. This complex tripartite tripartite structure itself mediates the space between God, nature, and the world of spirit. Furthermore, though the analysis in the "Stuttgart Seminars" is presented in a linear fashion, it is essential not to take the account as a whole as the linear unfolding of a predetermined process. Hegel explains the journey taken by the Idea throughout the *Encyclopedia of the Philosophical Sciences* as follows: "The absolute idea may in this respect be compared to the old man who utters the same creed as the child, but for whom it is pregnant with the significance of a lifetime."[115] Something similar can be said of the A^3 in Schelling's account of the alienation and possible redemption of the human spirit entangled in the world of nature and the world of spirit. Remember that A^3 in all cases is untouched by any temporal constraint. It is the eternal that provides the unity of finite and infinite. Though there are pockets of linearity, just as there are localized instances of mechanistic causality in nature, this linear model cannot be generalized to the account as a whole. History is but a cut in the Absolute. However, the healing of this wound means that at the "end" of its journey the Absolute itself is somehow is changed.

Schelling never abandons key components of the philosophy of identity, and in particular, those that arise from his critique of Spinoza. The actuality of revelation and redemption is possible only by virtue of an absolute identity in which real and ideal exist in a play of mutual penetration. The dynamic of human freedom can only play itself out in the muddy and messy space opened by the rejection of any parallelism between conceptually and casually distinct attributes. What Schelling calls the "organic unity of all things" is premised upon the conflict, mutual interpenetration, and dynamic saturation of thinking and being. It is at this point that we are returned to the beginning of the "Stuttgart Seminars." There, Schelling had opened with a discussion of the relation between a system of philosophy and first principles. "What is the principle of my system?" Schelling asks. He responds by noting that in his work this principle has multiple expressions. He then lists three, (1) "as the principle of absolute [and] unconditioned identity, to be well distinguished from an absolute indifference [*Einerleiheit*]; the identity that we refer to is an *organic* unity of all things"; (2) "[t]his principle, then, found its more specific expression as the absolute identity of the *Real* and the *Ideal*"; and (3) "I expressed the principle of my philosophy in straightforward manner as the *absolute* or *God*."[116] It is at the conclusion of the seminars that this principle is realized within each individual potency. Consequently, the Absolute, or God, is present in all things. Thus, at this point "God is in all actuality everything, and pantheism will have become true."[117]

Conclusion

The Poverty of Thought and the Madness of Living Well

A core orienting principle of this book is that the pantheism controversy never came to a conclusion. The relation between rationality and totality remains an unresolved crisis that has become embedded within the very possibility of philosophy. There have been a number of studies both recent and not so recent that have returned to Jacobi and the pantheism controversy in an attempt to make the case for the relevance of German Idealism to contemporary Anglo-American philosophy. Franks's influential work ends with some poignant remarks on the relation between the history of philosophy and contemporary philosophical interests and concerns. He writes, "Studies of German idealists often claim contemporary interest on the ground that some reconstructed version of German idealism fits a description with acknowledged contemporary appeal, such as 'non-reductive naturalism.'"[1] Franks acknowledges that this kind of study is not without importance, but the value of the history of philosophy cannot be reduced to this approach. To this, Franks adds, "If, in the history of philosophy, we seek to recognize ourselves in the other, this is worthwhile only if we also recognize the other in ourselves."[2] We can still find in ourselves the fear that petrified Jacobi to his bones. Philosophy often moves like a pendulum. Throughout its history, we see the vacillation between opposing philosophical worldviews. In the present study, I began with a vacillation between idealism and realism best articulated by way of Schelling's early characterization of dogmatism and criticism. On the one hand, dogmatism was the illegitimate termination of synthetic activity on the side of the object. As a result, subjectivity was engulfed by objectivity and consequently erased. Criticism, on the other hand, through the same illegitimate termination of synthesis, swallowed the object in the subject. This once again resulted in an erasure, but this time of the objective world. In our current attempt not to be overwhelmed by the world, we seem to have lost it all together. Consequently, many contemporary realists have once again sought refuge in the world and thereby abandoned the subject that comes to know this world.

We cannot take for granted the role that this positioning of German Idealism as a response to Jacobi and the pantheism controversy plays in reestablishing the relevance of Schelling in relation to contemporary continental philosophy. The trauma of Spinozism must be recognized as continuing to constitute our philosophical milieu regarding the interconnection of our natural existence and our highest moral aspirations. Various projects such as New Realism, New Materialism, speculative realism, and other forms of postcontinental philosophies can be read as responses to problems articulated by postanalytic philosophies understood broadly as a set of coherentist epistemological projects that entail the threat of antirealism insofar as they exclude immediate access to the nonconceptual. In an attempt to combat this antirealist threat, postcontinental philosophy turns back to the real, to the world, and to immanence. This return is a significant turn back to pre-Kantian metaphysical projects, and most notably that of Spinoza. Thus, if it is the case Spinozism is the poverty of thought around which everything remains entrapped, as Schelling claims, this troubled relation between totality, rationality, reality, morality, and nature is the vortex in which we still tumble. Spinozism remains the historical bone in the throat of contemporary philosophical debates that we must recognize and wrestle with. This inheritance of the poverty of thought brings along with it a Trojan horse within the battlements of these new realisms. In order to return to the real and to the world, many contemporary realisms are explicitly or implicitly anti-idealisms. These new realisms are correct in their attempted return to realism; the world cannot be well lost. The problem, however, is that they do so in such a way that they forget the lessons of idealism. In short, the problem is a return to objectivity at the expense of any thick account of subjectivity. To exit this vortex of dogmatic realism, we need the robust resources of a systematic criticism of the core of Spinozism. It is these resources that I have attempted to construct by way of Schelling's engagement with Spinoza. First is the idea of an existence monism that accounts for ontic plurality through the notion of degrees of existence or what Schelling called quantitative differentiation. The particularity of things is the result of their nonbeing (the quantitative affirmation of the Absolute's nonidentity) and not of their qualitatively identical being. Schelling agrees with Spinoza that only one thing exists, but against the letter of the *Ethics* this one thing (the Absolute) cannot be said to exist fully.[3] For Schelling, the Absolute is not a simple identity. Instead, as I have emphasized, it is an identity of identity and nonidentity or a unity of unity and bifurcation. Consequently, the Absolute sits uncomfortably with itself; it is what it is, but it is also what it is not, and it is internally driven to resolve this apparent contradiction. The second resource we can gather from Schelling's engagement with Spinoza is the rejection of any kind of clean parallelism between the real and ideal. When we reject the doctrine of strict parallelism we open the space for a dynamic interpenetration of real and ideal more capable of accounting for the messiness of nature and mindedness without appeal to the categories of immanence and transcendence. Both of these positions are made possible by the restriction of the PSR's applicability. As Schelling argues, the net of intelligibility must itself come into being. This is how we can resolve the tension between our ability to know and describe the world of things while maintaining the unprethinkability of the Absolute from which things are eternally born and to which they maintain a specific relation.

Schelling, like Hegel, is exemplary in his approach to his philosophical predecessors. This is in large part because he endeavors to reveal the truth of his predecessors instead of just highlighting their errors. In doing so, Schelling philosophizes in such a way that he is able to spur forward philosophical discourse through an iterative historical analysis, a practice that is at its very essence of what Hegel calls the education of the Idea. This is to say, with Sellars, that "philosophy without the history of philosophy, if not empty or blind, is at least dumb."[4] I hope to have given some evidence as to why any return to realism that draws from Schelling must equally be a return to his idealism. A proper invocation of Schelling's realism necessarily requires a simultaneous return to Schelling's idealism, because, as he himself argued, neither realism nor idealism can be philosophical without the other. If we extract from Schelling realism alone, we still return to Spinozism, even against our best intentions. We can find rich resources in Spinoza's monism, but if we uncritically accept the universal scope of the PSR and Spinoza's attribute parallelism, we render ourselves incapable of accounting for the coming to be of both nature and spirit. We must embrace the messiness that follows from the rejection of parallelism if we are to make room for an account of emergence that does not presuppose that which emerges. In short, if we are to return to Schelling (and as I have argued we must if we are to exit the Spinozist vortex of contemporary realism), we must return to Schelling's ideal-realism by passing through and learning from the hyphen that binds and separates real and ideal in a relation that can only be called absolute, thereby holding open the space in which human freedom plays itself out. Otherwise, we return to nothing but a corpse.

At both the beginning and the end of the passage through Spinozism lies nothing less than madness. Schelling wrote *Philosophy and Religion* as a response to Eschenmayer's 1803 *Die Philosophie in ihrem Übergang zur Nichtphilosophie*. Therein, Eschenmayer appeals to faith in an attempt to reconcile transcendental philosophy and naturephilosophy. Of this attempt Schelling critically observes that

> it is quite impossible, on the one hand, to credit a doctrine with being a philosophy, and a complete one at that, and on the other, to declare it in need of being complemented by faith; this contradicts and nullifies its concept because its essence consists in possessing clear knowledge and intuitive cognition of that which nonphilosophy means to grasp in faith.[5]

According to Schelling, a doctrine cannot remain philosophical if it holds either that faith is necessary in order to maintain the primordial unity of transcendental philosophy and the philosophy of nature (think of Jacobi's fideistic realism of transcendence) or that faith is necessary for bridging some gap between the two disciplines. Comments such as these put Schelling's reader in an unbearably tight spot: How is it possible for Schelling to reject "faith" as a relevant philosophical category, while he comes to increasingly invoke theosophical and theological language, speaking of God, the Son, revelation etc.? Schelling's 1811 remark dismissing Jacobi's "doctrine of know nothing" cited in chapter

1 shows us that his position regarding faith as a sufficient replacement of reason in relation to the Absolute is consistent with the above 1804 condemnation of philosophies such as Eschenmayer's. Yet, once again, how are we to take seriously both Schelling's rejection of faith and his claim that only intellectual intuition or some other form of immediate, nonsensible, and nonconceptual construction of the real can articulate the systematic unity of knowledge and world? Is it not the case that Schelling has correctly identified a problem (that faith has no place in philosophy) while at the same time offering a solution (intellectual intuition) that misunderstands the question to which it is responding? The answer to these concerns lies in Schelling's expansive and pluralistic notion of what is demanded from thinking and living well.

Schelling's explicit response to the problem of faith engages not with the mode of access to the Absolute but instead with the nature of the Absolute itself. As discussed in chapter 3, for Schelling the Absolute is identical with and not separable from reason. It is only insofar as reason is absolute that it is real and only insofar as the Absolute is real that it can be rational. Further, insofar as the identity philosophy denies the primacy of the subject-object distinction, it is able to dismiss the problem of epistemic access as a schema of correspondence between subject and object. Consequently, the task of philosophy is not to articulate the correspondence between subjective knowing and objective being, or to bridge a gap between the real and the ideal. The problem of access is merely a red herring embraced by those who take the subject-object distinction as absolute. In 1801, Schelling tells us that

> [t]he standpoint of philosophy is the standpoint of reason, its kind of knowing is a knowing of things as they are in themselves, i.e., as they are in reason. It is the nature of philosophy to completely suspend all secession and externality, all difference of time and everything which mere imagination mingles with thought, in a word, to see in things only that aspect by which they express absolute reason, not insofar as they are objects of reflection, which is subject to the laws of mechanism and has duration in time.[6]

Only philosophy in its speculative form allows one to grasp the Absolute as an organic unity, and in doing so it comes to know the being of things irreducible to time and the mechanistic laws to which reflection is beholden. Consequently, there is no need of an absolute relation to an Absolute that is itself inscrutable or beyond the reproach of rationality. There is nothing inherently irrational about intellectual intuition when we follow Schelling's recasting of it as creative reason understood as an expansive practice grounded in practical rationality that is capable of expanding the scope of theoretical reason's applicability. By extension, for Schelling intellectual intuition does not play the role of passive, mystical access to the already existing; it is instead an enterprise of construction of what is, what could be, and what ought to be. Further, as we saw in Schelling's 1797 discussion of spirit, in the identity philosophy, this creative reasoning is transposed away from the subject and grounded in the absolute indifference between subject and object. It is grounded in the function of the hyphen itself, and it is through the hyphen that creative reason is able to function as a living process of self-organization.

In the *Freedom* essay—which Schelling believed to be a clearer articulation of the "unclear" *Philosophy and Religion* and its relation to idealism[7]—Schelling writes, "A system in which reason really recognized itself, would have to unify all demands of spirit as well as those of the heart and those of the moral feeling as well as those of the most rigorous understanding."[8] A system reliant on faith, feeling, or any other category impervious or external to reason alone would fail to be a system at all. It would fail to articulate the formal possibility and actual content of freedom itself. However, Schelling's antidote for the madness Jacobi fears is not some kind of sober, hyperrationalist sanity. Instead, he proposes we embrace a kind of mad rationalism, or rational madness. In fact, as discussed in chapter 6, for Schelling, "What we call the *understanding,* if it is to be an actual, living, and active understanding, is therefore properly nothing other than a *coordinated* madness."[9] This is because the "most profound essence of the human spirit—*nota bene*: only when considered in separation from the soul and thus from God—is *madness.*"[10] Madness is profound because it captures the struggle of freedom in the human: to find again the center from which they have been divided, to once again reunite their soul with the Absolute, to erase the negation of nothingness upon which both their freedom and finitude are grounded. This activity of self-reflective decomposition is primordial *as well as* coextensive with the unfolding of the real and ideal orders. It is the regulative yet real locus of organization in nature *and* in transcendental philosophy; both are united by their mutual, interpenetrating becomings (the becoming natural of the transcendental and the becoming transcendental of nature). What exactly are the elements of the coordinated madness that is the profoundest essence of the human soul? These elements would have to be a play of the four demands isolated in the previous quote from the *Freedom* essay: Namely, the demands of (1) the spirit, (2) the heart, (3) "moral feeling," and (4) "most rigorous understanding." Only in meeting *each* of these demands can thinking find satisfaction. Through coordinating madness, we come alive, and we come to know. This coordination of madness is a mirror of its own primordial origin through which reason comes to know itself; it is only through this coordinated madness that reason can find itself, to come to know itself *as* reason. This process is the Absolute's coming to know itself as actualized following its fall into itself through self-sundering auto-affection. Thus, in order to become an organ of the system of the world, we must cast aside our finitude in order to become one with the madness of the Absolute.

Notes

Introduction: A Crack in the Abyss

1. F. W. J. Schelling, *System of Transcendental Idealism*, trans. Peter Heath (Charlottesville: University Press of Virginia, 1978), 41. (I/3, 386).

2. Schelling also uses this term in the 1801 essay "On the True Concept of Philosophy of Nature and the Correct Way of Solving its Problems." F. W. J. Schelling, "On the True Concept of Philosophy of Nature and the Correct Way of Solving its Problems," in *The Schelling-Eschenmayer Controversy, 1801: Nature and Identity*, ed. Benjamin Berger and Daniel Whistler, trans. Judith Kahl and Daniel Whistler (Edinburgh: Edinburgh University Press, 2020), 50. (I/4, 86).

3. In the later lectures on revelation and positive philosophy Schelling shifts his rhetoric to focus on rationalism and empiricism instead of just realism and idealism. Though I will not make this argument herein, I think the general thematic laid down in the earlier philosophy can be demonstrated to be continuous with the later work despite this rhetorical shift.

4. G. W. F. Hegel, *Lectures on the History of Philosophy the Lectures of 1825–1826: Volume III Medieval and Modern Philosophy*, ed. Robert F. Brown, trans. R. F. Brown, J. M. Stewart, H. S. Harris (Berkeley/Los Angeles/ Oxford: University of California Press, 1990), 155.

5. Schelling, *System of Transcendental Idealism*, 17. (I/3, 356).

6. Ibid.

7. See Immanuel Kant. *Critique of Pure Reason*, trans. Norman Kemp Smith (New York: Palgrave Macmillan, 2003), A543/B571: "Were we to yield to the illusion of transcendental realism, neither nature nor freedom would remain." What exactly Kant means by "transcendental realism" is (still) up for dispute. But as we will see when discussing the Antinomies of Pure Reason, there is good reason to believe Spinoza is the transcendental realist par excellence.

8. In the 1799 *First Outline of a System of the Philosophy of Nature*, Schelling even claims that "the philosophy of nature is seen to be the Spinozism of physics." F. W. J. Schelling, *First Outline of a System of the Philosophy of Nature*, trans. Keith R. Peterson (Albany: State University of New York Press, 2004), 117 fn ★ (I/3, 160 fn 2).

9. F. W. J. Schelling, *On the History of Modern Philosophy*, trans. Andrew Bowie (Cambridge: Cambridge University Press, 1994), 65.

10. My choice here is mainly motivated by my argument that the writings of this period (roughly from late 1800 to somewhere around 1804) do not form a coherent system. To call this period of Schelling's work a single system instead of a broader philosophical endeavor covers over important distinctions that emerge and play a central role in his critique of Spinoza.

11. Daniel Whistler's *Schelling's Theory of Symbolic Language: Forming the System of Identity* (Oxford: Oxford University Press, 2013) is a notable exception here.

12. Immanuel Kant, *Opus Postumum*, trans. Eckart Förster and Michael Rosen, ed. Eckart Förster (Cambridge: Cambridge University Press, 1993), 254.

13. See ibid., 274, n. 89.

14. Ibid., 255.

15. Ibid.; emphasis mine.

16. Grant directly associates Kant's remark in the margins and Schelling's *1800 System of Transcendental Idealism*. Though in the end I agree there is a connection between the two, I believe the direct association drawn by Grant is a bit too hasty. See Grant, "Prospects for Post-Copernican Dogmatism: The Antinomies of Transcendental Naturalism," in *Collapse: Philosophical Research and Development Volume V*, ed. Damian Veal (Falmouth: Urbanomic Press, 2009), 415.

17. Schelling, *System of Transcendental Idealism*, 41. (I/3, 386).

18. G. W. F. Hegel, *The Difference Between Fichte's and Schelling's Systems of Philosophy*, trans. H. S. Harris and Walter Cerf (Albany: State University of New York Press, 1977), 155.

19. This includes Grant, Woodard, Berger, Whistler, Wirth, and for different reasons Alderwick.

20. Ben Woodard, *Schelling's Naturalism: Motion, Space, and the Volition of Thought* (Edinburgh: Edinburgh University Press, 2019). Grant is perhaps the most well-known advocate of this approach. He has argued that through and through Schelling's philosophical concerns are best understood in relation to the naturephilosophical tradition. See Iain Hamilton Grant, *Philosophies of Nature after Schelling* (London: Continuum, 2006). What is interesting and possibly problematic about the continuity thesis is that it operates on two levels. The first is internal to Schelling's texts; there is a fundamental continuity in the content and subject matter to Schelling's project. The second level has to do

with the continuity of philosophy with naturephilosophy. That is, philosophy must "explore how nature philosophizes, and how thinking nature is impossible without a concept of nature as thinking through us." Woodard, *Schelling's Naturalism*, 7. I think that taking continuity as a methodological commitment threatens to form a vicious circle between content and philosophical framework.

21. See Benjamin Berger and Daniel Whistler's commentaries in *The Schelling-Eschenmayer Controversy, 1801*.

22. Michael Vater, "Schelling's Philosophy of Identity and Spinoza's *Ethico more geometrico*," in *Spinoza and German Idealism*, ed. Eckart Förster and Yitzhak Y. Melamed (New York: Cambridge University Press, 2012), 156.

23. Jeffery A. Bernstein, "On the Relation between Nature and History in Schelling's *Freedom* Essay and Spinoza's *Theological-Political Treatise*," in *The Barbarian Principle: Merleau-Ponty, Schelling, and the Question of Nature*, ed. Jason M. Wirth and Patrick Burke (Albany: State University of New York Press, 2013), 78.

24. Joseph P. Lawrence, "Spinoza in Schelling: Appropriation through Critique," *Idealistic Studies*, 33, no. 2–3 (2003): 175.

25. F. W. J. Schelling, "Presentation of My System of Philosophy," in *The Philosophical Rupture between Fichte and Schelling: Selected Texts and Correspondence (1800–1802)*, trans. and ed. Michael G. Vater and David W. Wood (Albany: State University of New York Press, 2012), 143. (I/4, 110).

26. Unlike Hegel's reading of Spinoza, to which a number of book-length works have been dedicated, the majority of recent work on Spinoza and Schelling can be found in book chapters and articles. For example, Joseph P. Lawrence, "Spinoza in Schelling: Appropriation through Critique," *Idealistic Studies* 33, no. 2/3 (2003); Franz Knappik "What Is Wrong with Blind Necessity? Schelling's Critique of Spinoza's Necessitarianism in the Freedom Essay," *Journal of the History of Philosophy*, 57, no. 1 (2019); Dalia Nassar, "Spinoza in Schelling's Early Conception of Intellectual Intuition," in *Spinoza and German Idealism*, ed. Eckart Förster and Yitzhak Y. Melamed (Cambridge: Cambridge University Press, 2012); Michael Vater "Schelling's Philosophy of Identity and Spinoza's *Ethica more geometrico*," in *Spinoza and German Idealism* ed. Eckart Förster and Yitzhak Y. Melamed (Cambridge: Cambridge University Press, 2012); Jeffrey A. Bernstein, "On the Relation Between Nature and History"; Boris van Meurs, "Deep Ecology and Nature: Naess, Spinoza, and Schelling," *The Trumpeter* 35, no. 1 (2019); Yitzhak Y. Melamed, "*Deus Dive Vernuft*: Schelling's Transformation of Spinoza's God," in *Schelling's Philosophy: Freedom, Nature, and Systematicity*, ed. G. Anthony Bruno (Oxford: Oxford University Press, 2020); Errol E. Harris, "Schelling and Spinoza: Spinozism and Dialectic," in *Spinoza Issues and Directions: Proceedings from the Chicago Spinoza Conference*, ed. Edwin Curley and Pierre-François Moreau. (Leiden/New York/København/Köln:

E. J. Brill, 1990); Daniel Dragićević, "Schelling with Spinoza on Freedom," in *A Companion to Spinoza*, ed. Yizhak Y. Melamed (Hoboken: Wiley Blackwell, 2021).

27. Vater and Nassar isolate the role of Spinoza in Schelling's early philosophy—namely the essay "Of the I," and the *Presentation of My System of Philosophy*. Alternatively, Knappik and Bernstein focus in on Schelling's *Philosophical Investigations into the Essence of Human Freedom*.

28. A notable exception here is chapter 9 ("The Early Schelling: Between Fichte and Spinoza") in Nassar's *The Romantic Absolute: Being and Knowing in Early German Romantic Philosophy, 1795–1804* (Chicago: University of Chicago Press, 2014). Therein Nassar artfully presents Schelling's critique of Spinoza that takes place between his early essay "Of the I" and the subsequent "Philosophical Letters on Dogmatism and Criticism."

29. Robert J. Richard, *The Romantic Conception of Life: Science and Philosophy in the Age of Goethe* (Chicago: University of Chicago Press, 2002), 11.

30. Giles Deleuze, *Expressionism in Philosophy: Spinoza*, trans. Martin Joughin (New York: Zone Books, 1990), 118.

31. Martin Heidegger, *Schelling's Treatise on the Essence of Human Freedom*, trans. Joan Stambaugh (Athens: Ohio University Press, 1985), 34. Heidegger's claim here is more focused on the structure rather than the actual content of Schelling's philosophy in relation to that of Spinoza. For Heidegger, the *Ethics* is the example par excellence of the Modern conception of a philosophical system originating in Descartes and drawing its model from the mathematics of the time. Further, one cannot deny the possibility of anti-Semitism in Heidegger's exclusion of any thorough consideration of Spinoza's influence on Schelling.

32. Jason M. Wirth, *Schelling's Practice of the Wild: Time, Art, Imagination* (Albany: State University of New York Press, 2015).

33. Andrew Bowie, *Schelling and Modern European Philosophy: An Introduction* (London/New York: Routledge, 1993).

34. Nassar, *The Romantic Absolute*; Woodard, *Schelling's Naturalism*.

35. I avoid an extended engagement with Schelling's essay *On the World Soul* due to the minimal role Spinoza (explicitly) plays therein.

36. F. W. J. Schelling, *Philosophical Investigations into the Essence of Human Freedom*, trans. Jeff Love and Johannes Schmidt (Albany: State University of New York Press, 2006), 20. (I/7, 349).

37. Franz Knappik provides a detailed analysis of Schelling's criticism of Spinoza's necessitarianism in the *Freedom* essay by linking it to Leibniz's critique of Spinoza's necessitarianism as well as to the themes of divine love and divine personality in Schelling's earlier works. However, he does not extensively detail the continuity of the *Freedom* essay's critique with Schelling's previous engagements with Spinoza. "What is Wrong with Blind

Necessity? Schelling's Critique of Spinoza's Necessitarianism in the *Freedom Essay*." Therein Knappik also makes the claim relevant to the aims of this book that in Schelling's early work "Spinozism mainly figures there (a) as the most consequent version of dogmatism" (a claim not unique to Schelling), "(b) as a precursor to Schelling's own ideal-realism or his philosophy of nature," and finally "(c) as inspiration for an account of the Absolute as pure activity that is free in the sense that it only follows its own nature" (Knappik, "What Is Wrong with Blind Necessity?" 132). Because (a) is a commitment shared by most of the German Idealists, (b) and (c) will be of primary importance throughout this book.

38. Schelling, *Philosophical Investigations into the Essence of Human Freedom*, 21. (I/7, 350).

39. F. W. J. Schelling, *The Philosophy of Art*, ed. and trans. Douglas W. Stott (Minneapolis: University of Minnesota Press, 1989) 30. (I/5, 383) Stott translates "*Wechseldurchdringung*" as "mutual interpenetration."

40. Schelling, *Philosophical Investigations into the Essence of Human Freedom*, 20. (I/7, 349).

41. Ibid., 21–22. (I/7, 351).

42. Ibid., 22. (I/7, 352).

43. Ibid., 26. (I/7, 356).

44. Ibid.

45. Ibid., 20. (I/7, 349).

46. See Grant's *Philosophies of Nature after Schelling* for a more extended discussion of the problems of somatism as they relate to the division between metaphysics and physics, as well as the according of primacy to being over becoming.

47. F. W. J. Schelling, "Stuttgart Seminars," in *Idealism and the Endgame of Theory: Three Essays by F. W. J. Schelling*, trans. Thomas Pfau (Albany: State University of New York Press, 1994), 215. (I/7, 444).

48. Schelling, *First Outline for a System of the Philosophy of Nature*, 32. (I/3, 39).

49. Schelling, *System of Transcendental Idealism*, 127. (I/3, 496).

50. Schelling, *Philosophical Investigations into the Essence of Human Freedom*, 63. (I/7, 400).

51. F. W. J. Schelling, *Ages of the World*, 1815, trans. Jason M. Wirth (Albany: State University of New York Press, 2000), 90. (I/8, 321).

52. F. W. J. Schelling, "On the World Soul," trans. Iain Hamilton Grant, in *Collapse: Philosophical Research and Development Vol. V1* (Falmouth: Urbanomic, 2010), 85. (I/2, 390).

53. It is possible that Schelling's inspiration for this characterization of life is more theological than philosophical. See Matthews for the theosophical roots of Schelling's understanding of life. See chapter 2 of Bruce Matthews,

Schelling's Organic Form of Philosophy (Albany: State University of New York Press, 2012).

54. Schelling, *Philosophical Investigations into the Essence of Human Freedom*, 61. (I/7, 397).

55. F. H. Jacobi "David Hume on Faith or Idealism and Realism," in *The Main Philosophical Writings and the Novel Allwill*, trans. George Di Giovanni (Montreal and Kingston: McGill-Queens University Press, 2009) 303.

56. Stuart Brock and Edwin Mares, *Realism and Anti-Realism* (Durham: Acumen, 2007), 2.

57. See Markus Gabriel, *Fields of Sense: A New Realist Ontology* (Edinburgh: Edinburgh University Press, 2015); Maurizio Ferraris, *Manifesto of New Realism* (Albany: State University of New York Press, 2014).

58. W. V. O. Quine, "Two Dogmas of Empiricism," in *From a Logical Point of View* (Cambridge: Harvard University Press, 1980).

59. Ludwig Wittgenstein, *Philosophical Investigations*, trans. G. E. M. Anscombe, P. M. S. Hacker, and Joachim Schulte (Oxford: Wiley-Blackwell, 2009).

60. Donald Davidson, "On the Very Idea of a Conceptual Scheme," in *Inquiries into Truth and Interpretation* (Oxford: Oxford University Press, 2009).

61. Richard Rorty, *Philosophy and the Mirror of Nature* (Princeton: Princeton University Press, 1981) and, "The World Well Lost," in *Journal of Philosophy* 69, no. 19 (1972).

62. Christopher Norris, *New Idols of the Cave: On the Limits of Anti-Realism* (Manchester: Manchester University Press, 1997), 117.

63. Rom Harré and Roy Bhaskar, "How to Change Reality: Story V. Structure—A Debate between Rom Harré and Roy Bhaskar," in *After Postmodernism: An Introduction to Critical Realism*, ed. José López and Garry Potter (London/New York: The Athlone Press, 2001), 28.

64. Jacques Derrida, "White Mythology: Metaphor in the Text of Philosophy," *New Literary History* 6, no. 1, On Metaphor (Autumn 1974).

65. John Ó Maoilearca [as John Mullarkey], *Post-Continental Philosophy: An Outline* (London: Continuum, 2006), 1.

66. Ibid., 2.

67. Namely, Giles Deleuze, *The Fold: Leibniz and the Baroque*, trans. Tom Coneley (Minneapolis: University of Minnesota Press, 1993); Alain Badiou, *Being and Event*, trans. Oliver Feltham (London/New York: Continuum, 2005); Michel Henry, *Seeing the Invisible: On Kandinsky*, trans. Scott Davidson (London/New York: Continuum, 2005); and a public discussion between Derrida and Laruelle published under the title "Controversy over the Possibility of a Science of Philosophy," in *The Non-Philosophy Project: Essays by François Laruelle*, ed. Gabriel Alkon and Boris Gunjevic (New York: Telos Press, 2012).

68. Published as "Speculative Realism (Annex to *Collapse II*)," in *Collapse: Philosophical Research and Development Vol. II*, ed. Robin Mackay (Falmouth: Urbanomic Press, 2007).

69. Jacques Derrida, *Of Grammatology*, trans. Gayatri Chakravorty Spivak (Baltimore: Johns Hopkins University Press, 2016), 172.

70. Hilary Putnam, *The Many Faces of Realism: The Paul Carus Lectures* (Chicago/La Salle: Open Court, 1987), 16. Later in his life, Putnam himself was included by Ferraris and Gabriel as a "New Realist," largely due to his notion of internal realism.

71. Deborah Goldgaber, *Speculative Grammatology: Deconstruction and the New Materialism* (Edinburgh: Edinburgh University Press, 2021).

72. This return to realism and particularly the relation between the four thinkers listed above is by no means a homogeneous body of literature. In fact, they are largely divided regarding the status of something like epistemology when understood broadly as the relation between subjective mindedness and the objective world. On the one hand, Harman openly rejects epistemology altogether. Alternatively, though he does not reject epistemology outright, Meillassoux's reliance on (1) a pre-Kantian notion of intellectual intuition, and (2) the constitutive nature of what he calls the Principle of Unreason threatens his own epistemology according to which only the primary mathatizable qualities of objects are knowable as objectively real. On the other hand, Ray Brassier's work turns to Sellars in an attempt to fully develop a post-Kantian, naturalist epistemology capable of incorporating a unique brand of neuro-scientific eliminitivism in the wake of continental Heideggerianisms. Finally, Grant's work finds a similar interest in the philosophy of nature. Following Schelling, Grant asks, How is it possible to have a philosophy of nature? Or, more precisely, what is nature such that it philosophizes?

73. Meillassoux explains, "Correlationism consists in disqualifying the claim that it is possible to consider the realms of subjectivity and objectivity independently of on another." Quentin Meillassoux, *After Finitude: An Essay on the Necessity of Contingency*, trans. Ray Brassier (London: Continuum, 2008), 5. The aspect of this doctrine that attracted the ire of the speculative realists is the assumption that the objective world can only be known in subjective terms or in relation to a subject however broadly understood.

74. Keith Robinson, "Whitehead, Post-Structuralism, and Realism," in *Secrets of Becoming: Negotiating Whitehead, Deleuze, and Butler*, ed. Roland Faber and Andrea M. Stephenson (New York: Fordham University Press, 2011), 54.

75. Tyler Tritten, *The Contingency of Necessity: Reason and God as Matter of Fact* (Edinburgh: Edinburgh University Press, 2019), 52.

76. John Foster, *The Case for Idealism* (London: Routledge and Kegan Paul, 1982), 3.

77. It is almost impossible to find an actual articulation of the kind of radical constructivism that Ferraris believes to be omnipresent in contemporary philosophical discourse. I cannot honestly think of a philosopher who would need to be reminded, for example, that mountains are not social constructs: "This negativity, however, triggered an uncontrollable process, and in particular the idea that everything, including lakes and mountains, is socially constructed." Maurizio Ferraris, *Introduction to New Realism*, trans. Sarah De Sanctis (London: Bloomsbury, 2015), 17.

78. For example, Spinoza claims, "God's intellect, insofar as it is conceived as constituting God's essence, is in actual fact the cause of things, in respect both of their essence and their existence." Benedict de Spinoza, "Ethics," in *Spinoza: Complete Works*, ed. Michael L. Morgan, trans. Samuel Shirley (Indianapolis/Cambridge: Hackett, 2002), EIp17 Schol. If it is the case that God's intellect is the cause of both the essence and the existence of things, and only one thing exists, then reality is both wholly mental and wholly real. Della Rocca argues against this kind of conclusion based upon Spinoza's understanding of the parallelism between attributes (understood as their causal independence which follows from their conceptual independence). See Michael Della Rocca, *Spinoza* (New York: Routledge, 2008), 103–104.

79. This opposition also scaffolds much of Allison's reading of Kant's transcendental idealism. The idea is that transcendental realism is somehow the absolute opposite of transcendental idealism. Absolute realism is broader frame of transcendentalism in which this strict opposition between the transcendental variants of idealism and realism is rendered a real, but *local* opposition. Henry E. Allison, *Kant's Transcendental Idealism: An Interpretation and Defense* (New Haven/London: Yale University Press, 2004).

80. Ibid., 3.

81. Ibid., xiv.

82. The problem of what Kant calls "transcendental illusion."

83. Andrew Bowie, *Schelling and Modern European Philosophy: An Introduction* (London/New York: Routledge, 1993), 3.

84. Dale E. Snow, *Schelling and the End of Idealism* (Albany: State University of New York Press, 1996), 3.

85. Frederick C. Beiser, *German Idealism: The Struggle Against Subjectivism 1781–1801* (Cambridge: Harvard University Press, 2008), 3.

86. Jeremy Dunham, Iain Hamilton Grant, and Sean Watson, *Idealism: The History of a Philosophy* (Montreal and Kingston: McGill-Queen's University Press, 2011), 3.

87. Ibid., 4.

88. Ibid.

89. Ibid., 8.

90. Schelling, "Philosophical Letters on Dogmatism and Criticism," 176. (I/1, 311–12).

91. See F. W. J. Schelling, *Philosophy of Revelation (1841–1842) and Related Texts*, trans. Klaus Ottmann (Putnam: Spring Publications, 2020), 69.

Chapter 1. Reason, Realism, and Faith in Jacobi and Kant

1. See also Paul W. Franks, *All or Nothing: Systematicity, Transcendental Arguments, and Skepticism in German Idealism* (Cambridge/London: Harvard University Press, 2005); Dieter Henrich, *Between Kant and Hegel: Lectures on German Idealism*, ed. David S. Pacini (Cambridge/London: Harvard University Press, 2003); Fredrick C. Beiser, *German Idealism: The Struggle Against Subjectivism 1781–1801*; and Manfred Frank, *Philosophical Foundations of Early German Romanticism*, trans. Elizabeth Millán-Zaibert (Albany: State University of New York Press, 2008).

2. Schelling subsequently composed a lengthy criticism of this work with the equally lengthy title *Denkmal der Schrift von den göttlichen Dingen etc des Herrn Friedrich Heinrich Jacobi und der ihm in derselben gemachten Beschuldigung eines absichtlich täuschenden, Lüge redenden Atheismus* (I/8, 19–136). Schelling's general attack against Jacobi therein is that his understanding of philosophy is itself so impoverished that he cannot but conclude all philosophy to be fatalism and atheism. For more on the *Denkmal* see McGrath's *The Philosophical Foundations of the Late Schelling*, 63–71.

3. *Aus Schellings Leben, In Briefen, Zweiter Band., 1803–1820*, ed. G. L. Plitt (Leipzig: S. Hirzel, 1870), 270. Cited in Lewis S. Ford "The Controversy Between Schelling and Jacobi," *Journal of the History of Philosophy* 3, no. 1 (April 1963): 81. For a discussion of this exchange see Dale Snow's *Schelling and the End of Idealism*, 205–13.

4. Beiser nicely details and dramatizes the complex set of events that occurred in a brief span of time following the publication of Jacobi's 1785 work in Frederick C. Beiser, *The Fate of Reason: German Philosophy from Kant to Fichte* (Cambridge/London: Harvard University Press, 1987), so I refer the reader there if it is a more historical retelling of the events they seek.

5. Ibid., 48–61.

6. Ibid., 74. Beiser suggests that public debates over whether Jacobi was responsible for the death of the much beloved Mendelssohn were what brought so much public attention to what had initially been a private affair.

7. Ibid., 44.

8. Ibid., 47.

9. The forgotten history of nihilism before Nietzsche has played a significant role in this. However, more recently a growing amount of attention has been paid to the impact of Jacobi on the history of German idealism by scholars attempting to reframe post-Kantian philosophy as a more explicit response to Jacobi's provocations as well as by the theological school of Radical

Orthodoxy that seeks to rehabilitate Jacobi's criticism of philosophy and direct it against what they call "liberal theology."

10. Beiser, *The Fate of Reason*, 82.

11. David Janssens, "The Problem of Enlightenment: Strauss, Jacobi, and the Pantheism Controversy," *The Review of Metaphysics* 56, no. 3 (Mar. 2003): 611.

12. With this in mind, we can view Jacobi as a precursor to social theory of the twentieth century that views the Enlightenment's faith in reason and valorization of a particular type of rationality as detrimental to more than just philosophy.

13. F. H. Jacobi, "Concerning the Doctrine of Spinoza in Letters to Herr Moses Mendelssohn (1795)," in *The Main Philosophical Writings and the Novel Allwill*, trans. George di Giovanni (Montreal and Kingston: McGill-Queen's University Press, 2009), 181.

14. Ibid.

15. The view of Spinozism as irreligious was by no means shared by all those who embraced his work. Beiser suggests that "[w]hat was true of Spinozism in the late seventieth century did not cease to be true in the late eighteenth: it was Lutheranism without the Bible." Beiser, *The Fate of Reason*, 61.

16. Pierre Bayle, *Historical and Critical Dictionary: Selections*, trans. Richard H. Popkin (Indianapolis/Cambridge: Hackett, 1991), 288.

17. Ibid., 300–301 note N.

18. Ibid., 296–97.

19. Jacobi, "Concerning the Doctrine of Spinoza in Letters to Herr Moses Mendelssohn (1795)," 201.

20. Jacobi, "David Hume on Faith," 288.

21. Jacobi, "Concerning the Doctrine of Spinoza in Letters to Herr Moses Mendelssohn (1785)," 205.

22. Quoted in Rene Koekkoek, "Carl Schmitt and the Challenge of Spinoza's Pantheism between the World Wars," *Moral and Intellectual History* 11, issue 2 (August 2014): 333.

23. F. H. Jacobi "Concerning the Doctrine of Spinoza in Letters to Moses Mendelssohn (1789)," 372; italics removed.

24. Ibid.

25. Ibid., 370.

26. Ibid.

27. Ibid., 387.

28. Ibid., 376.

29. Ibid., 370.

30. John Milbank, "The Theological Critique of Philosophy in Hamann and Jacobi," in *Radical Orthodoxy: A New Theology*, ed. John Milbank, Catherine Pickstock, and Graham Ward (London: Routledge, 1999), 26.

31. For further discussion of McDowell and Jacobi see G. Anthony Bruno, "Jacobi's Dare: McDowell, Meillassoux, and Consistent Idealism," in *Idealism, Relativism, and Realism: New Essays on Objectivity Beyond the Analytic-Continental Divide*, ed. Dominik Finkelde and Paul M. Livingston (Berlin/Boston: De Gruyter, 2020).

32. John McDowell, *Mind and World* (Cambridge: Harvard University Press, 1996), 11.

33. Jacobi, "David Hume on Faith," 306.

34. Ibid; emphasis added. It should be noted in passing that the three sources of truth to which Jacobi here refers are Kant's Ideas of reason listed in reverse order: Ourselves (the soul), Nature (the world), and God.

35. Ibid.

36. Kant, *Critique of Pure Reason*, A307/B364.

37. Ibid., A307–308/B364.

38. See Michelle Grier, *Kant's Doctrine of Transcendental Illusion* (Cambridge: Cambridge University Press, 2001).

39. Ibid., 124.

40. In reference to the relationship between Kant's critical project and transcendental realism Grier explains that "in the *Critique*, Kant ultimately links the error exhibited by both Locke and Leibniz (that of taking appearances for things-in-themselves) up to the position he refers to as 'transcendental realism.' Although Kant's explicit references to 'transcendental realism' are scant, it does seem clear that he wishes to characterize it as an erroneous position that takes the subjective conditions of space and time, and therefore also spatiotemporal *objects* (appearances), to be given 'in themselves' independently of our sensibility." Ibid., 98.

41. Kant, *Critique of Pure Reason*, A543/B571.

42. See, for example, Ṣādiq Jalāl 'Aẓm, *The Origins of Kant's Arguments in the Antinomies* (Oxford: Oxford University Press, 1972).

43. I return to all these themes in relation to Schelling in chapter 5.

44. Omri Boehm, *Kant's Critique of Spinoza* (Oxford: Oxford University Press, 2014), 1.

45. Ibid., 91.

46. Ibid.

47. Franks, *All or Nothing*, 98–108.

48. Boehm, *Kant's Critique of Spinoza*, 132.

49. Ibid., 150.

50. Ibid., 153.

51. Ibid.

52. Ibid.

53. Ibid., 185.

54. Kant, *Critique of Pure Reason*, A444/B472.
55. Ibid., A445/B473.
56. Ibid., A466/B494.
57. Milbank, "The Theological Critique of Philosophy in Hamann and Jacobi," 32.
58. Ibid.
59. Benjamin D. Crowe, "F. H. Jacobi on Faith, or What it Takes to Be an Irrationalist," *Religious Studies*, 45, no. 3 (Sept. 2009): 311.
60. Ibid., 317.
61. Ibid., 321.
62. Ibid., 311.
63. Ibid., 323.
64. Jacobi, "David Hume on Faith," 255.
65. Ibid.
66. Milbank, "The Theological Critique of Philosophy in Hamann and Jacobi," 26.
67. Jacobi, "David Hume on Faith," 256.
68. Bruno, "Jacobi's Dare," 39.
69. Jacobi, "David Hume on Faith," 291.
70. Ibid., 290.
71. Ibid., 291.
72. Ibid., 322.
73. Ibid., 316.
74. Ibid., 322.
75. Ibid., 323.
76. Ford, "The Controversy Between Schelling and Jacobi," 86.
77. Jacobi, "Concerning the Doctrine of Spinoza in Letters to Moses Mendelssohn (1789)," 348.
78. Jay M. Bernstein, "Remembering Isaac: On the Impossibility and Immorality of Faith," in *The Insistence of Art: Aesthetic Philosophy After Early Modernity*, ed. Paul A. Kottman (New York: Fordham University Press, 2017), 265.
79. Ferraris, *Introduction to New Realism*, 43.
80. Schelling, *Philosophy of Revelation*, 78. For a discussion of abstraction particularly in relation to Schelling's philosophy of identity, see Berger and Whistler's *The Schelling-Eschinmeyer Controversy, 1801*, 162–83.
81. Jacobi, "Concerning the Doctrine of Spinoza in Letters to Herr Moses Mendelssohn (1785)," 188.
82. Ibid., 189.
83. Ibid.
84. Jeremy Proulx, *The Provocation of Nihilism: Practical Philosophy and Aesthetics in Jacobi, Kant, and Schelling*, Unpublished Dissertation (https://macsphere.mcmaster.ca/handle/11375/19361), 25–26.

85. Ibid., 26.
86. Karin Nisenbaum, *For the Love of Metaphysics: Nihilism and the Conflict of Reason from Kant to Rosenzweig* (Oxford: Oxford University Press, 2018), 37.
87. Ibid., 42–43.
88. Ibid., 45.
89. Jacobi, "David Hume on Faith," 322.
90. Ibid.

Chapter 2. Weak Weapons in the Fight against Dogmatism

1. F. W. J. Schelling, *Historisch-Kritische Ausgabe* (Stuttgart: Frommann-Holzboog, 1976–), 3/I:22.
2. F. W. J. Schelling, "Of the I as Principle of Philosophy, or On the Unconditional in Human Knowledge," in *The Unconditional in Human Knowledge: Four Early Essays (1794–1796)*, trans. Fritz Marti (Lewisburg: Bucknell University Press, 1980), 64. (I/1, 151).
3. Ibid., 69. (I/1, 159).
4. "Of the I" contains a critique of Spinoza similar to that of the *Philosophical Letters on Dogmatism and Criticism*, but the latter text systematizes this critique in relation to realism and idealism more generally. Consequently, I have decided to begin with this later 1795 essay. See Dalia Nassar's "Spinoza in Schelling's Early Conception of Intellectual Intuition" for further discussion of Spinoza's role in "Of the I."
5. F. W. J. Schelling, "Philosophical Letters on Dogmatism and Criticism," in *The Unconditional in Human Knowledge: Four Early Essays (1794–1796)*, trans. Fritz Marti (Lewisburg: Bucknell University Press, 1980), 156. (I/1, 283).
6. Ibid., 169. (I/1, 303).
7. Ibid., 161. (I/1, 290).
8. Ibid., 175–76. (I/1, 311–12).
9. Ibid., 157–58. (I/1, 285).
10. Ibid., 158. (I/1, 286).
11. Ibid., 158–59. (I/1, 287).
12. Ibid., 169. (I/1, 301–302).
13. Ibid., 165; italics removed. (I/1, 296).
14. Ibid.; italics removed.
15. Ibid.
16. Kant, *Critique of Pure Reason*, B19.
17. Ibid., A6/ B10.
18. Schelling, "Philosophical Letters on Dogmatism and Criticism,"165. (I/1, 296).
19. Kant, *Critique of Pure Reason*, B131.

20. Ibid., B133.
21. Schelling, "Philosophical Letters on Dogmatism and Criticism," 164. (I/1, 294).
22. Ibid., 163. (I/1, 293).
23. Ibid., 166. (I/1, 297).
24. Ibid., 165. (I/1, 296).
25. Ibid.; italics removed.
26. Ibid.; italics removed.
27. J. G. Fichte, *The Science of Knowledge*, ed. and trans. Peter Heath and John Lachs (Cambridge: Cambridge University Press, 1982), 120.
28. Kant, *Critique of Pure Reason*, A497/B525.
29. Grier systematizes this process in the following syllogism:

i. If the conditioned is given, the entire series of conditions is likewise given.

ii. Objects of the senses are given as conditioned.

iii. Therefore, the entire series of all conditions of objects of the senses is already given.

Grier, *Kant's Doctrine of Transcendental Illusion*, 175.
30. Schelling, "Philosophical Letters on Dogmatism and Criticism," 166. (I/1, 297).
31. Ibid. (I/1, 298).
32. Ibid.
33. Ibid., 169. (I/1, 302).
34. Ibid., 166. (I/1, 298).
35. Ibid., 166–67. (I/1, 298).
36. Ibid., 166. (I/1, 298).
37. Ibid., 173–74. (I/1, 306).
38. Immanuel Kant, *Critique of Practical Reason*, trans. Werner S. Pluhar (Indianapolis: Hackett, 2002), 129.
39. J. G. Fichte, *Science of Knowledge: With the First and Second Introductions*, trans. Peter Heath and John Lachs (Cambridge: Cambridge University Press, 1982), 117.
40. Novalis, "Miscellaneous Observations," in *Philosophical Writings*, ed. and trans. Margaret Mahony Stoljar (Albany: State University of New York Press, 1997), 23.
41. Schelling, "Philosophical Letters on Dogmatism and Criticism," 174. (I/1, 310).
42. J. G. Fichte *Introductions to the* Wissenschaftslehre *and Other Writings (1797–1800)*, trans. and ed. Daniel Breazeale (Indianapolis: Hackett, 1994), 98.

43. Ibid.
44. Schelling, "Philosophical Letters on Dogmatism and Criticism," 177. (I/1, 313).
45. Ibid.
46. Ibid. (I/1, 314).
47. Ibid.
48. Ibid. 178. (I/1, 315).
49. Ibid. (I/1, 316).
50. Ibid. (I/1, 315).
51. Ibid.
52. Ibid.
53. Kant explains, "We then assert that the conditions of the *possibility of experience* in general are likewise conditions of the *possibility of the objects of experience,* and that for this reason they have objective validity in synthetic *a priori* judgment." Kant, *Critique of Pure Reason*, A158/B197.
54. Ibid., A92/B124.
55. Ibid., A92/B125.
56. Ibid., B274.
57. Ibid., B275.
58. Rene Descartes, "Meditations on First Philosophy," in *The Philosophical Writings of Descartes Volume II*, trans. John Cottingham, Robert Stoothoff, and Dugald Murdoch (Cambridge: Cambridge University Press, 1984), 17; emphasis added.
59. Kant, *Critique of Pure Reason*, B275.
60. Ibid.
61. Ibid., B276.
62. Ibid.; emphasis added.
63. Beiser, *German Idealism*, 106.
64. Ibid., 110.
65. Kant, *Critique of Pure Reason*, B276.
66. Ibid., B278.
67. Ibid., A228/B280.
68. Schelling, *Philosophy of Revelation*, 73–75.
69. Kant, *Critique of Pure Reason*, B71.
70. Ibid., B 307.
71. Nassar, *The Romantic Absolute*, 6.
72. Kant, *Critique of Pure Reason*, Bxl.
73. Nassar, *The Romantic Absolute*, 7.
74. Schelling, "Philosophical Letters on Dogmatism and Criticism," 180–81. (I/1, 318).
75. Ibid., 181. (I/1, 318–19).
76. Ibid. (I/1, 319).
77. Fichte, *Introductions to the* Wissenschaftslehre *and Other Writings*, 99 fn.

78. F. W. J. Schelling, *Ideas for a Philosophy of Nature as Introduction to the Study of This Science*, trans. Errol E. Harris and Peter Heath (Cambridge: Cambridge University Press, 1988), 27. (I/2, 36).

79. In his 1810 "Stuttgart Seminars," given one year after the *Letters*'s second publication, Schelling nicely recapitulates the ultimate shortcoming in Spinoza's system as outlined initially in the Letters. "To be sure," he writes, "Spinoza claims that thinking and substance (= the Ideal and the Real) both belong to the same substance and function as its attributes; he altogether fails, however, to think with any precision this very substance of which they are considered attributes, determining it through the empty concept of an identity (empty because of the lack of opposition), which is tantamount to ignoring it rather than making *it* the principal object of his philosophy. *Precisely* at this point, which Spinoza does not investigate any further, precisely here the concept of a living God can be found, namely, God as the supreme personality. Hence it is altogether true [to say] that Spinoza at the very least ignores the personality of the supreme Being, if he does not positively deny it." F. W. J. Schelling, "Stuttgart Seminars," in *Idealism and the Endgame of Theory: Three Essays by F. W. J. Schelling*, ed. and trans. Thomas Pfau (Albany: State University of New York Press, 1994), 214. (I/7, 443–444). Though Spinoza understands that the real and ideal must somehow be united in a larger unity, he is unable to posit a real opposition between the two. He is unable to account for the genesis of the real and the ideal. Right beyond the reach of Spinoza's thought is the concept of a living God.

80. Schelling, "Philosophical Letters on Dogmatism and Criticism," 161. (I/1, 290).

81. Ibid., 167. (I/1. 299).

82. Ibid., 158. (I/1, 286).

83. Ibid., 175. (I/1, 310).

84. Ibid., 175. (I/1, 311).

85. Snow, *Schelling and the End of Idealism*, 54.

86. Immanuel Kant, *Groundwork for the Metaphysics of Morals*, ed. and trans. Allen W. Wood (New Haven/London: Yale University Press, 2002), 63.

87. Kant, *Critique of Practical Reason*, 134.

88. Ibid., 203; italics removed.

89. Schelling, "Philosophical Letters on Dogmatism and Criticism," 156–57. (I/1,284).

90. Ibid., 185. (I/1,325).

91. Ibid., 189. (I/1, 331).

92. Ibid., 188. (I/1, 330).

93. Derrida, *Of Grammatology*, 157.

94. J. G. Fichte, "[First] Introduction to the *Wissenschaftslehre*," in *Introductions to the* Wissenschaftslehre *and Other Writings (1797–1800)*, ed. and trans. Daniel Breazeale (Indianapolis/Cambridge: Hackett, 1994), 20.

95. Schelling, "Philosophical Letters on Dogmatism and Criticism," 171–72. (I/1, 306).

Chapter 3. Spinoza and Schelling on Identity and Difference

1. F. W. J. Schelling, *The Ages of the World (1815)*, trans. Jason M. Wirth (Albany: State University of New York Press, 2000), 104. (I/8, 339).

2. Ibid. (I/1, 339–40). Malamed utilizes this quotation to make a similar point, yet admits he is unclear of the dark feeling to which Schelling refers. "*Deus sive Vernuft*: Schelling's Transformation of Spinoza's God," 96.

3. F. W. J. Schelling, "Presentation of My System of Philosophy (1801)," in *The Philosophical Rupture between Fichte and Schelling: Selected Texts and Correspondence (1800–1802)*, trans. and ed. Michael G. Vater and David W. Wood (Albany: State University of New York Press, 2012), 144. (I/4, 112).

4. Schelling, "Philosophical Letters on Dogmatism and Criticism," 163. (I/1, 293).

5. Ibid., (I/1, 294).

6. Interestingly, Schelling himself refuses to do this. In his lectures on the Philosophy of Revelation, he insists that the "only one certifiably acknowledged" articulation of the identity philosophy "by the author as authentic" is the 1801 "Presentation of My System of Philosophy" as published in Volume 2 Issue 2 of the *Zeitschrift für [Spekulative] Physik*. See Schelling, *Philosophy of Revelation*, 73.

7. F. W. J. Schelling, *Philosophy and Religion*, trans. Klaus Ottmann (Putnam: Spring Publications, 2014), 8. (I/6. 17).

8. For a more historically sensitive reconstruction of Spinoza's definitions, axioms, and arguments more generally see Martin Lin, *Being and Reason: An Essay on Spinoza's Metaphysics* (Oxford: Oxford University Press, 2019).

9. Much of the current literature on the theme of identity in Spinoza focuses on the identity of mind and body as it relates to contemporary debates in the philosophy of mind and the cognitive sciences. As Michael Pauen notes, "Spinoza develops his theory of mind from his own fundamental conceptual presuppositions concerning the essence of substance and its attributes." Michael Pauen, "Spinoza and the Theory of Identity (2P1–13)," in *Spinoza's Ethics: A Collective Commentary*, ed. Michael Hampe, Ursula Renz, Robert Schnepf (Leiden: Brill, 2011), 82. The present chapter takes the larger view of identity in Spinoza by articulating these conceptual presuppositions. Further, Pauen makes the claim that "there is a long and winding road which leads from Spinoza through Schelling, Oken, Fechner and Alois Riehl to one of the founders of 20th century identity theory: Herbert Feigl," "Spinoza and the Theory of Identity (2P1–13)," 94.

10. Schelling, "Of the I," 72. (I/1, 163).
11. Friedrich Hölderlin, "Judgment Being Possibility (1795)," in *Classic and Romantic German Aesthetics*, ed. J. M. Bernstein. (Cambridge: Cambridge University Press, 2003).
12. Schelling, *First Outline of a System of the Philosophy of Nature*, 27, note ✶. (I/3. 31 note 1).
13. Ibid., 28. (I/3, 33).
14. Schelling, "Of the I," 64. (I/1, 151).
15. Schelling, "Presentation of My System of Philosophy," 141. (I/4, 107).
16. Ibid.
17. Ibid. (I/4, 108).
18. Ibid., 142–43. (I/4, 110).
19. Ibid., 145. (I/1, 113).
20. Vater, "Schelling's Philosophy of Identity and Spinoza's *Ethica more geometrico*," 158.
21. Melamed, "*Deus Sive Vernuft*: Schelling's Transformation of Spinoza's God," 94.
22. Spinoza, *Ethics*, Id4.
23. Ibid., Id5.
24. See Michael Della Rocca, "A Rationalist Manifesto: Spinoza and the Principle of Sufficient Reason," *Philosophical Topics* 31, nos. 1&2 (Fall 2003).
25. Spinoza, Letter 76 to Alfred Burg, 949. "For I do not presume to have found the best philosophy, but I know that what I understand is the true one." Cited in, F. W. J. Schelling, *Statement on the True Relationship of the Philosophy of Nature to the Revised Fichtean Doctrine: An Elucidation of the Former*, trans. Dale E. Snow (Albany: State University of New York Press, 2018), 9.
26. Della Rocca, *Spinoza*, 4.
27. Ibid., 5.
28. Ibid., 6.
29. Alderwick's recent book correctly emphasizes the role of monism in the identity philosophy but does not connect it directly back to the PSR and the issue of explicability. See Charlotte Alderwick, *Schelling's Ontology of Powers* (Edinburgh: Edinburgh University Press, 2021).
30. Michael Della Rocca, "Rationalism, Idealism, Monism, and Beyond," in *Spinoza and German Idealism*, ed. Yizhak Y. Melamed (Cambridge: Cambridge University Press, 2012), 16.
31. Ibid.
32. Jonathan Schaffer. "Monism: The Priority of the Whole," *Philosophical Review* 119, no. 1 (2010): 33.
33. Benedict de Spinoza, "Letter 12," in *Spinoza: Complete Works*, trans. Samuel Shirley, ed. Michael L. Morgan (Indianapolis: Hackett, 2002), 788.

34. Terry Hogan and Matjaž Potrč, "Existence Monism Trumps Priority Monism," in *Spinoza on Monism*, ed. Phillip Goff (Hampshire: Palgrave Macmillan, 2012), 51–52.

35. Terry Hogan and Matjaž Potrč, *Austere Realism: Contextual Semantics Meets Minimal Ontology* (Cambridge/London: The MIT Press, 2008), 3.

36. Ibid., 189.

37. Ibid., 1.

38. Schelling, "Presentation of My System of Philosophy," 147. (I/4, 116).

39. Errol E. Harris, "Schelling and Spinoza: Spinozism and Dialectic," in *Spinoza: Issues and Directions*, ed. Edwin Curley and Pierre-François Moreau (Linden/New York/København/Köln: E. J. Brill, 1990).

40. Schelling, "Presentation of My System of Philosophy," 145. (I/4, 114).

41. Ibid., 146. (I/4, 115).

42. Vater, "Schelling's Philosophy of Identity and Spinoza's *Ethica more geometrico*," 162.

43. Schelling, "Presentation of My System of Philosophy," 146. (I/4, 115).

44. Ibid.

45. Ibid., 147. (I/4, 116).

46. Spinoza, EId3.

47. Schelling, "Presentation of My System of Philosophy," 147. (I/4, 116).

48. Ibid., 150. (I/4, 121).

49. Berger and Whistler, *The Schelling-Eschenmayer Controversy, 1801*, 137.

50. F. W. J. Schelling, *Bruno or On the Natural and the Divine Principle of Things*, ed. and trans. Michael G. Vater (Albany: State University of New York Press, 1984), 136. (I/4, 236).

51. Hegel, *The Difference Between Fichte's and Schelling's Systems of Philosophy*, 156.

52. Manfred Frank, "'Identity of identity and non-identity': Schelling's Path to the "Absolute System of Identity,'" trans. Ian Alexander Moore, in *Interpreting Schelling: Critical Essays* ed. Lara Ostric (Cambridge: Cambridge University Press, 2014), 120.

53. Michael G. Vater, "Introduction," in F. W. J. Schelling, *Bruno or On the Natural and the Divine Principle of Things*, ed. and trans. Michael G. Vater (Albany: State University of New York Press, 1984), 25.

54. Nassar, *The Romantic Absolute*.

55. Schelling, *Bruno*, 136. (I/4, 236).

56. Ibid., 137. (I/4, 236–37).

57. Vater, "Introduction," 25.

58. F. W. J. Schelling, "System of Philosophy in General and of the Philosophy of Nature in Particular," in *Idealism and The Endgame of Theory:*

Three Essays by F. W. J. Schelling, trans. Thomas Pfau (Albany: State University of New York Press, 1994), 146. (I/6, 145).

59. Ibid., 141. (I/6, 137).

60. Schelling, "Of the I," 71. (I/1, 162).

61. Ibid.

62. Schelling, "System of Philosophy in General and of the Philosophy of Nature in Particular," 141. (I/6, 138).

63. Ibid., 142. (I/6, 139).

64. Ibid., 143. (I/6, 140).

65. Ibid. (I/6, 141).

66. Ibid., 146. (I/6, 145).

67. Ibid. (I/6, 146).

68. Ibid., 148. (I/6, 148).

69. Ibid., 156. (I/6, 160).

70. Ibid. (I/6, 161).

71. Matthews, *Schelling's Organic Form of Philosophy*, 185.

72. Iain Hamilton Grant, "Everything is Primal Germ or Nothing Is: The Deep Field Logic of Nature," *Symposium* 19, issue 1 (Spring 2015): 115.

73. Grant, *Philosophies of Nature After Schelling*, 176.

74. Schelling, *Philosophical Investigations into the Essence of Human Freedom*, 17. (I/7, 345).

75. Ibid. (I/7, 345–46).

76. Manfred Frank, *"Reduplikative Identität": Der Schulüssel zu Schillings reifer Philosophie* (Stuttgart: Frommann-Holzboog, 2018), 107.

77. Ibid., 108.

78. Ibid., 104–10.

79. Ibid., 107.

80. Bayle, *Historical and Critical Dictionary*, 296–97.

81. Alderwick, *Schelling's Ontology of Powers*, 117.

82. Schelling, *Philosophy of Revelation*, 73.

83. Ibid.

84. For a brilliant analysis of this see Ursula Renz, *The Explicability of Experience: Realism and Subjectivity in Spinoza's Theory of the Human Mind* (Oxford: Oxford University Press, 2018).

85. See ibid., iv.

86. Knox Peden, *Spinoza contra Phenomenology: French Rationalism from Cavaillès to Deleuze* (Stanford: Stanford University Press, 2014), 6.

87. This debate is incredibly complex. In the following, I will only focus in broad strokes upon the issue of the existence of finite particulars. This question regards not just how finite particulars exists, but if they even exist at all.

88. Yitzhak Y. Melamed, *Spinoza's Metaphysics: Substance and Thought* (Oxford: Oxford University Press, 2013), 4.

89. Lin offers the following "noncomprehensive" list of possible objections:

"(1) the definition of mode makes no mention of causality and instead describes them as states (*affectiones*); (2) Spinoza argues for the causal relation between substance and mode in 1p15 and 1p16, which would be odd if modes causally depended on God by definition; (3) God would not be omniscient, indeed wouldn't have any ideas at all, if his relationship to ideas was merely causal and they didn't inhere in him; and (4) if modes did not inhere in God then they wouldn't be immanently caused by him contrary to what Spinoza asserts in 1p18" Lin, *Being and Reason*, 106.

90. Spinoza, "Letter 12," 788.
91. Melamed, *Spinoza's Metaphysics*, 48.
92. Ibid., 7.
93. Lin, *Being and Reason*, 113.
94. Ibid., 128.
95. Deleuze, *Expressionism in Philosophy*, 197.
96. Róbert Mátyási, "Spinoza on Composition, Monism, and Beings of Reason," *Journal of Modern Philosophy* 2, no. 1 (2020): 1.
97. Benedict de Spinoza, "Short Treatise on God, Man, and His Well-Being," in *Spinoza: Complete Works* trans. Samuel Shirley, ed. Michael L. Morgan (Indianapolis: Hackett, 2002), 44.
98. Della Rocca, "Rationalism, Idealism, Monism, and Beyond," 16.
99. "Finally, a Being of Reason is nothing but a mode of thinking, which serves the more easily to retain, explain, and imagine things that are understood." Benedict de Spinoza, "Principles of Cartesian Philosophy *and* Metaphysical Thoughts," in *Spinoza: Complete Works* trans. Samuel Shirley, ed. Michael L. Morgan (Indianapolis: Hackett, 2002), 178.
100. Schelling, "Presentation of My System of Philosophy," 151. (I/4, 123).
101. Ibid.
102. Ibid., 155. (I/4, 131).
103. Though Schelling at times artfully avoids the anthropomorphizing practice of attributing pronouns to God, the texts under consideration in this section do not. I will follow Schelling's usage of pronouns largely for the sake of clarity.
104. Schelling, "System of Philosophy in General and of the Philosophy of Nature in Particular," 162. (I/6, 169).
105. Ibid., 186. (I/6, 203).

106. Christopher Lauer, *The Suspension of Reason in Hegel and Schelling* (London/New York: Continuum, 2010), 89.
107. Schelling, "System of Philosophy in General and of the Philosophy of Nature in Particular," 186–87. (I/6, 203–204).
108. Ibid., 187. (I/6, 204).
109. Ibid.
110. Schelling, "Presentation of My System of Philosophy," 158. (I/4, 136).
111. Spinoza, "Letter 50," 892.
112. James Dodd "Expression in Schelling's Early Philosophy," *Graduate Faculty Philosophy Journal* 27, no. 2 (2006): 125–26.
113. Ibid., 131.
114. Ibid., 134.
115. Ibid.
116. Ibid., 137.
117. Schelling, "System of Philosophy in General and of the Philosophy of Nature in Particular," 176. (I/6, 189).
118. Dodd, "Expression in Schelling's Early Philosophy," 135.
119. Schelling, "System of Philosophy in General and of the Philosophy of Nature in Particular," 177. (I/6, 191).
120. Ibid., 178. (I/6, 192).
121. Ibid., 192. (I/6, 211).
122. Dodd, "Expression in Schelling's Early Philosophy," 136.
123. Slavoj Žižek, *Sex and the Failed Absolute* (London/New York: Bloomsbury Academic, 2020), 123.
124. Lauer, *The Suspension of Reason in Hegel and Schelling*, 91.
125. Thomas Pfau, "Identity before Subjectivity: Schelling's Critique of Transcendentalism, 1974–1810," in *Idealism and the Endgame of Theory: Three Essays by F. W. J. Schelling*, trans. and ed. by Thomas Pfau (Albany: State University of New York Press, 1994), 43.

Chapter 4. Realism, Idealism, and Parallelism

1. Schelling, "Presentation of My System of Philosophy," 142. (I/4, 108–109).
2. Schelling, *Philosophy and Religion*, 12. (I/6, 22).
3. Ibid.
4. Schelling, *Philosophical Investigations into the Essence of Human Freedom*, 20. (I/7, 349).
5. F. W. J. Schelling, *The Grounding of Positive Philosophy: The Berlin Lectures*, trans. Bruce Matthews (Albany: State University of New York Press, 2007), 126. (II/3, 54).

6. F. H. Jacobi, "Letter to Fichte," in *The Main Philosophical Writings and the Novel* Allwill, trans. George di Giovanni (Montreal and Kingston: McGill-Queen's University Press, 2009), 502.

7. Fichte, for example, writes in the second introduction to the *Wissenschaftslehre*, "For the idealist, nothing is positive but freedom, and, for him, being is but a negation of freedom. . . . In contrast, the dogmatist believes that his system possesses a secure foundation in being, which he considers to be something that cannot be further examined and that requires no further ground for foundation; hence he finds the idealist's claim to be a folly and a horror, for it—and it alone—threatens his very existence." Fichte, "Second Introduction to the *Wissenschaftslehre* for Readers Who Already Have a Philosophical System of Their Own," in *Introductions to the* Wissenschaftslehre *and Other Writings (1797–1800)*, ed. and trans. Daniel Breaseale (Indianapolis/Cambridge: Hackett, 1994), 84.

8. J. G. Fichte and F. W. J. Schelling, "Correspondence 1800–1802," in *The Philosophical Rupture between Fichte and Schelling: Selected Texts and Correspondence (1800–1802)*, ed. and trans. Michael G. Vater and David W. Wood (Albany: State University of New York Press, 2012), 42.

9. In *Philosophies of Nature after Schelling*, Grant goes to great lengths to show how an opposition to Fichtean philosophy is constitutive of Schelling's philosophy of nature. See chapter 3 "Antiphysics and Neo-Fichteanism."

10. Fichte and Schelling, "Correspondence 1800–1802," 62.

11. Ibid., 73.

12. Ibid.

13. Ibid., 75.

14. Ibid.

15. Schelling, *Statement on the True Relationship of the Philosophy of Nature to the Revised Fichtean Doctrine*, 49. (I/7, 53–54).

16. Ibid., 8. (I/7, 11).

17. We must acknowledge that this appeal, though it does not explicitly mention Jacobi, is possibly motivated by a kind of mean-spiritedness on the part of Schelling. Jacobi's open letter to Fichte, which likewise speaks of the phantoms generated by Fichte's philosophy, caused a great deal of problems for Fichte professionally. It of course fueled the atheism controversy that pushed Fichte from Jena to Berlin.

18. Schelling, "On the True Concept of Philosophy of Nature and the Correct Way of Solving its Problems," 53. (I/4, 91).

19. Fichte and Schelling, "Correspondence 1800–1802," 75.

20. Schelling, "Presentation of My System of Philosophy," 142. (I/4, 109).

21. Ibid.

22. Ibid.

23. Schelling, *System of Transcendental Idealism*, 14. (I/3, 352).

24. Schelling, "On the True Concept of Philosophy of Nature and the Correct Way of Solving its Problems," 50. (I/4, 86).

25. Grant, "Everything is Primal Germ or Nothing is: The Deep Field Logic of Nature, 124.

26. Schelling, "On the True Concept of Philosophy of Nature and the Correct Way of Solving its Problems," 48. (I/4, 84).

27. Schelling, *HKA*, 3/1:22.

28. Against this self-assessment, Whistler suggest that there is a continuity between Schelling and Spinoza regarding the Idea: "In fact, the Platonic terminology hides a Spinozist meaning as well. Spinozan ideas are acts by which substance affirms itself ideally; they are immanent affirmations of substance in thought. The same is true for Schelling: ideas are productions of essence in determinate forms. The major difference between Schelling and Spinoza here is that Spinozan ideas are purely ideal, whereas Schellingian ideas are defined as the identity or indifference of ideal and real. They are metaphysical entities, not purely epistemological ones." Whistler, *Schelling's Theory of Symbolic Language*, 95.

29. Schelling, "System of Philosophy in General and of the Philosophy of Nature in Particular," 172. (I/6, 183).

30. Della Rocca, *Spinoza*, 90.

31. Schelling, *Bruno*, 143. (I/4, 244).

32. Ibid. (I/4, 243).

33. Ibid., 155; emphasis mine. (I/4, 255).

34. Grant, *Philosophies of Nature After Schelling*, 189.

35. Schelling, "Presentation of My System of Philosophy," 142–43. (I/4, 109–10).

36. Ibid., 144. (I/4, 111–12).

37. Schelling, *Ideas for a Philosophy of Nature*, 15. (I/2, 20).

38. Ibid., 54. (I/2, 71–72).

39. Schelling *Ages of the World (1815)*, 105. (I/8, 340).

40. "Attributes are univocal conditions of God's existence, and also of his action." Deleuze, *Expressionism in Philosophy*, 102.

41. Ibid., 100.

42. *Spinoza*, 101–102.

43. On Della Rocca's own account, Spinoza can be read as an idealist, but only in a very limited sense. Della Rocca claims that if "[t]he nature of each thing consists, at least in part, in the thing's availability to thought," then Spinoza can be taken as a kind of idealist. Della Rocca, "Rationalism, Idealism, Monism, and Beyond," 13. Insofar as the order and connection of ideas is the same as the order and connection of things, one cannot give a reason for why a thing would exist for which there is no corresponding idea. That is, for something to exist *and* be fundamentally unintelligible is

impossible. Further, Della Rocca takes a hardline stance on Spinoza's account of the relation between conception and causation, namely, he maintains that conception *is* causation and to be caused is just to be conceived. This of course ties back to the role of the PSR and the prohibition against sharp breaks in reality; if there is no conceivable, articulable *reason* for the division between two things, this division is not just epistemologically inconceivable, it is ontologically impossible as well. Della Rocca uses this reasoning to argue against a more generalized reading of Spinoza's idealism. If idealism is the commitment that "mind and body are identical and, more generally, that physical things just are mental things, and also holds that the mental properties of a thing explain and are more fundamental than its physical properties," then Spinoza cannot be an idealist. Della Rocca, *Spinoza*, 103. This is because the conceptual independence of thought and extension excludes the possibility of reducing one to the other. Consequently, just as Spinoza is not an idealist in this sense, he is not a reductive physicalist either.

44. Lin, *Being and Reason*, 74.

45. Noa Shein, "The False Dichotomy Between Objective and Subjective Interpretations of Spinoza's Theory of Attributes," *British Journal for the History of Philosophy* 17, no. 3 (2009): 506.

46. Schelling, *Fernere Darstellungen aus dem System der Philosophie* (I/4, 372–90). In his discussion of Spinoza in the *Further Presentation*, Schelling turns to intellectual intuition and the Idea in an attempt to reconcile the duality of Spinoza's attributes in the unity of substance. It seems safe to assume based on his work following this 1802 addendum to the *Presentation* that Schelling viewed this as a failed attempt.

47. Lin, *Being and Reason*, 75.

48. Schelling, "Presentation of My System of Philosophy," 145. (I/4, 114).

49. Ibid., 147. (I/4, 116).

50. F. W. J. Schelling, "Treatise Explicatory of the Idealism in the *Science of Knowledge*," in *Idealism and the Endgame of Theory: Three Essays by F. W. J. Schelling*, trans. and ed. Thomas Pfau (Albany: State University of New York Press, 1994), 65. (I/1, 350).

51. Ibid.

52. Ibid., 66. (I/1, 350).

53. Karl Ameriks, *Kantian Subjects: Critical Philosophy and Late Modernity* (Oxford: Oxford University Press, 2019), 159–60.

54. Ibid., 160.

55. Schelling, "Treatise Explicatory of the Idealism in the *Science of Knowledge*," 82. (I/1, 372).

56. Ibid.

57. Ibid., 78–79. (I/1, 367).

58. Ibid., 82. (I/1, 372).

59. Ibid., 89–90. (I/1, 382).
60. Ibid., 92. (I/1, 386).
61. Ibid.
62. Ibid., 93 (I/1, 338).
63. Ibid., 111. (I/1, 413–14).
64. Schelling, "System of Philosophy in General and the Philosophy of Nature in Particular," 144. (I/6, 143).
65. In the 1815 *Weltalter*, Schelling writes, "Instead of the living conflict between the unity and duality of both the so-called attributes and substance being the main object, Spinoza only occupies himself with them as both opposed, indeed, with each for itself, without their unity coming into language as the active, living copula of both substance and attribute. Hence the lack of life and progression in his system." Schelling, *Ages of the World (1815)*, 105. (I/8, 340).
66. Ibid.
67. Schelling, *Statement on the True Relationship of the Philosophy of Nature to the Revised Fichtean Doctrine*, 14. (I/7, 19).
68. Ibid., 32. (I/7, 33–34).
69. Ibid., 48. (I/7, 52).
70. Schelling, *Philosophical Investigations into the Essence of Human Freedom*, 21. (I/7, 350).
71. Ibid.
72. Ibid.
73. Ibid.

Chapter 5. Divine Indigestion

1. Schelling, *Philosophy and Religion*, 8. (I/6, 17).
2. F. W. J. Schelling and Slavoj Žižek, *The Abyss of Freedom/Ages of the World (1813)*, trans. Judith Norman (Ann Arbor: The University of Michigan Press, 1997), 4.
3. Alderwick, *Schelling's Ontology of Powers*, 113.
4. Whistler, *Schelling's Theory of Symbolic Language*.
5. Berger and Whistler, *The Schelling-Eschenmayer Controversy, 1801: Nature and Identity*.
6. Grant, *Philosophies of Nature after Schelling*, 5.
7. Schelling, *Philosophy of Revelation*, 57.
8. Ibid., 63.
9. Ibid., 60.
10. Ibid., 67.
11. Ibid., 68–69; italics removed.

12. Schelling, *The Grounding of Positive Philosophy*, 149.

13. Schelling, *Philosophy of Revelation*, 68.

14. There is much more to be discussed regarding the overall relation between Spinoza and Schelling's later Positive philosophy. A thorough consideration of this relation is outside of the scope of the present work, but Schelling makes several intriguing retrospective observations. For example, "I wrote in my 'Letter on Dogmatism and Criticism' (1795) that a mightier, more majestic dogmatism would rise up against Kantian Criticism, and that this was positive philosophy. Thus, *the notion of a positive philosophy* has been inscribed in me for a long time." Schelling, *Philosophy of Revelation*, 88.

15. Markus Gabriel, "Schelling on the Compatibility of Freedom and Systematicity," in *Schelling's Philosophy: Freedom, Nature, and Systematicity*, ed. G. Anthony Bruno (Oxford: Oxford University Press, 2020), 141.

16. Edward Allen Beach, *The Potencies of God(s): Schelling's Philosophy of Mythology* (Albany: State University of New York Press, 1994), 84–91. Though this characterization is somewhat helpful in articulating a difference between Hegel and Schelling, it relies on a simplistic understanding of negativity in Hegel's dialectic as well as an overemphasis on linearity in Schelling's own metaphysics and ontology.

17. Ibid., 86.

18. This is not to say that doubling plays no role in Hegel's work. For example, the notion plays a large role in Michael Marder's *Hegel's Energy: A Reading of the Phenomenology of Spirit* (Evanston: Northwestern University Press, 2021).

19. Schelling, "Stuttgart Seminars," 200. (I/7, 424–25).

20. For a discussion of the notion of doubling in Schelling and his relation to Boehme see S. J. McGrath, *The Dark Ground of Spirit: Schelling and the Unconscious* (London/New York: Routledge, 2012), 49.

21. Wittgenstein, *Philosophical Investigations*, 62e.

22. Kant, *Critique of Pure Reason*, A426/B454.

23. Ibid.

24. Ibid., A427/B455.

25. Ibid., A445/B473–A446/B474.

26. Ibid., A 446/B 474.

27. Ibid., A447/B475.

28. This logic connects to Spinoza's argument for why things with nothing in common with one another cannot be conceived or caused through each other.

29. Kant, *Critique of Pure Reason*, A452/B480.

30. Ibid.

31. Ibid.

32. Ibid., A453/B481.

33. Ibid.
34. Ibid.
35. Ibid., A455/B483.
36. Reza Negarestani *Intelligence and Spirit* (Falmouth/New York: Urbanomic/Sequence Press, 2018), 232.
37. Žižek, *The Indivisible Remainder: An Essay on Schelling and Related Matters* (London: Verso, 1996), 16.
38. Cixin Liu, *Death's End*, trans. Ken Liu (New York: Tom Doherty Associates, 2016), 28.
39. Tritten, *The Contingency of Necessity*, 45.
40. F. W. J. Schelling, *On the History of Modern Philosophy*, trans. Andrew Bowie (Cambridge: Cambridge University Press, 1994), 147.
41. Slavoj Žižek, *The Indivisible Remainder*, 16.
42. Robert B. Brandom, *Articulating Reasons: An Introduction to Inferentialism* (Cambridge: Harvard University Press, 2000), 80.
43. Ibid., 81.
44. Markus Gabriel, *The Limits of Epistemology*, trans. Alex Englander and Markus Gabriel (Cambridge: Polity Press, 2020), 225–26.
45. Tritten, *The Contingency of Necessity*, 91.
46. Schelling, "Presentation of My System of Philosophy," 149. (I/4, 119–20).
47. Kant, *Critique of Pure Reason*, A505/B533.
48. Adrian Johnston, *A New German Idealism: Hegel, Žižek, and Dialectical Materialism* (New York: Columbia University Press, 2019), 15.
49. Slavoj Žižek, *The Parallax View* (Cambridge: The MIT Press, 2006), 240. Žižek places "reality" in quotation marks in order to differentiate it from the Lacanian Real.
50. Adrian Johnston, *Prolegomena to Any Future Materialism Volume Two: A Weak Nature Alone* (Evanston: Northwestern University Press, 2019), 58–59.
51. Ibid., 61.
52. Gregor Moder, *Hegel and Spinoza: Substance and Negativity* (Evanston: Northwestern University Press, 2017), 8.
53. Schelling, *On the History of Modern Philosophy*, 65.
54. Moder, *Hegel and Spinoza*, 19.
55. David Farrell Krell, *The Tragic Absolute: German Idealism and the Languishing of God* (Bloomington: Indiana University Press, 2005).
56. McGrath, *The Dark Ground of Spirit*.
57. Berger and Whistler, *The Schelling-Eschenmayer Controversy, 1801*, 133.
58. Ibid., 135.
59. For more on intussusception in the *Critique of Pure Reason*, see Jennifer Mensch, *Kant's Organicism: Epigenesis and the Development of Critical Philosophy* (Chicago/London: The University of Chicago Press, 2013).

60. Kant, *Critique of Pure Reason*, A833/B861.
61. Schelling, "Stuttgart Seminars," 198; translation modified. (I/7, 421).
62. Ibid.
63. Ibid.
64. Schelling, "Presentation of My System of Philosophy," 147. (I/4, 117).
65. Schelling, "Stuttgart Seminars," 201. (I/7, 425).
66. Schelling, "Stuttgart Seminars," 198, translation modified. (I/7, 421).
67. Ibid.
68. Ibid., 197. (I/7, 421).
69. Schelling, "System of Philosophy in General," 144. (I/6, 143).
70. Schelling, *First Outline of a System of the Philosophy of Nature*, 94. (I/3, 127).
71. Ibid., 7. (I/3, 7).
72. Ibid., 121. (I/3, 166).
73. Ibid.
74. Ibid., 10. (I/3, 10).
75. Ibid., 121 fn. ★. (I/3, 166 fn. 1).
76. Ibid., 94. (I/3, 127).
77. Schelling, "Presentation of My System of Philosophy," 195. (I/4, 196).
78. Schelling, *First Outline of a System of the Philosophy of Nature*, 37–38 fn ★ (I/3, 46, fn. 1).
79. Ibid., 48 and footnote ★. (I/3, 61).
80. Catherine Malabou, *Before Tomorrow: Epigenesis and Rationality* (Malden: Polity Press, 2016), 16. For more on preformation, epigenesis, and Schelling's naturephilosophy see Elena Casetta, "Preformation vs. Epigenesis: Inspiration and Haunting Within and Outside Contemporary Philosophy of Biology," *Rivista di estetica* 74 (2020).
81. Malabou, *Before Tomorrow*, 17.
82. McGrath, *The Dark Ground of Spirit*, 120–21.
83. Ibid., 121.
84. Krell, *The Tragic Absolute*, 124.
85. Ibid., 178.
86. Žižek, *Indivisible Remainder*, 24. Žižek provides an in-depth analysis of the relation between the account of symbolic castration in Lacan and the creation of the divine word out of a kind of self-cutting. See *Indivisible Remainder*, 42–49.
87. Ibid., 20–21.
88. Heidegger, *Schelling's Treatise on the Essence of Human Freedom*, 9.
89. Woodard, *Schelling's Naturalism*, 132.
90. Adrian Johnston, *Žižek's Ontology* (Evanston: Northwestern University Press, 2008), 77.
91. Schelling, *On the World Soul*, 74. (I/2, 381).

274 | Notes to Chapter 6

92. Schelling, "Stuttgart Seminars," 214. (I/7, 443).
93. Ibid.
94. Ibid.
95. Ibid., 201. (I/7, 425).
96. F. W. J. Schelling, *Ages of the World (1811)*, trans. Joseph P. Lawrence (Albany: State University of New York Press, 2019), 58.
97. Ibid., 174. The 1813 *Ages of the World* reiterates this claim while combining Schelling's two distinct framings in the 1811 draft. Schelling, *The Abyss of Freedom/Ages of the World*, 114.
98. Ibid., 128.
99. Ibid., 115–16.
100. Ibid., 157.
101. Frank, "'Identity of Identity and Non-identity,'" 131.
102. Ibid., 137.
103. Ibid., 140.
104. Matthews, *Schelling's Organic Form of Philosophy*, 57.
105. Ibid., 54.
106. Schelling, *The Ages of the World (1815)*, 6. (I/8, 212).
107. Ibid., 12. (I/8, 219).
108. Žižek, *Sex and the Failed Absolute*, 119.
109. Schelling, *Ages of the World (1811)*, 122.

Chapter 6. From Freedom to Pantheism

1. For a detailed discussion of the potencies and their role in Schelling's metaphysics and methodology, see Beach, *The Potencies of God(s)*, and Woodard, *Schelling's Naturalism*.
2. Günnter Zöller, "Church and State: Schelling's Political Philosophy of Religion," in *Interpreting Schelling: Critical Essays*, ed. Lara Ostric (Cambridge: Cambridge University Press, 2014).
3. Kirill Chepurin, "Indifference and the World: Schelling's Pantheism of Bliss," *Sophia* 58 (2019).
4. Schelling, "Stuttgart Seminars," 224. (I/7, 457).
5. Ibid., 243. (I/7, 484).
6. Ibid., 224. (I/7, 457).
7. Ibid.
8. Ibid. (I/7, 458).
9. Ibid., 225. (I/7, 458).
10. Ibid.
11. Ibid., 226. (I/7, 4460).

12. Schelling, *On the World Soul*, 69. (I/2, 349).
13. Ibid., 70. (I/2, 350).
14. Schelling, "Stuttgart Seminars," 225. (I/7, 458–59).
15. It seems to me that attempts to read Schelling's work as naturalism or naturephilosophy through and through can only do so through an abstract generalization of the notion of nature. This is one reason why I have emphasized Schelling's realism over and above his naturalism.
16. Schelling, "Stuttgart Seminars," 225. (I/7, 459).
17. Ibid., 225–26.
18. Ibid., 226. (I/7, 460).
19. Ibid., 225. (I/7, 459).
20. Ibid., 226. (I/7, 460).
21. Slavoj Žižek The Indivisible Remainder: On Schelling and Related Matters (London/New York: Verso, 1996), 40.
22. Ibid., 41.
23. Ibid.
24. Schelling, "Stuttgart Seminars," 227. (I/7, 461).
25. Anonymous, "The Oldest Systematic Program of German Idealism," in *Philosophy of German Idealism* ed. Ernst Behler, trans. Diana I. Behler (New York: Continuum, 1987), 161.
26. Schelling, "Stuttgart Seminars," 227. (I/7, 461).
27. F. W. J. Schelling, "System of Philosophy in General and the Philosophy of Nature in Particular (1804)," trans. Lydia Azadpour and Daniel Whistler, in *The Schelling Reader* ed. Benjamin Berger and Daniel Whistler (London/New York: Bloomsbury Academic, 2021), 400. (I/6, 575).
28. Ibid., 401. (I/6, 575).
29. Ibid., 402. (I/6, 576).
30. Anonymous, "The Oldest Systematic Program of German Idealism," 162.
31. Ibid.
32. Schelling, "Stuttgart Seminars," 228. (I/7, 462).
33. F. W. J. Schelling, "Presentation of the Purely Rational Philosophy (c. 1847)," trans. Kyla Bruff, in *The Schelling Reader*, ed. Benjamin Berger and Daniel Whistler (London/New York: Bloomsbury Academic, 2021), 408. (II/1, 533).
34. Ibid.
35. Ibid. (II/1, 532).
36. "[O]nly in the state does he find and acquire real freedom." Ibid., 411. (II/1, 537).
37. Ibid., 412. (II/1, 538).
38. Ibid., 417. (II/2, 548).

39. Ibid. (II/1, 548–49).
40. "The state is that which raises the individual to a person." Ibid., 416. (II/1, 546).
41. Ibid., 419. (II/1, 552).
42. Schelling, "Stuttgart Seminars," 228. (I/7, 463).
43. "Christ was the lord of nature by virtue of His *mere* will, and *He* entered into that magic relation with nature that man was originally meant to assume." Ibid.
44. Ibid.
45. Ibid., 229. (I/7, 464).
46. Schelling, *Philosophy of Revelation* (1841–42), 322.
47. Schelling, "Stuttgart Seminars," 229. (I/7, 465).
48. For a discussion of how Schelling's philosophy of revelation pushes beyond out contemporary understanding of theocracy, see Sean McGrath, "Populism and the Late Schelling on Mythology, Ideology, and Revelation," *Analecta Hermeneutica* 9 (2017).
49. Schelling, "Stuttgart Seminars," 229. (I/7, 465).
50. Ibid., 229–30. (I/7, 465).
51. Ibid., 230. (I/7, 465) Here Schelling uses "*Geist*" to describe the second power of the human spirit, but he will later use the French "*l'esprit*" in order to differentiate this power from *Geist* more generally.
52. Ibid.
53. Ibid.
54. Ibid. (I/7, 466).
55. Ibid. (I/7, 465).
56. Ibid.
57. Ibid.
58. Ibid. (I/7, 465–66).
59. Ibid. (I/7, 466).
60. Ibid.
61. Ibid.
62. Ibid.
63. Ibid., 231.
64. Ibid. (I/7, 467).
65. Ibid.
66. Ibid.
67. Ibid., 232. (I/7, 468).
68. Ibid.
69. Ibid. (I/7, 469).
70. Ibid.
71. Ibid., 234. (I/7, 471).
72. Ibid.

73. Ibid.
74. Ibid.
75. Ibid.
76. Ibid.
77. Ibid. (I/7, 472).
78. Ibid.
79. Ibid., 235. (I/7, 472).
80. Ibid.
81. Ibid.
82. Ibid. (I/7, 472–73).
83. Ibid. (I/7, 473).
84. Ibid.
85. Ibid., 236. (I/7, 473).
86. McGrath, "Populism and the Late Schelling on Mythology, Ideology, and Revelation," 1.
87. Ibid., 16.
88. Schelling, "Stuttgart Seminars," 236. (I/7, 474).
89. Ibid.
90. Ibid.
91. Spinoza, *EIIp40 Schol.2*.
92. Kant, *Critique of Practical Reason*, 155.
93. Ibid.
94. Schelling, "Stuttgart Seminars," 236. (I/7, 474).
95. Ibid.
96. Ibid., 237. (I/7, 475).
97. Ibid. (I/7, 476).
98. Ibid., 238. (I/7, 477).
99. Ibid., 239. (I/7, 478).
100. Charlotte Alderwick, "Atemporal Essence and Existential Freedom in Schelling," *British Journal for the History of Philosophy* 23, issue 1 (2015): 128.
101. Ibid.: 133.
102. Schelling, "Stuttgart Seminars," 238. (I/7, 476–77).
103. F. W. J. Schelling, *Clara or, On Nature's Connection to the Spirit World*, trans. Fiona Steinkamp (Albany: State University of New York Press, 2002), 55. (I/9, 77).
104. Chepurin, "Indifference and the World: Schelling's Pantheism of Bliss," 615.
105. Schelling, "Stuttgart Seminars," 238. (I/7, 477).
106. Ibid.
107. Ibid., 239. (I/7, 478).
108. Ibid.
109. Ibid., (I/7, 478–79).

110. Ibid. (I/7, 479).
111. Ibid., 240–41 (I/7, 480)
112. Ibid., 242. (I/7, 482).
113. Ibid., 240. (I/7, 480).
114. Schelling, *Clara*, 55. (I/9, 77).
115. G. W. F. Hegel, *Hegel's Logic: Being Part One of the* Encyclopedia of the Philosophical Sciences *(1830)*, trans. William Wallace (Oxford: Oxford University Press, 1975), 293.
116. Schelling, "Stuttgart Seminars," 198–99. (I/7, 422–23).
117. Ibid., 243. (I/7, 484).

Conclusion: The Poverty of Thought and the Madness of Living Well

1. Franks, *All or Nothing*, 392.
2. Ibid., 392–93.
3. For more on this point see Della Rocca, "Rationalism, Idealism, Monism, and Beyond."
4. Wilfrid Sellars, *Science and Metaphysics: Variations on Kantian Themes* (London: Routledge, 1968), 1.
5. Schelling, *Philosophy and Religion*, 8. (I/6, 18).
6. Schelling, "Presentation of My System of Philosophy," 146. (I/4,115).
7. Schelling, *Philosophical Investigations into the Essence of Human Freedom*, 4. (I/7, 334).
8. Ibid., 75. (I/7. 413).
9. Schelling, "Stuttgart Seminars," 233. (I/7, 470).
10. Ibid.

Bibliography

Schelling Primary

Sämmtliche Werke. Stuttgart/Ausburg: J. C. Cotta'sscher Verlag, 1856–61.

System of Transcendental Idealism. Translated by Peter Heath. Charlottesville: University Press of Virginia, 1978.

"Of the I as Principle of Philosophy, or On the Unconditional in Human Knowledge." In *The Unconditional in Human Knowledge: Four Early Essays (1794–1776)*, translated by Fritz Marti, 59–150. Lewisburg: Bucknell University Press, 1980.

"Philosophical Letters on Dogmatism and Criticism." In *The Unconditional in Human Knowledge: Four Early Essays (1794–1776)*, translated by Fritz Marti, 151–218. Lewisburg: Bucknell University Press, 1980.

Bruno or On the Natural and the Divine Principle of Things. Edited and translated by Michael G. Vater. Albany: State University of New York Press, 1984.

Ideas for a Philosophy of Nature as Introduction to the Study of This Science. Translated by Errol E. Harris, and Peter Heath. Cambridge: Cambridge University Press, 1988.

The Philosophy of Art. Edited and translated by Douglas W. Stott. Minneapolis: University of Minnesota Press, 1989.

On the History of Modern Philosophy. Translated by Andrew Bowie. Cambridge: Cambridge University Press, 1994.

"Treatise Explicatory of the Idealism in the *Science of Knowledge*." In *Idealism and the Endgame of Theory: Three Essays by F. W. J. Schelling*, edited and translated by Thomas Pfau, 61–138. Albany: State University of New York Press, 1994.

"System of Philosophy in General and of the Philosophy of Nature in Particular." In *Idealism and The Endgame of Theory: Three Essays by F. W. J. Schelling*, edited and translated by Thomas Pfau, 139–94. Albany: State University of New York Press, 1994.

"Stuttgart Seminars." In *Idealism and The Endgame of Theory: Three Essays by F. W. J. Schelling*, edited and translated by Thomas Pfau, 195–243. Albany: State University of New York Press, 1994.

The Ages of the World (1815). Translated by Jason M. Wirth. Albany: State University of New York Press, 2000.
Clara or, On Nature's Connection to the Spirit World. Translated by Fiona Steinkamp. Albany: State University of New York Press, 2002.
First Outline of a System of the Philosophy of Nature. Translated by Keith R. Peterson. Albany: State University of New York Press, 2004.
Philosophical Investigations into the Essence of Human Freedom. Translated by Jeff Love and Johannes Schmidt. Albany: State University of New York Press, 2006.
"On the World Soul." In *Collapse: Philosophical Research and Development Vol. VI*, translated by Iain Hamilton Grant, edited by Robin Mackay, 67–95. Falmouth: Urbanomic Press, 2010.
"Correspondence 1800–1802." In *The Philosophical Rupture between Fichte and Schelling: Selected Texts and Correspondence (1800–1802)*, edited and translated by Michael G. Vater and David W. Wood, 21–76. Albany: State University of New York Press, 2012.
"Presentation of My System of Philosophy (1801)." In *The Philosophical Rupture between Fichte and Schelling: Selected Texts and Correspondence (1800–1802)*, edited and translated by Michael G. Vater and David W. Wood, 141–205. Albany: State University of New York Press, 2012.
Philosophy and Religion. Translated by Klaus Ottmann. Putnam: Spring Publications, 2014.
Statement on the True Relationship of the Philosophy of Nature to the Revised Fichtean Doctrine: An Elucidation of the Former. Translated by Dale E. Snow. Albany: State University of New York Press, 2018.
The Ages of the World (1811). Translate by Joseph P. Lawrence. Albany: State University of New York Press, 2019.
"On the True Concept of Philosophy of Nature and the Correct way of Solving Its Problems." In *The Schelling-Eschenmayer Controversy, 1801: Nature and Identity*, edited by Benjamin Berger and Daniel Whistler; translated by Judith Kahl and Daniel Whistler, 46–62. Edinburgh: Edinburgh University Press, 2020.
Philosophy of Revelation (1841–1842) and Related Texts. Translated by Klaus Ottmann. Putnam: Spring Publications, 2020.
"System of Philosophy in General and the Philosophy of Nature in Particular (1804)." Translated by Lydia Azadpour and Daniel Whistler. In *The Schelling Reader*, edited by Benjamin Berger and Daniel Whistler, 400–402. London/New York: Bloomsbury Academic, 2021.
"Presentation of the Purely Rational Philosophy (c. 1847)." Translated by Kyla Bruff. In *The Schelling Reader*, edited by Benjamin Berger and Daniel Whistler, 406–19. London/New York: Bloomsbury Academic, 2021.
Historisch-Kritische Ausgabe. Stuttgart: Frommann-Holzboog, 1976–Present.

Other

Alderwick, Charlotte. "Atemporal Essence and Existential Freedom in Schelling." *British Journal for the History of Philosophy* 23, issue 1 (2015): 115–37.

———. *Schelling's Ontology of Powers*. Edinburgh: Edinburgh University Press, 2021.

Allison, Henry E. *Kant's Transcendental Idealism: An Interpretation and Defense*. New Haven/London: Yale University Press, 2004.

Ameriks, Karl. *Kantian Subjects: Critical Philosophy and Late Modernity*. Oxford: Oxford University Press, 2019.

Anonymous. "The Oldest Systematic Program of German Idealism." In *Philosophy of German Idealism*, edited by Ernst Behler; translated by Diana I. Behler, 161–63. New York: Continuum, 1987.

'Aẓm, Ṣādiq Jalāl. *The Origins of Kant's Arguments in the Antinomies*. Oxford: Oxford University Press, 1972.

Bayle, Pierre. *Historical and Critical Dictionary: Selections*. Translated by Richard H. Popkin. Indianapolis/Cambridge: Hackett, 1991.

Badiou, Alain. *Being and Event*. Translated by Oliver Feltham. London/New York: Continuum, 2005.

Beach, Edward Allen. *The Potencies of God(s): Schelling's Philosophy of Mythology*. Albany: State University of New York Press, 1994.

Beiser, Frederick C. *The Fate of Reason: German Philosophy from Kant to Fichte*. Cambridge/London: Harvard University Press, 1987.

———. *German Idealism: The Struggle against Subjectivism 1781–1801*. Cambridge: Harvard University Press, 2008.

Bernstein, Jay M. "Remembering Isaac: On the Impossibility and Immorality of Faith." In *The Insistence of Art: Aesthetic Philosophy after Early Modernity*, edited by Paul A. Kottman, 257–58. New York: Fordham University Press, 2017.

Bernstein, Jeffery A. "On the Relation between Nature and History in Schelling's *Freedom* Essay and Spinoza's *Theological-Political Treatise*." In *The Barbarian Principle: Merleau-Ponty, Schelling, and the Question of Nature*, edited by Jason M. Wirth and Patrick Burke, 77–100. Albany: State University of New York Press, 2013.

Bhaskar, Roy, and Rom Harré. "How to Change Reality: Story V. Structure—A Debate between Rom Harré and Roy Bhaskar." In *After Postmodernism: An Introduction to Critical Realism* edited by José López and Garry Potter, 22–39. London/New York: The Athlone Press, 2001.

Boehm, Omri. *Kant's Critique of Spinoza*. Oxford: Oxford University Press, 2014.

Bowie, Andrew. *Schelling and Modern European Philosophy: An Introduction*. London/New York: Routledge, 1993.

Brandom, Robert B. *Articulating Reasons: An Introduction to Inferentialism*. Cambridge: Harvard University Press, 2000.

Brock, Stuart, and Edwin Mares. *Realism and Anti-Realism*. Durham: Acumen Publishing Limited, 2007.

Casetta, Elena. "Preformation vs. Epigenesis: Inspiration and Haunting Within and Outside Contemporary Philosophy of Biology." *Rivista di estetica* 74 (2020): 119–38.

Chaćon, Rodrigo. "On a Forgotten Kind of Grounding: Strauss, Jacobi, and the Phenomenological Critique of Modern Rationalism." *The Review of Politics* 76, issue 4 (Fall 2014): 589–617.

Chepurin, Kirill. "Indifference and the World: Schelling's Pantheism of Bliss." *Sophia* 58 (2019): 613–30.

Crowe, Benjamin D. "F. H. Jacobi on Faith, or What it Takes to Be an Irrationalist." *Religious Studies* 45, no. 3 (September 2009): 309–24.

Davidson, Donald. "On the Very Idea of a Conceptual Scheme." In *Inquiries into Truth and Interpretation*, 183–98. Oxford: Oxford University Press, 2009.

Deleuze, Gilles. *Expressionism in Philosophy: Spinoza*. Translated by Martin Joughin. New York: Zone Books, 1990.

———. *The Fold: Leibniz and the Baroque*. Translated by Tom Coneley. Minneapolis: University of Minnesota Press, 1993.

Della Rocca, Michael. "A Rationalist Manifesto: Spinoza and the Principle of Sufficient Reason." *Philosophical Topics* 31, nos. 1&2 (Fall 2003): 75–93.

———. *Spinoza*. New York: Routledge, 2008.

———. "Rationalism, Idealism, Monism, and Beyond." In *Spinoza and German Idealism*, edited by Yizhak Y. Melamed, 7–26. Cambridge: Cambridge University Press, 2012.

Derrida, Jacques. "White Mythology: Metaphor in the Text of Philosophy." *New Literary History* 6, no. 1 (Autumn 1974): 5–74.

———. *Of Grammatology*. Translated by Gayatri Chakravorty Spivak. Baltimore: Johns Hopkins University Press, 2016.

Descartes, Rene. "Meditations on First Philosophy." In *The Philosophical Writings of Descartes Volume II*, translated by John Cottingham, Robert Stoothoff, Dugald Murdoch, 1–62. Cambridge: Cambridge University Press, 1984.

Dodd, James. "Expression in Schelling's Early Philosophy." *Graduate Faculty Philosophy Journal* 27, no. 2 (2006): 109–39.

Dragićević, Daniel. "Schelling with Spinoza on Freedom." In *A Companion to Spinoza*, edited by Yizhak Y. Melamed, 538–47. Hoboken: Wiley Blackwell, 2021.

Dunham, Jeremy, Iain Hamilton Grant, and Sean Watson. *Idealism: The History of a Philosophy*. Montreal and Kingston: McGill-Queen's University Press, 2011.

Ferraris, Maurizio. *Manifesto of New Realism*. Albany: State University of New York Press, 2014.

———. *Introduction to New Realism*. Translated by Sarah De Sanctis. London: Bloomsbury, 2015.

Fichte, J. G. *The Science of Knowledge*. Edited and translated by Peter Heath and John Lachs. Cambridge: Cambridge University Press, 1982.

———. "[First] Introduction to the *Wissenschaftslehre*." In *Introductions to the Wissenschaftslehre and Other Writings (1797–1800)*, edited and translated by Daniel Breazeale, 7–35. Indianapolis/Cambridge: Hackett, 1994.

———. "Second Introduction to the *Wissenschaftslehre* For readers Who Already Have a Philosophical System of Their Own." In *Introductions to the Wissenschaftslehre and Other Writings (1797–1800)*, edited and translated by Daniel Breazeale, 36–105. Indianapolis/Cambridge, Hackett, 1994.

Ford, Lewis S. "The Controversy between Schelling and Jacobi." *Journal of the History of Philosophy* 3, no. 1 (April 1963): 75–89.

Foster, John. *The Case for Idealism*. London: Routledge and Kegan Paul, 1982.

Frank, Manfred. *Philosophical Foundations of Early German Romanticism*. Translated by Elizabeth Millán-Zaibert. Albany: State University of New York Press, 2008.

———. "'Identity of Identity and Non-identity': Schelling's Path to the "Absolute System of Identity.'" Translated by Ian Alexander Moore. In *Interpreting Schelling: Critical Essays*, edited by Lara Ostric, 120–44. Cambridge: Cambridge University Press, 2014.

———. "*Reduplikative Identität*": *Der Schulüssel zu Schillings reifer Philosophie*. Stuttgart: Frommann-Holzboog, 2018.

Franks, Paul W. *All or Nothing: Systematicity, Transcendental Arguments, and Skepticism in German Idealism*. Cambridge/London: Harvard University Press, 2005.

Gabriel, Markus. *Fields of Sense: A New Realist Ontology*. Edinburgh: Edinburgh University Press, 2015.

———. "Schelling on the Compatibility of Freedom and Systematicity." In *Schelling's Philosophy: Freedom, Nature, and Systematicity*, edited by G. Anthony Bruno, 137–53. Oxford: Oxford University Press, 2020.

———. *The Limits of Epistemology*. Translated by Alex Englander and Markus Gabriel. Cambridge: Polity Press, 2020.

Goldgaber, Deborah. *Speculative Grammatology: Deconstruction and the New Materialism*. Edinburgh: Edinburgh University Press, 2021.

Grant, Iain Hamilton. *Philosophies of Nature after Schelling*. London: Continuum International Publishing Group, 2006.

———. "Prospects for Post-Copernican Dogmatism: The Antinomies of Transcendental Naturalism." *Collapse: Philosophical Research and Development Volume V*. Edited by Damian Veal, 413–51. Falmouth: Urbanomic Press, 2009.

———. "Everything Is Primal Germ or Nothing Is: The Deep Field Logic of Nature." *Symposium* 19, no. 1 (2015): 106–24.

———. "Nature after Nature, or Naturephilosophical Futurism." In *Idealism, Relativism, and Realism: New Essays on Objectivity beyond the Analytic-*

Continental Divide, edited by Dominik Finkelde and Paul M. Livingston, 99–112. Berlin/ Boston: De Gruyter, 2020.
Grier, Michelle. *Kant's Doctrine of Transcendental Illusion*. Cambridge: Cambridge University Press, 2001.
Harris, Errol E. "Schelling and Spinoza: Spinozism and Dialectic." In *Spinoza Issues and Directions: Proceedings from the Chicago Spinoza Conference*, edited by Edwin Curley and Pierre-François Moreau, 359–72. Leiden/New York/København/Köln: E. J. Brill, 1990.
Harman, Graham. *The Quadruple Object*. Laurel House: Zero Books, 2011.
———, Ray Brassier, Quentin Meillassoux, and Iain Hamilton Grant. "Speculative Realism (Annex to *Collapse II*)." In *Collapse: Philosophical Research and Development Vol. II*. edited by Robin Mackay, 307–450. Falmouth: Urbanomic Press, 2007.
Hegel, G. W. F. *Hegel's Logic: Being Part One of the* Encyclopedia of the Philosophical Sciences *(1830)*. Translated by William Wallace. Oxford: Oxford University Press, 1975.
———. *The Difference between Fichte's and Schelling's Systems of Philosophy*. Translated by H. S. Harris and Walter Cerf. Albany: State University of New York Press, 1977.
———. *Lectures on the History of Philosophy the Lectures of 1825–1826: Volume III Medieval and Modern Philosophy*. Edited by Robert F. Brown, translated by R. F. Brown, J. M. Stewart, and H. S. Harris. Berkeley/Los Angeles/Oxford: University of California Press, 1990.
Heidegger, Martin. *Schelling's Treatise on the Essence of Human Freedom*. Translated by Joan Stambaugh. Athens: Ohio University Press, 1985.
Henrich, Dieter. *Between Kant and Hegel: Lectures on German Idealism*. Edited by David S. Pacini. Cambridge/London: Harvard University Press, 2003.
Henry, Michel. *Seeing the Invisible: On Kandinsky*. Translated by Scott Davidson. London/New York: Continuum, 2005.
Hogan, Terry, and Matjaž Potrč. *Austere Realism: Contextual Semantics Meets Minimal Ontology*. Cambridge/London: The MIT Press, 2008.
———. "Existence Monism Trumps Priority Monism." In *Spinoza on Monism*, edited by Phillip Goff, 51–76. Hampshire: Palgrave Macmillan, 2012.
Hölderlin, Friedrich. "Judgment Being Possibility (1795)." In *Classic and Romantic German Aesthetics*, edited by J. M. Bernstein, 91–92. Cambridge: Cambridge University Press, 2003.
Jacobi, F. H. "Concerning the Doctrine of Spinoza in Letters to Herr Moses Mendelssohn (1785)." In *The Main Philosophical Writings and the Novel* Allwill, translated by George di Giovanni, 173–252. Montreal and Kingston: McGill-Queen's University Press, 2009.
———. "David Hume on Faith, or Idealism and Realism, A Dialogue (1787)." In *The Main Philosophical Writings and the Novel* Allwill, translated by

George di Giovanni, 253–338. Montreal and Kingston: McGill-Queen's University Press, 2009.
———. "Concerning the Doctrine of Spinoza in Letters to Moses Mendelssohn (1789)." In *The Main Philosophical Writings and the Novel* Allwill, translated by George di Giovanni, 339–78. Montreal and Kingston: McGill-Queen's University Press, 2009.
———. "Letter to Fichte." In *The Main Philosophical Writings and the Novel* Allwill, translated by George di Giovanni, 497–536. Montreal and Kingston: McGill-Queen's University Press, 2009.
Janssens, David. "The Problem of Enlightenment: Strauss, Jacobi, and the Pantheism Controversy." *The Review of Metaphysics* 56, no. 3 (March 2003): 605–31.
Johnston, Adrian. *Žižek's Ontology*. Evanston: Northwestern University Press, 2008.
———. "'Off with their thistleheads!' Against Neo-Spinozism." In *Adventures in Transcendental Materialism: Dialogues with Contemporary Thinkers*, 50–64. Edinburgh: Edinburgh University Press, 2014.
———. *A New German Idealism: Hegel, Žižek, and Dialectical Materialism*. New York: Columbia University Press, 2019.
———. *Prolegomena to Any Future Materialism: A Weak Nature Alone (Volume II)*. Evanston: Northwestern University Press, 2019.
Kant, Immanuel. *Opus Postumum*. Translated by Eckart Förster and Michael Rosen, edited by Eckart Förster. Cambridge: Cambridge University Press, 1993.
———. *Groundwork for the Metaphysics of Morals*. Edited and translated by Allen W. Wood. New Haven/London: Yale University Press, 2002.
———. *Critique of Practical Reason*. Translated by Werner S. Pluhar. Indianapolis/Cambridge: Hackett, 2002.
———. *Critique of Practical Reason*. Translated by Werner S. Pluhar. Indianapolis/Cambridge: Hackett, 2002.
Knappik, Franz. "What Is Wrong with Blind Necessity? Schelling's Critique of Spinoza's Necessitarianism in the Freedom Essay." *Journal of the History of Philosophy* 57, no. 1 (2019): 129–57.
Koekkoek, Rene. "Carl Schmitt and the Challenge of Spinoza's Pantheism between the World Wars." *Moral and Intellectual History* 11, no. 2 (August 2014): 333–57.
Krell, David Farrell. *The Tragic Absolute: German Idealism and the Languishing of God*. Bloomington: Indiana University Press, 2005.
Laruelle, François. "Controversy over the Possibility of a Science of Philosophy." In *The Non-Philosophy Project: Essays by François Laruelle*, edited by Gabriel Alkon and Boris Gunjevic, 74–92. New York: Telos Press, 2012.
Lauer, Christopher. *The Suspension of Reason in Hegel and Schelling*. London/New York: Continuum, 2010.

Lawrence, Joseph P. "Spinoza in Schelling: Appropriation Through Critique." *Idealistic Studies* 33, no. 2–3 (2003): 175–93.
Lin, Martin. *Being and Reason: An Essay on Spinoza's Metaphysics.* Oxford: Oxford University Press, 2019.
Liu, Cixin. *Death's End.* Translated by Ken Liu. New York: Tom Doherty Associates, 2016.
Malabou, Catherine. *Before Tomorrow: Epigenesis and Rationality.* Malden: Polity Press, 2016.
Maoilearca, John Ó [as John Mullarkey]. *Post-Continental Philosophy: An Outline.* London: Continuum, 2006.
Marder, Michael. *Hegel's Energy: A Reading of the Phenomenology of Spirit.* Evanston: Northwestern University Press, 2021.
Matthews, Bruce. *Schelling's Organic Form of Philosophy: Life as the Schema of Freedom.* Albany: State University of New York Press, 2012.
Mátyási, Róbert. "Spinoza on Composition, Monism, and Beings of Reason." *Journal of Modern Philosophy* 2, no. 1 (2020): 1–16.
McDowell, John. *Mind and World.* Cambridge: Harvard University Press, 1996.
McGrath, Sean J. *The Dark Ground of Spirit: Schelling and the Unconscious.* London/New York: Routledge, 2012.
———. "Populism and the Late Schelling on Mythology, Ideology, and Revelation." *Analecta Hermeneutica* 9 (2017): 1–20.
———. *The Philosophical Foundations of the Late Schelling: The Turn to the Positive.* Edinburgh: Edinburgh University Press, 2021.
Meillassoux, Quentin. *After Finitude: An Essay on the Necessity of Contingency.* Translated by Ray Brassier. London: Continuum, 2008.
Melamed, Yitzhak Y. *Spinoza's Metaphysics: Substance and Thought.* Oxford: Oxford University Press, 2013.
———. "*Deus Dive Vernuft*: Schelling's Transformation of Spinoza's God." In *Schelling's Philosophy: Freedom, Nature, and Systematicity*, edited by G. Anthony Bruno, 93–114. Oxford: Oxford University Press, 2020.
Mensch, Jennifer. *Kant's Organicism: Epigenesis and the Development of Critical Philosophy.* Chicago/London: The University of Chicago Press, 2013.
Meurs, Boris van. "Deep Ecology and Nature: Naess, Spinoza, and Schelling." *The Trumpeter* 35, no. 1 (2019): 3–21.
Milbank, John. "The Theological Critique of Philosophy in Hamann and Jacobi." In *Radical Orthodoxy: A New Theology*, edited by John Milbank, Catherine Pickstock, and Graham Ward, 21–37. London: Routledge, 1999.
Moder, Gregor. *Hegel and Spinoza: Substance and Negativity.* Evanston: Northwestern University Press, 2017.
Nassar, Dalia. "Spinoza in Schelling's Early Conception of Intellectual Intuition." In *Spinoza and German Idealism*, edited by Eckart Förster and Yitzhak Y. Melamed, 136–55. Cambridge University Press, 2012.

---. *The Romantic Absolute: Being and Knowing in Early German Romantic Philosophy, 1795–1804*. Chicago: University of Chicago Press, 2014.

Negarestani, Reza. *Intelligence and Spirit*. Falmouth/New York: Urbanomic/Sequence Press, 2018.

Nisenbaum, Karin. *For the Love of Metaphysics: Nihilism and the Conflict of Reason from Kant to Rosenzweig*. Oxford: Oxford University Press, 2018.

Norris, Christopher. *New Idols of the Cave: On the Limits of Anti-Realism*. Manchester: Manchester University Press, 1997.

Pauen, Michael. "Spinoza and the Theory of Identity (2P1–13)." In *Spinoza's Ethics: A Collective Commentary*, edited by Michael Hampe, Ursula Renz, and Robert Schnepf, 79–98. Leiden: Brill, 2011.

Pfau, Thomas. "Identity Before Subjectivity: Schelling's Critique of Transcendentalism, 1974–1810." In *Idealism and the Endgame of Theory: Three Essays by F. W. J. Schelling*, translated and edited by Thomas Pfau, 24–44. Albany: State University of New York Press, 1994.

Proulx, Jeremy. *The Provocation of Nihilism: Practical Philosophy and Aesthetics in Jacobi, Kant, and Schelling*, Unpublished Dissertation, https://macsphere.mcmaster.ca/handle/11375/19361.

Putnam, Hilary. *The Many Faces of Realism: The Paul Carus Lectures*. Chicago/La Salle: Open Court, 1987.

Quine, W. V. O. "Two Dogmas of Empiricism." In *From a Logical Point of View: Nine Logico-Philosophical Essays*, 20–46. Harvard: Harvard University Press, 1980.

Renz, Ursula. *The Explicability of Experience: Realism and Subjectivity in Spinoza's Theory of the Human Mind*. Oxford: Oxford University Press, 2018.

Richard, Robert J. *The Romantic Conception of Life: Science and Philosophy in the Age of Goethe*. Chicago: University of Chicago Press, 2002.

Robinson, Keith. "Whitehead, Post-Structuralism, and Realism." In *Secrets of Becoming: Negotiating Whitehead, Deleuze, and Butler*, edited by Roland Faber and Andrea M. Stephenson, 53–69. New York: Fordham University Press, 2011.

Rorty, Richard. "The World Well Lost." *Journal of Philosophy* 69, no. 19 (1972): 649–65.

---. *Philosophy and the Mirror of Nature*. Princeton: Princeton University Press, 1981.

Schaffer, Jonathan. "Monism: The Priority of the Whole." *Philosophical Review* 119, no. 1 (2010): 31–76.

Sellars, Wilfrid. *Science and Metaphysics: Variations on Kantian Themes*. London: Routledge, 1968.

Shein, Noa. "The False Dichotomy between Objective and Subjective Interpretations of Spinoza's Theory of Attributes." *British Journal for the History of Philosophy* 17, no. 3 (2009): 505–32.

Snow, Dale E. *Schelling and the End of Idealism*. Albany: State University of New York Press, 1996.
Spinoza, Benedict de. "Short Treatise on God, Man, and His Well-Being." In *Spinoza: Complete Works*, translated by Samuel Shirley, edited by Michael L. Morgan, 31–107. Indianapolis/Cambridge: Hackett, 2002.
———. "Principles of Cartesian Philosophy *and* Metaphysical Thoughts." In *Spinoza: Complete Works*, translated by Samuel Shirley, edited by Michael L. Morgan, 108–212. Indianapolis/Cambridge: Hackett, 2002.
———. "Ethics." In *Spinoza: Complete Works*, translated by Samuel Shirley, edited by Michael L. Morgan, 212–382. Indianapolis/Cambridge: Hackett, 2002.
———. "Letter 12." In *Spinoza: Complete Works*, translated by Samuel Shirley, edited by Michael L. Morgan, 787–91. Indianapolis/Cambridge: Hackett, 2002.
———. "Letter 50." In *Spinoza: Complete Works*, translated by Samuel Shirley, edited by Michael L. Morgan, 891–92. Indianapolis/Cambridge: Hackett, 2002.
———. "Letter 76." In *Spinoza: Complete Works*, translated by Samuel Shirley, edited by Michael L. Morgan, 947–95. Indianapolis/Cambridge: Hackett, 2002.
Tritten, Tyler. *The Contingency of Necessity: Reason and God as Matter of Fact*. Edinburgh: Edinburgh University Press, 2019.
Vater, Michael G. "Introduction." In *Bruno or On the Natural and the Divine Principle of Things*, edited and translated by Michael G. Vater, 3–107. Albany: State University of New York Press, 1984.
———. "Schelling's Philosophy of Identity and Spinoza's *Ethica more geometrico*." In *Spinoza and German Idealism*, edited by Eckart Förster, and Yitzhak Y. Melamed, 156–74. New York: Cambridge University Press, 2012.
Whistler, Daniel. *Schelling's Theory of Symbolic Language: Forming the System of Identity*. Oxford: Oxford University Press, 2013.
Wittgenstein, Ludwig. *Philosophical Investigations*. Translated by G. E. M. Anscombe, P. M. S. Hacker, and Joachim Schulte. Oxford: Wiley-Blackwell, 2009.
Woodard, Ben. *Schelling's Naturalism: Motion, Space, and the Volition of Thought*. Edinburgh: Edinburgh University Press, 2019.
Žižek, Slavoj. *The Indivisible Remainder: An Essay on Schelling and Related Matters*. London: Verso, 1996.
———. *The Parallax View*. Cambridge: The MIT Press, 2006.
———. *Sex and the Failed Absolute*. London/New York: Bloomsbury Academic, 2020.
Zöller, Günter. "Church and State: Schelling's Political Philosophy of Religion." In *Interpreting Schelling: Critical Essays*, edited by Lara Ostric, 200–15. Cambridge: Cambridge University Press, 2014.

Index

Absolute, the, 3, 5, 10–11, 24, 25–26, 59, 62–63, 68–69, 87–88, 92, 101, 105–108, 110–11, 117, 119–27, 129–31, 134–35, 151, 153–55, 159–61, 167, 170, 172, 176, 178–82, 184, 186–86, 189–90, 194, 197–98, 200, 205, 223–24, 226, 234, 236, 239, 241–43. *See also* God; substance; unconditioned, the
Alderwick, C., 112, 168, 230, 246n19, 262n29
Allison, H. E., 20–21
Ameriks, K., 155
antirealism, 4, 13, 15, 18, 19–22, 25, 29, 56, 73, 182, 238
atheism, 30, 32, 34–36, 47, 69, 112, 116, 154, 253n2
attribute, 24, 96, 99–100, 113, 122, 129–31, 134, 142, 144–52, 153, 170, 195, 199, 203, 234, 236, 269n46. *See also* parallelism

Bayle, P., 33–35, 112, 115
Beach, E. A., 170, 274n1
Beiser, F. C., 21, 31–32, 55, 76
Berger, B., 106, 168, 186, 246n19, 256n80

Berkeley, G., 17, 75
Bernstein, J. A., 6
Bernstein, J. M., 52
Bhaskar, R., 15
blobject, *see* blobjectivism
blobjectivism, 102–103, 116, 119
Boehm, O., 31, 41–45
Bowie, A., 7, 21
Brandom, R., 179, 200
Brassier, R., 17, 251n72
Bruno, G. A., 49, 255n31

Chepurin, K., 204, 231
church, the, 203–204, 214–15, 224, 229
conflict, 12–13, 81, 85, 129, 146, 153, 187, 193. *See also* life
conatus, 96, 125
contraction, 186, 190–92, 194, 196
correlationism, 17, 20, 109, 251n73
creative reason (*realisirenden Vernunft*), 23–24, 58–69, 73–74, 80, 83–84, 131, 139, 153–54, 160, 172, 188, 242
criticism, 58–61, 72, 81, 85, 95, 133, 137, 237–38
Crowe, B. D., 47, 50
Curley, E., 114

Davidson, D., 15, 20
death, 52, 137–38, 162, 193, 204, 226, 229–32, 234
Deleuze, G., 7, 116, 119, 148
Della Rocca, M., 29, 98, 100–101, 118, 150, 152, 184, 252n78, 268–69n43
Derrida, J., 15, 17, 86
Descartes, R., 54, 75
Divine, the, *see* God
Dodd, J., 123–25
dogmatism, 1, 57–69, 72, 81, 84–85, 91, 95, 133, 237
doubling, 25, 105, 119, 126, 170–71, 184–89, 193–94, 196–200
Dunham, J., 21–22

Eschenmayer, A. C. A., 168, 240–41
emergence, 25, 42, 71, 124, 126, 141, 152, 163, 169, 171–73, 175–82, 184–86, 190–91, 200, 208, 240
evil, 25, 205, 209, 211, 220–21, 228, 231–32

faith, 25–26, 32, 42, 46–49, 52–56, 61, 225, 240–42
fatalism, 30, 32, 69, 253n2
Ferraris, M., 19, 52, 252n77
Fichte, J. G., 2, 10, 24, 29, 33, 52, 54, 65, 68–70, 80–81, 87, 106, 131–39, 141, 151, 160, 168, 188, 267n7, 267n17
Ford, L. S., 51
Foster, J., 19, 21
Frank, M., 55, 106, 111, 199
Franks, P. W., 43, 257
freedom, 23, 25, 37, 41–42, 54, 58, 67, 70, 82, 84, 87, 126, 168, 173–74, 176–77, 193–94, 200, 204–208, 210, 212–16, 220–21, 226, 233, 236, 240, 242

Frege, G., 111

Gabriel, M., 169–70, 179
God, 10–11, 25, 34–38, 45, 51, 54–55, 60, 69–72, 78–86, 103–105, 107, 109, 115, 117, 120–22, 125–26, 142, 145, 147–49, 154, 157, 169–70, 178–81, 185–86, 190, 192–94, 196–98, 200–201, 203–207, 209–11, 214, 216, 225, 227–28, 232–33, 235–36, 240, 255n34, 260n79, 265n103. *See also* Absolute, the; substance
Goldgaber, D., 17
Grant, I. H., 17, 21–22, 110, 140–41, 143–44, 168, 182, 246n16, 246n20, 249n46, 251n72, 267n9
Grier, M., 41, 255n38, 255n40, 258n29

Habermas, J., 210
Harris, E. E., 103
Harman, G., 17, 251n72
Hegel, G. W. F., 1–4, 46, 57, 106, 123, 141, 156, 170–71, 182–87, 189, 236, 239
Heidegger, M., 7, 194, 248n31
Hogan, T., 102–103, 116
Hölderlin, F., 94
Hume, D., 47, 111
hyphen, 1, 4, 160–62, 201, 203, 240, 242
hyphenated unity, 4, 25, 105, 160, 162

Idea, the, 22, 125, 132, 141–43, 151, 191, 201, 236, 239
ideal-realism, 1–5, 11, 13, 25, 141, 204, 240
idealism, 1–2, 4, 6, 8–10, 13–15, 17–22, 23–26, 29–30, 38–39,

44, 48–49, 55–61, 63, 67, 72–75, 77–79, 85–86, 92, 129–34, 136–41, 144, 153–54, 160, 162–63, 172, 182, 237–39, 268–69n43
immanence, 4, 11, 16, 18, 20, 181–83, 201, 238–39
indifference, 4, 105–106, 108, 120, 160, 221, 233, 242
intellectual intuition, 7, 23, 55, 59, 72, 74, 77–81, 83, 85, 112, 118, 189, 241–42, 251n72
intussusception, 25, 187, 189–92, 194, 196
irrationalism, 14, 47, 53–54

Jacobi, F. H., 2, 13–14, 23, 29–39, 41, 45–56, 58, 68–69, 80–81, 93, 95, 98, 112, 115, 132, 137, 157, 161, 174, 185, 192, 200, 237–38, 240, 242, 253n2, 254n12, 267n17; *salto mortale*, 23, 29–31, 52–55, 61
Janssens, D., 33
Johnston, A., 182–84, 194, 200

Kant, I., 2, 17, 20–21, 29–30, 32, 34, 45–46, 56, 57–58, 64, 68, 72, 135, 171, 176, 177, 180, 187, 191, 213, 222, 226
  Critique of Practical Reason, 60, 68, 84, 223, 227
  Critique of Pure Reason, 23, 30, 59, 60–61, 63, 66, 74, 182, 191; Antinomies of Pure Reason, 39, 58, 171–76, 179, 181–83, 245n7; Architectonic of Pure Reason, 187; First Antinomy, 42–43, 172–73, 181; Fourth Antinomy, 174–75; Refutation of Idealism, 59, 73–77, 79, 84, 137; Transcendental Deduction, 74; Transcendental Deduction (B edition), 62; Transcendental Dialectic, 25, 31, 36, 39, 45, 65, 181; Transcendental Doctrine of Method, 187; Third Antinomy, 42–45, 82, 173–74
  Groundwork for the Metaphysics of Morals, 83
  Opus postumum, 2–3, 72
Knappik, F., 248–49n37
Krell, D. F., 185, 192–93

Lacan, J., 193
Lauer, C., 121, 126
Leibniz, G. W., 41, 111, 248n37
life, 11–12, 23, 25, 49–50, 52, 61, 80–81, 85, 110, 129, 132, 138, 146, 153, 158–59, 161–63, 170, 193, 195, 198, 204, 218, 225, 229–30, 233–34
Lin, M., 116, 150–52, 261n8, 265n89
Liu, C., 177
love, 55, 185, 198, 227–28

Malabou, C., 191–92
Maoilearca, J. Ó., 15–18
Marder, M., 271n18
Matthews, B., 110, 199, 249–50n53
Mátyási, R., 117
McDowell, J., 38
McGrath, S. J., 185, 192, 225, 253n2, 271n20, 276n48
Melamed, Y. Y., 96–97, 114–15, 151, 261n2
Meillassoux, Q., 17, 251n72, 251n73
mode, 99, 113–16, 118, 145, 149
Moder, G., 185
monism, 2, 4, 6, 11–13, 30, 33–35, 38, 41, 43, 71, 96–97, 99, 101, 104, 112, 127, 129, 136, 147, 170, 195, 200, 240; existence,

monism *(continued)*
  93, 97, 101–103, 111–14, 116–18, 129, 147, 149, 152, 170, 181, 185, 198, 239; priority, 101–102, 112, 114
Milbank, J., 37, 46, 48
mutual saturation (*Wechseldurchdringung*), 4, 8–9, 24, 131, 153, 160, 223, 230

Nassar, D., 7, 78, 80, 106, 248n28, 257n4
natura naturans, 121
natura naturata, 121
naturalism, 5, 22, 29, 100, 152–53, 172, 182, 184, 208, 232, 275n15; liberal, 201; reductive, 68–69, 109, 201
Negarestani, R., 176
negative philosophy, 63
New Realism, 238. *See also* Ferraris, M.
nihilism, 23, 30, 32–33, 48, 53, 55, 69, 77, 253–54n9
Nisenbaum, K., 53–55
Nostalgia (*Sehnsucht*), 218–19, 232
Norris, C., 15–18
Novalis, 69

opposition, 12, 61, 67, 72, 81, 84–87, 92, 106–107, 137–38, 158, 162, 188, 195, 201

pain, 185–86, 190, 192, 194
pantheism, 9, 11–12, 25, 115–16, 132, 161–62, 174, 204, 207, 225
pantheism controversy (*Pantheismusstreit*), 6, 31–32, 56, 70, 237–38
parallelism, 6, 24, 122, 129, 131, 134–35, 142, 147, 149–50, 161, 172, 199, 203, 223, 229–30, 234, 236, 239–40, 252n78. *See also* attribute
Peden, K., 113
Pfau, T., 126
Plato, 141, 199
postcontinental philosophy, 14–16, 18, 238
positive philosophy, 7, 210
Potrč, M., 102–103, 116
Principle of Sufficient Reason (PSR), 23–24, 29–30, 34–47, 68, 70, 92, 97–103, 110–11, 119, 126, 129, 151, 159, 170, 172–73, 175–79, 181–82, 184, 208, 239, 268–69n43
Proulx, J., 53, 55
Putnam, H., 17

Quine, W. V. O., 15

rationalism, 29, 36, 97, 100, 112–13, 119, 153
realism, 1–5, 6, 8–10, 13–15, 17–20, 22–26, 29–30, 44, 46, 53, 55–61, 67, 72, 85–86, 92, 95, 129–33, 137–38, 140–41, 144–45, 147, 153–54, 160, 162–63, 172, 182, 237–40
reason, 25, 29–32, 36–41, 44–50, 52–55, 61, 65, 69, 71, 97, 103–105, 107–109, 120, 124, 151–52, 160, 162, 178, 181–83, 213, 222–23, 227, 241–43; practical, 23, 54–56, 58–61, 74, 82–83, 227, 242; system of, 60, 189; theoretical, 30, 37, 45, 55–56, 58–61, 66, 71, 82, 228, 242; tragic fate of, 65–66, 183
Renz, U., 113, 264n84

revelation, 10–11, 193, 203–205, 212, 214, 218, 225, 231–32, 236, 240
Robinson, K., 18–19
Rorty, R., 15, 20

Schaffer, J., 101–102, 115
Schelling, F. W. J.
  Ages of the World (1811), 186, 196–99
  Ages of the World (1813), 193
  Ages of the World (1815), 11–12, 91, 146, 200
  Bruno or On the Natural and the Divine Principle of Things, 106–107, 129, 135, 143
  Clara or, On Nature's Connection to the Spirit World, 231–32, 235
  First Outline of a System of the Philosophy of Nature, 11, 94, 189–91
  Further Presentation from the System of Philosophy, 151, 269n46
  Ideas for a Philosophy of Nature, 81, 145–46
  "*J. G. Fichte/F. W. J. Schelling: Correspondence 1800–1802*," 133–36
  Of the I as the Principle of Philosophy, or On the Unconditional in Human Knowledge, 57, 94, 108, 141, 257n4
  On the History of Modern Philosophy, 2, 178
  "On the True Concept of Philosophy of Nature and the Correct Way of Solving its Problems," 6, 138, 140–41, 154, 168, 245n2
  On the World Soul, 12, 194, 207
  Philosophical Investigations into the Essence of Human Freedom, 8–11, 24–25, 111, 129, 131–32, 161–63, 169, 176, 193, 195, 203, 205, 210, 242–43
  Philosophical Letters on Dogmatism and Criticism, 7, 23–24, 57–64, 66–68, 70–72, 74, 79–82, 84–87, 92, 94–95, 135, 137–39, 141, 153–54, 173, 227, 257n4
  Philosophy and Religion, 7, 92, 113, 130–31, 151, 160, 167, 169, 240, 242
  Philosophy of Revelation (1841–42), 168–67, 215, 271n14
  Philosophy of Art, 8
  Presentation of My System of Philosophy, 6, 24, 92, 94–97, 103–106, 108, 119–20, 122, 126–27, 129–30, 138–39, 144, 151–52, 160, 191, 241
  "Presentation of the Purely Rational Philosophy," 212–13
  Statement on the True Relationship of the Philosophy of Nature to the Revised Fichtean *Doctrine*, 136–37, 161
  "Stuttgart Seminars," 11, 25, 169, 171, 176, 186–88, 195–96, 203–11, 213–26, 228–36
  System of Philosophy in General and the Philosophy of Nature in Particular, 24, 108–10, 112–13, 120–22, 124–27, 142, 160, 178, 211–12
  System of Transcendental Idealism, 1–3, 9, 11, 91, 95, 123, 138–39, 157
  The Grounding of Positive Philosophy, 132, 169
  "Treatise Explicatory of the Idealism in the *Science of Knowledge*," 131, 153–59, 242

Schmitt, C., 35
Sellars, W., 179–80, 200, 239, 251n72
Shein, N., 150
Snow, D., 21, 55, 83, 253n3
speculative realism, 17, 238, 251n72, 251n73
Spinoza, B.
 Ethics, *E*Id2, 113; *E*Id6, 103, 148; *E*Ia2, 148; *E*Ia3, 98; *E*Ia5, 98; *E*Ia6, 148; *E*Ip1, 99; *E*Ip3, 98; *E*Ip4, 99; *E*Ip7, 99; *E*Ip8, 100; *E*Ip9, 148; *E*Ip10, 148; *E*Ip11, 98; *E*Ip15, 104; *E*Ip16, 150; *E*Ip17, 252n78; *E*IId1, 113, 148; *E*IId3, 113–14, 142, 148; *E*IId7, 114; *E*IIa5, 113; *E*IIp1, 149; *E*IIp2, 149; *E*IIp4, 142; *E*IIp5, 142; *E*IIp7, 146–47, 149; *E*IIp13, 117; *E*IIp40, 118, 226; *E*IIIp7, 125; *E*Vp23, 226; *E*Vp25, 226; *E*Vp29, 226; *E*Vp30, 226–27; *E*Vp36, 227; *E*Vp37, 228; *E*Vp38, 228
 "Letter 12," 102, 115
 "Letter 50," 123
 "Letter 76," 100
 Principles of Cartesian Philosophy and *Metaphysical Thoughts*, 117–18
 Short Treatise on God, Man, and His Well-Being, 117–18
spirit, 26, 59, 72, 131, 140, 144, 153–59, 161, 163, 179, 186, 188–89, 200–201, 201, 210, 240, 242, 243; human, 25, 203–204, 208, 212, 214–17, 222, 224–26, 228–31, 234–35; *l'esprit*, 220–21
spirit world, 208, 229–35
state, the, 203–204, 210–15, 229

substance, 11, 36, 38, 41, 72, 84, 96, 104–105, 114–17, 119, 125, 134–35, 145, 147–53, 178, 180, 187, 195, 198, 269n46
synthesis, 59, 61–67, 69, 72, 95, 124, 153, 160–61, 238; absolute, 4, 153. *See also* mutual saturation

temperament (*Gemüth*), 217–24, 226, 232, 233
"The Oldest Systematic Program of German Idealism," 211–12, 215
totum analyticum, 36, 42–43, 71, 102, 110, 115, 178, 180, 185
totum syntheticum, 42, 44
transcendence, 4, 16, 18, 20, 29, 56, 112, 172, 174, 185–86, 192, 201, 228, 239–40
transcendental idealism, 20, 23, 30, 45, 55, 68, 73–74, 76–77, 95
transcendental realism, 21, 41–45, 137, 245n7
Tritten, T., 18, 178, 180–81

unconditioned, the, 66, 68, 72, 79, 205; in Kant, 40, 65, 71, 83, 174. *See also* Absolute, the; God; substance
understanding, 26, 154, 156, 178, 183, 220–23, 242–43; discursive, 20, 78

Vater, M. G., 6, 96–97, 104, 106–107

Watson, S., 21–22
Whistler, D., 106, 168, 186, 246n11, 258n80 268n28
will, 83–84, 120, 220–24; as primal Being (*Ur-sein*), 163; God's, 51, 185

Wittgenstein, L., 15, 171
Wirth, J. M., 7, 246n19
Woodard, B., 7, 168, 194, 246n 19, 246–47n20, 274n1

Zöller, G., 204.
Žižek, S., 126, 168, 178, 182–84, 192–93, 194, 200, 210, 213

www.ingramcontent.com/pod-product-compliance
Lightning Source LLC
Chambersburg PA
CBHW021937140625
28084CB00014B/49